For the Love
OF

by Elwood McQuaid

For the Love OF Zion

by Elwood McQuaid

The Friends of Israel Gospel Ministry, Inc.
P.O. Box 908 • Bellmawr, NJ 08099

FOR THE LOVE OF ZION

Elwood McQuaid

Our thanks to Nonie Darwish, who gave us permission to use her letter to the Public Broadcasting System.

Printed in the United States of America
Library of Congress Catalog Card Number: 2006938234
ISBN 10-0-915540-78-9
     13-978-0-915540-78-5

Cover design by Waveline Direct Inc., Mechanicsburg, PA.

Visit our Web site: *foi.org*.

DEDICATION

In grateful memory of Morris V. Brodsky. For well over the half-century of our relationship, Morrie exemplified the purest virtues of Christian commitment, charity, and dedication to God's Word and His servants worldwide. His mentoring, wise counsel, and better-than-a-friend encouragement sustained this author and his family through many of the make-or-break tests that demand wisdom, honesty, and generosity beyond the scope of one's own abilities. For this, and so much more, I'm thankful to have called him my friend.

ACKNOWLEDGMENT

Although the fact is not often acknowledged, authors—without exception—are indebted to the many hands and skills necessary to bring a finished product into the lives of readers. I am no different. Foremost among this invaluable cast of colleagues is Lorna Simcox, editor-in-chief of *Israel My Glory* magazine, who spent many hours and days editing and contributing advice and material in the preparation phase of the publication. To Lorna and the many encouragers who endured the process, I trust the appreciation of readers will bring a sense of gratification for a job well done.

TABLE OF CONTENTS

PREFACE

As this book goes to press, Israel and the Middle East are once again in a period of flux. Longtime observers of the region are aware that this is not a new phenomenon. Israel and its people are at the epicenter of world events and will continue to occupy that trauma-inducing position until the consummation. This book, therefore, is not intended to be a commentary on the news events that seem to fluctuate with every passing day. On these pages you will discover the broad scope of the controversies that lie behind the headlines. You'll see the real issues that are seldom clarified in the struggle between Israel and its entrenched and perpetual enemies. Thus, whatever are the upheavals and changes in the political winds that ruffle the pages of contemporary history, the story remains the same. For this reason, it is imperative to gain an understanding that goes beyond the evening news and elitist, secular media sources and to sort out the truth. Once you have accomplished this, you will be better equipped to view the big picture and understand where history is taking us—and what we can do about it.

INTRODUCTION

How does one describe Zion? Certainly, it is a place—a singularity of landscape that stands apart from every mound, mountain, plain, and plateau on the face of this planet. But what makes it so? And how can this Zion we talk and sing of be framed in words or inscribed on pallid sheets of paper? Capturing its essence is impossible. For Zion, you see, represents so many shades and shadows, texts and textures that deftly escape the powers of human explanation.

I suppose that may be so because Zion cannot be compressed into merely a place. It is surpassingly encompassing in scope, application, and appeal. For Christians of other generations, who delighted in lyrically "Marching to Zion," it represented a triumphal expedition through fields that yield "a thousand sacred sweets" by way of "Immanuel's ground," along heavenly byways. They were on their journey to "walk the golden streets" in "fairer worlds on high"—the heavenly Zion, that "beautiful city of God."

For Jewish people, Zion meant something else. Through all their years of wandering as foot-weary, temporary sojourners in realms they knew were not their own, Zion represented home. Often it lay far, far away, on the other side of oceans and across indescribable encounters with privation, fear, and suffering. But somehow, it was never far from the hearts of these pilgrim people forcibly estranged from their Zion. Their longing may have been described best, with all its heart-gripping pathos, by the Jewish psalmist on the shores of Babylon:

> By the rivers of Babylon, there we sat down, yea, we wept when we remembered Zion. We hung our harps upon the willows in the midst of it. For there those who carried us away captive asked of us a song, and those who plundered us requested mirth, saying, "Sing us one of the songs of Zion!" How shall we sing the LORD's song in a foreign land? (Ps. 137:1–4).

Nebuchadnezzar's fabled hanging gardens, Ishtar Gate, and deep-flowing rivers held no appeal for these Israelites dwelling as strangers in a far-off land. Zion was home—always and forever.

To other generations walking other roads, Zion was the dream at the end of a thousand hellish nightmares. The dream was, as the lyricist of "Hatikva" wrote, to dwell in peace "upon the hills of Zion and Jerusalem." That dream motivated Jewish pioneers to drain the malaria-infested swamps of a Holy Land ruled by the Ottoman Turks and then Great Britain. That dream fired the political Zionism that was to blaze a path for the rush of bedraggled World War II survivors who sought refuge in their ancestral homeland when the fires of the Holocaust confirmed once and for all that only one legitimate haven of rest and security existed for them on Earth. That sanctuary was their beloved Zion, deeded to them forever by God with the promise of the long-sought peace they have never fully known.

I suppose one could say that Zion is as much a provision for our hearts as it is soil, ancient structures, narrow streets, picturesque paths, and gardens. It is people, conflict, and a myriad of issues yet to be settled. There is no place on Earth that embodies more of the stuff that invades, inspires, and confronts us with the inescapable issues of our time than Zion and its people. Nothing can be even remotely compared to it. It stands alone.

In the end, all believers long for that city "whose builder and maker is God" (Heb. 11:10). And that city graces the summit of our Zion:

> *But you have come to Mount Zion and to the city of the living God, the heavenly Jerusalem* (12:22).

So why do we write and sing and pray for peace to reign in Jerusalem or talk of matters "for the love of Zion"? For very good reasons, my friends—reasons we are about to share.

—Elwood McQuaid

CHAPTER 1

◦✦◦

THE PEACE PROCESS—
IS IT BECOMING A BAD DREAM?

From where I sit, things don't look promising for Israel. I'm doing a considerable amount of head-scratching these days, and I'm not alone. Many Christians who are deeply committed to Israel's best interests cannot ignore our gut feelings. Although we don't make it part of our daily routines to question decisions made by Jerusalem, which is, of course, where decisions about the future of the nation should be made, and we realize that government leaders always possess information we do not, many questions are grinding away at us. Is Israel giving away the store in exchange for nothing? Are Israel's Arab enemies interpreting its concessions, such as its unilateral pullout in 2005 from Gaza and parts of the West Bank, as a signal that the embattled Jewish nation has lost its taste for survival? Are Israel's enemies merely biding their time as they gear up for a yet more vicious "throw them into the sea" campaign? Is little Israel being sucked in by an Arab strategy to carve the Jewish state up one slice at a time?

These fundamental questions are being asked by evangelical Christians, whom the late Israeli Prime Minister Menachem Begin once called one of Israel's "two solid friends in the world," the other being "some of our own people." Although we're certainly not trying to discredit the Israeli government's efforts, concessions in the form of unilateral withdrawals are encouraging Israel's enemies.

Although the Israeli government denies it, Palestinian militants and their radical Muslim bedfellows feel that terrorism has been successful in causing Israel to retreat.

In August 2005, while Israel was traumatically evacuating its 21 towns in the Gaza Strip, Hamas leader Khaled Mashaal boasted on Arab television, "The resistance and the steadfastness of our people forced the Zionists to withdraw. The resistance is capable of ending the Israeli occupation. . . . The armed struggle is the only strategy that Hamas possesses."[1]

"You are leaving Gaza in shame today," said bombmaker Muhammad Deif on a videotape Hamas released days after the Gaza expulsion. "Today you are leaving hell. But we promise you that tomorrow all Palestine will be hell for you."[2]

Mahmoud Zahar, Hamas's leader there, told the London-based Arab daily *Asharq al-Awsat*, "Now, after the victory in the Gaza Strip, we will transfer the struggle first to the West Bank and later to Jerusalem."[3]

But not even Jerusalem is the final destination. "Neither the liberation of the Gaza Strip, nor the liberation of the West Bank or even Jerusalem will suffice us. Hamas will pursue the armed struggle until the liberation of all our lands," Zahar said.[4]

To Muslims, the words *occupied territory* refer to any land that has ever been in Muslim hands but now is not. In an interview on Hezbollah's al-Manar TV, Sheikh Muhammad Ali, director of the Palestinian Clerics Association, explained: "Any land, any piece of land, over which flies the banner of 'There is no god but Allah, and Muhammad is His Messenger,' and which at a certain point belonged to the Muslims . . . it is the duty of the Muslims to liberate."

"Allah willing," he said, "we will enter [Israel] as conquerors and liberators, not through negotiations, but through Jihad and resistance, because the hadith goes: 'And the Muslims would kill the Jews'—there is killing involved."[5]

As Israel pulled out from Gaza, Abdel Al, another

Palestinian leader, vowed, "We will transfer two-thirds of our budget to the West Bank. Our rockets have a range of 18 kilometers. This means that if we fire them from Kalkilya, they will hit the occupied city of Tal al-Rabi [Tel Aviv]."[6]

Israel is at the epicenter of a profound worldwide battle over power, politics, and religion. And those of us who know our theology know that religion is not ancillary; it is the fulcrum of the struggle. Christians and Jews worship Jehovah, or Yahweh (YHWH). Muslims worship Allah, revealed through the teachings of Muhammad, who was born in A.D. 570 in Mecca in what is today Saudi Arabia. Jehovah and Allah are nothing alike. Consequently, neither are their followers.

Muslims believe all Israel belongs to them because they once occupied it and are, therefore, obligated to win it back for Allah. As evangelical Christians, we believe Israel belongs to the Jewish people because it was given to them by God.

Christians and the Bible

When it comes to Israel, Bible-believing Christians and Bible-believing Jews have little to argue about. We both believe the Jewish people have a fundamental right to their God-given homeland in the Middle East:

> And the LORD said to Abram, after Lot had separated from him: 'Lift your eyes now and look from the place where you are—northward, southward, eastward, and westward; for all the land which you see I give to you and your descendants forever' (Gen. 13:14–15).

Furthermore, under the Messiah, Israel's ultimate destiny is to live in peace within greater Israel—a land spanning an area east and west from the little river of Egypt to the Euphrates: "On the same day the LORD made a covenant with

Abram, saying: 'To your descendants I have given this land, from the river of Egypt to the great river, the River Euphrates'" (15:18).

The "seed" receiving these covenant land promises was to come through Abraham's son, the Jewish patriarch Isaac, not through his son Ishmael: "Sarah your wife shall bear you a son, and you shall call his name Isaac; I [God] will establish My covenant with him for an everlasting covenant, and with his descendants after him" (17:19).

No one from our side of the line wants an Israeli expansionist crusade that will create the promised greater Israel at the expense of its current neighbors. The Messiah Himself will accomplish that feat. What we do firmly believe, however, and fervently support, is a Jewish homeland with defensible borders and the means to keep its rapidly encroaching enemies at a respectable distance.

Survival Through Strength

In America we hear a great deal about what politicians feel must be achieved quickly in the Middle East. They feel there must be some calculated risk-taking—gambles, if you will. We know, of course, that any peace process with the type of adversaries Israel faces is risky business. And those who become addicted to high-stakes gambling almost inevitably lose it all. When it comes to Israel's survival, political survival at the polls should not even be on the table.

The security of the State of Israel, a country legally established with the consent of the United Nations, is a bottom-line issue in the quest for peace. Any talk about safeguarding Syria and Lebanon from Israeli expansionism would be laughable if it were not being taken so seriously by wishful-thinking international peace brokers. To call Israel expansionist and a threat to the world is as ludicrous as it is irrational. Any nation that has taken land only in response to aggression and then, as it did with Egypt, given it back, is not expansionist. The only stability the Middle East will know, short- or long-term, will be predicated on Israel's security— and Israel's alone. Only when Israel's neighbors become convinced, as the Egyptians and Jordanians seem to have been so far, that Israel has the means, determination, and allied support it needs not only to survive but to rain retribution on those attempting to destroy it, will substantive negotiations over subsidiary issues with fair concessions from both sides be attainable.

Words and Deeds

America's naïveté about the nature and objectives of some of Israel's "peace partners," in and out of Washington, is incredible. Fundamentally, we are a nation of optimists. We are pluralistic, observe separation of church and state, and have no disposition toward killing and conquest in the name of religion. We are, therefore, willing to give almost everyone the benefit of the doubt.

The Middle East, however, is a different world. It is a world where ideologies of radical, religious Islamic elements run counter to Judeo-Christian perceptions of peace and goodwill. In the Qur'an, Allah commands his followers to perpetuate the religion by killing or subjugating all non-Muslims everywhere:

> *Fight and slay the Pagans wherever ye find them, and seize them, beleaguer them, and lie in wait for them in every stratagem [of war]* (surah 9:5).
>
> *Therefore, when ye meet the Unbelievers (in fight), smite at their necks; at length, when ye have thoroughly subdued them, bind a bond firmly (on them)* (surah 47:4).
>
> *Truly Allah loves those who fight in His Cause in battle array, as if they were a solid cemented structure* (surah 61:4).

These are a far cry from Jesus' commands: "Love your enemies, bless those who curse you, do good to those who hate you, and pray for those who spitefully use you and persecute you" (Mt. 5:44).

Moshe Sharon, a professor of Islamic history at Hebrew University in Jerusalem, shed light on some fundamental issues in an article titled "The Islamic Factor in Middle East Politics," published in the January 1994 issue of the monthly magazine *Midstream*. Sharon made a fascinating statement about Islamic "fundamentalism":

> *The term "fundamentalism," so frequently bandied about in connection with contemporary Islamic activity, has in fact, nothing to do with Islam.*
>
> *Fundamentalism emerges directly from the heart of Christian theology. The term applies to a religion based on belief in which the definitions of the articles of faith are essential for the salvation of each believer. The acceptance of the Bible as the true unchangeable words of God is the basis for the fundamental movements in Christianity. In Islam, however, such a problem does not exist. No Muslim who defines himself as a believer . . . would ever doubt that the Koran [Qur'an] is the exact written representation of the Word of Allah.*[7]

A fundamental Christian is one who accepts God's Word as it is, for what it is. Moshe Sharon's perceptive statement effectively counters the current practice of much of the news media and some politicians to throw fundamental Christians into the same pot with every radical terror group in the world. A friend in the Israeli Embassy in Washington, D.C., once forcefully corrected me on the matter. When I referred to Muslim terrorists as Islamic fundamentalists, he said, "No, Elwood, you should never refer to them as fundamentalists.

Fundamentalists are biblically oriented Christians. These people are fanatical Islamic radicals, not fundamentalists!"

"Islam," Sharon wrote, "is a legal system, not a religion based on articles of faith. The Muslim is not 'saved' because he believes in something; his religious credibility is defined by his adherence to Islamic practice. . . . Islam does not differentiate between the two realms of the sacred and the secular, between politics and religion, between church and state."[8]

Furthermore, he said, "The inferior position of the Jew and the Christian is defined by Islamic law, which clearly prevents Jews and Christians from participating in the life of the Islamic state in parity with Sunni Muslims."[9] Therefore, talk of "the establishment of a 'secular, democratic Palestinian Arab state' in which Muslims, Christians and Jews would share the same rights is a contradiction in terms." [10]

Muslim intransigence over the existence of Jewish settlements, or rather, communities, remaining in territories being ceded to the Arabs would bear this out. During a trip to Palestinian Jericho, I sensed from the looks of the Palestinian police that this would never again be the Jericho we had known. We do not need special revelation to perceive that Jewish people will not be welcome in Jericho, Gaza, or the West Bank once Palestinians have their state. Christian tourists will, in all likelihood, be tolerated for their currency deposits in restaurants and gift shops and for whatever largesse that showing a good face will bring from Western nations.

Another complicating factor is revisionist propaganda. Adolf Hitler's propaganda expert, Joseph Goebbels, said, "If you tell a lie big enough and keep repeating it, people will eventually come to believe it." Clearly, he was right. Truth is being swept into the dustbin. History is being rewritten. And historical illiterates in the Western world are swallowing the big lie that Islamic people predated Jewish people in the

Middle East and, therefore, qualify as displaced persons whose land was stolen by marauding descendants of Isaac. This is the same type of revisionism that is attempting to turn fantasy into history by contending that the Holocaust of World War II did not happen. In the revisionist model, Syrians are reinvented as direct descendants of the Old Aramaeans; Iraqis spring from the Summerians, Accadians, and Babylonians; and Jordanians are transformed into Moabites and Ammonites. Meanwhile the Palestinians are shouting that they are the true heirs of the Amorites, Canaanites, and Jebusites from whom David wrested control of Jerusalem.

As if that were not enough, Islam, which did not arise until the 7th century A.D., claims to be the first and only true religion and has rewritten history accordingly. For Islam, human history is regarded as Muslim history. Therefore, Adam has been made a Muslim prophet, along with Noah. Abraham becomes the forerunner of Muhammad and thus a great Muslim prophet. The great Muslim prophet Moses received a revelation identical to the Qur'an. And, for good measure, Jewish Kings David and Solomon have joined the ranks of Muslim prophets. Even Jesus was a Muslim prophet who produced a book like the Qur'an.

Is it any wonder then that the late Palestinian Authority (PA) chieftain and terrorist, Yasser Arafat, once told 300 reporters in Geneva, Switzerland, that Jesus Christ was a Palestinian freedom fighter who led a Palestinian revolt against the Romans? Ironically, the reporters applauded his preposterous statement.

Moshe Sharon concluded his enlightening article with an observation that bears directly on fundamental elements in the peace process today:

> *Islam does not rule out the possibility of a long*
> *period of truce with the enemy as part of its long-*

term policy of war. The enemy may understand such truce as peace.[11]

But in the Islamic scheme of things,

The only alibi for concluding a truce with the enemy, and de facto giving him some sort of legitimacy is when the enemy is too strong. Thus, a strong enemy is a necessary condition for concluding what amounts to peace with him; conversely, a weak enemy obliges the Muslim to renew the war against him.[12]

In Islamic eyes, peace agreements are only a postponement of what they see as the inevitable: the day when jihad will be resumed and the enemy destroyed.

So, with all the talk of "peace in our time," we must listen carefully to what has been said and watch what proponents of revisionist history are doing.

King Saud ibn Abdul Aziz, a king of Saudi Arabia, quoted by the Associated Press, January 9, 1954: "The Arab nations should sacrifice up to 10 million of their 50 million people, if necessary, to wipe out Israel. . . . Israel to the Arab world is like a cancer to the human body; and the only way of remedy is to uproot it, just like a cancer."

The late Syrian president, Hafez Assad, on Radio Damascus, October 16, 1973: "Our forces continue to pressure the enemy and will continue to strike at him until we recover the occupied territory [Golan Heights], and we will then continue until all the land is liberated."

Salah Khalaf (Abu Iyad), in Al-Safir, January 25, 1988: "The establishment of an independent Palestinian state on the West Bank and Gaza Strip does not contradict our ultimate strategic aim, which is the establishment of a democratic state in the entire territory of Palestine, but rather is a step in that direction."

Yasser Arafat, from the Algiers Voice of Palestine, May 13, 1991: "[W]e will continue our revolution and our resistance and our uprising until the banner of our revolution flies over holy Jerusalem and the walls of Jerusalem and the minarets of Jerusalem and the churches of Jerusalem."

Yasser Arafat, Johannesburg, South Africa, 1994, following his signing of the peace accord on the south lawn of the White House: "Join me in a 'Jihad' [holy war] to liberate Jerusalem from the Jews."

Jamal Abdel Hamid Yussef, explaining the military wing of Hamas, February 15, 1995: "Our suicide operations are a message . . . that our people love death. Our goal is to die for the sake of God, and if we live, we want to humiliate Jews and trample on their heads."

Predictably, Assad was tough in negotiations with Israel and the United States. His successor, son Bashar Assad, is as well. Syria's policy to promise nothing and expect everything continues. It seems that the more difficult tyrants are, the more apt they are to gain concessions for their intransigence. Despite Bashar Assad's professed willingness to talk peace, he continues to collaborate with the Iranians and support terrorist organizations, namely, Lebanon's Hezbollah. These people, he has said, are, in fact, "patriots and militants who fight for the liberty and independence of their country . . . such people cannot be called terrorists." It has been all but forgotten that these "freedom fighters" took Americans hostage and bombed U.S. Embassy and Marine barracks in 1983, costing 241 American lives. Their operations today continue from the Syrian-controlled Bekaa Valley in Lebanon, with a primary mission of killing innocent people in northern Israeli settlements.

Following the withdrawal of all Israeli troops from the South Lebanon security zone on May 24, 2000, Hezbollah, we were told, would become benign, peace-loving citizens, restoring the tranquility Israel and its Christian Southern

Lebanese Army collaborators had taken from the area. Considering Assad and Hezbollah's history, this scenario pushed the limits of credibility over the edge, and northern Israel is to this day living under a terrorist arsenal of immense proportions while being battered from time to time by Hezbollah's Katyushas. Although, in 2005, Syria (under U.S. pressure) moved out some of its 40,000 troops stationed in Lebanon, it is doubtful Assad plans to fully abandon the area he regards as a part of Greater Syria.

Finally, all hands were forced to admit that the corrupt, money-grubbing Yasser Arafat failed to be a trustworthy partner in the peace process. For starters, he steadfastly refused to do what he promised when he signed on in Oslo and Washington, namely, rescind the article in the Palestinian Covenant that is actually the basis of the covenant and calls for the destruction of Israel. He also gave little more than lip service to punishing terrorists and shutting down their operations from Gaza, Bethlehem, and Jericho. Of no little consequence to Israelis, who may be called on to undo some unwise commitments in the future, is that Arafat and his successors have amassed a police force seeded with known terrorists from organizations that refuse to relinquish their arms and will ostensibly serve as "peacekeepers" in an eventual Palestinian state.

Is it surprising that some of us are beginning to wonder if the peace process is becoming a bad dream? Christian Zionists, like me, who view these events from a distance, don't see much peace on the horizon.

With these considerations before us, we will look at the war against Israel and, by extension, the war against the West. And we will look at the State of Israel—past, present, and future—from an evangelical, biblical point of view. So even if you haven't been scratching your head along with the rest of us, hopefully you will better understand what is *really* happening in the Middle East and how the volatile situation there indisputably affects even those of us who live half a world away.

ENDNOTES

[1] Khaled Abu Toameh, "Mashaal: 'Beginning of end for Israel,'" August 18, 2005 <jpost.com/servlet/Satellite?pagename=JPost/JPArticle/ShowFull&cid=1124245484297&p=1101615860782>.

[2] "Alleged Hamas Bombmaker Resurfaces," The Associated Press, August 27, 2005 <cbsnews.com/stories/2005/08/26/world/main798705.shtml>.

[3] Toameh.

[4] Ibid.

[5] "Palestinian Clerics Association Deputy Director on Hizbullah's Al Manar TV: 'We Will Enter Palestine as Conquerors, Not Through Negotiations But Through Jihad'; According to Prophetic Tradition, All Palestine Will Be Liberated and The Zionist Entity Wiped Out," Special Dispatch Series No. 967, August 23, 2005 <http://memri.org/bin/latestnews.cgi?ID=SD96705>.

[6] Toameh.

[7] Moshe Sharon, "The Islamic Factor in Middle East Politics," *Midstream*, (January 1994), 7–8.

[8] Ibid., 8.

[9] Ibid.

[10] Ibid., 9.

[11] Ibid., 10.

[12] Ibid.

CHAPTER 2

⟡⟢

BOMBS IN THE MARKETPLACE

On July 30, 1997, two young Arab men embarked on a homicide mission with the intent to kill and maim as many innocent Israelis as possible. Their target was Jerusalem's Mahane Yehuda market, an open-air shopping strip jammed tightly between buildings in what looks somewhat like a wide alley. The place is perpetually crowded with people who come to pick the best of the fresh fruits and vegetables for their tables. It is the market where, for years, our friend Zvi's wife, Naomi, has gone every day of the week to do her shopping.

About 1:15 that afternoon, when the place was especially busy, the men got out of a car and walked casually into the market. Each carried a briefcase. They quickly stationed themselves within sight of each other among people more intent on selecting vegetables than eyeing their executioners.

Then they threw the toggle switches that set off their devices. Powerful bombs exploded, shredding their victims to pieces with screws and nails that had been packed into the devices to ensure maximum carnage. By the time rescuers arrived, they found nearly 200 people on the ground, buried under fruit, vegetables, and debris from the stalls that had collapsed from the force of the blast. A body count revealed 15 dead, including the two bombers, and 168 wounded.

It wasn't the first suicide bombing. But it was a harbinger of evil things to come—a vicious, Islamic war conducted against unarmed Israeli men, women, children, infants, the crippled, and the elderly. The intent is not only to kill but to cripple and demoralize the nation of Israel, as well as "recapture" the land "for Allah." The extreme extent of Muslim cruelty toward the Jewish people is often beyond comprehension.

For example, in 2004, 34-year-old Tali Hatuel, eight months pregnant, was driving with her four daughters—ages eleven, nine, seven, and two. Palestinian terrorists ambushed her car, pumped bullets into her stomach and face, then riddled the little girls' faces with bullets until all five in the car were dead. In 2001, 10-month-old Shalhevet Pass was in her stroller when a Palestinian terrorist deliberately aimed at her head, shot, and killed her.

From September 2000, when the current war began, to January 2006, terrorists killed 1,084 Israelis and injured 7,633, according to statistics from the Israel Defense Forces. To that point, Israel had endured 22,406 terrorist attacks, including those in the West Bank and what was Jewish Gaza. Statistically, that amounts to one attack a day in a country smaller than the state of New Jersey.

Hardly an Israeli is left who has not lost loved ones to terrorism. Many, in fact, have lost more than one person. And thousands have been crippled. It is common for a single family to have someone dead, plus a child who has lost a leg and another child who has lost an arm. When Israelis see someone who is disfigured, they don't think, *That person is sick.* They think, *That person was caught in a terrorist attack.*

Since the so-called peace process began, death and mayhem have only accelerated for the Jews. It is what they have come to expect from their "peace partners." Some say that what has transpired is more akin to a war process than a quest for peace. And the body count verifies that assessment. More Israelis have been killed and wounded during terrorist attacks than in any comparable period since the State of Israel was born in 1948.

The Silence Is Deafening

After the first official homicide bombing in October 1994, Warren Christopher, then U.S. secretary of state, was quoted as saying the United States was declaring "war" on terrorism. He was correct in asserting that a war was in progress. But we have yet to witness any significant response from the counterterrorists in the Western world. There is an abundance of tough rhetoric. However, as long as no tangible action accompanies it—severe action, that is, that proves there is a heavy price to pay for killing innocent people—terrorism will not subside.

Not only does the evil go virtually unpunished, but whenever such attacks occur, the world blames Israel and yells at it to give up more land and make concessions that no civilized nation should make when in a functional state of war. In the meantime, Islamic leaders continue to train, arm, and harbor young Muslim fanatics and send them to their deaths with impunity. There is no international outrage. On the contrary, there is silence. And the silence in the corridors of the United Nations is especially deafening.

Clearly, the UN is no friend of Israel. Books could be written on the subject. But one need go no further than to compare the UN's reaction to Israel's legitimate construction of a housing development—Har Homa—and the vicious bombing at the Mahane Yehuda market. It is a quick study because of the proximity of the events. Har Homa incorporated fewer than 460 acres and was not near any Arab populations. In fact, 75 percent of the land was expropriated from Jews.[1] Nevertheless, a nettled Yasser Arafat demanded veto power over every brick the Jews planned to lay in or around Jerusalem. And he was rewarded with a 131–3 UN vote to condemn the Israeli government for daring to stand by its decision to build. But when the bombs went off in Mahane Yehuda and the charred, bloodied, mangled bodies of

25

innocent Israelis were carried out, the UN kept quiet. The families of the dead would wait in vain for the international "keepers of world peace" to register a 130-plus vote to condemn those who conspire to drive screws and nails into unsuspecting Jews who are out for an afternoon of shopping.

While the UN persists in condemning Israel for protecting itself against those determined to destroy the Jewish state, it does nothing to condemn the Palestinians for the atrocities they commit "in the name of Allah." Shooting defenseless Israeli children in their beds and strollers apparently is okay with this world body of peacekeepers.

On the Sabbath morning of April 27, 2002, a terrorist burst into the bedroom of three small children in the Shefi family home in Adora. He shot five-year-old Danielle in her bed; shot her siblings, ages four and two; and shot her mother, who was trying desperately to protect them. Danielle died on the spot. The rest were wounded.[2]

On April 3, 2004, the Zagha family finished their evening meal and gathered in the living room to sing and enjoy a relaxing time exchanging pleasantries and stories. Later Esther Zagha put four of their six children to bed before she and her husband, Yaakov, retired for the night.

Hani, 14, the eldest, remained awake. At about 1 A.M. she got scared when she heard gunfire outside the house and ran to awaken her parents. Hani realized immediately that a terrorist had infiltrated the community, and she ran through the house screaming for the children to get under their beds. Even more terrifying was the sound of the terrorist attempting to break into their house through a window.

Yaakov, 40, an immigrant from Argentina, picked up his handgun and ran out the door to confront the intruder. Yaakov was immediately shot and killed. Meanwhile, Hani picked up her three-year-old sister and began running toward the secure area inside the house. Before she could reach the room, a bullet struck her. Despite her injuries, the 14-year-old managed to drag herself and her younger sister to safety.

The terrorist was finally shot as he ran up the street spraying bullets in every direction. Hamas quickly claimed responsibility and extolled the murderer as a martyr.

Esther, Hani, and the children stayed in the shelter 20 minutes waiting for Yaakov to return and tell them it was safe to come out. At the time they had no idea what had happened to him.

"He didn't return the whole time we were waiting," Hani said of her father. "Slowly I realized . . . " Her voiced trailed off.

While terrorists rejoiced, the seven remaining members of the Zagha family were left without a husband and father. And the legacy of that awful night will be with them for the remainder of their lives. Hani recalled the tragedy:

> We understood immediately that it was a terrorist and I screamed to my father. I tried to continue running for the shelter room, but I couldn't walk anymore because I was injured, so I fell down and crawled to the shelter, with my little sister Tehiya in my arms. If my father hadn't gone outside, maybe none of us would be alive. People tell me that I saved my little sister, but my father was a hero and saved the whole family.[3]

Such terrorism is not a cottage industry confined to Israel, the Middle East, or Africa. It has become a global business with tentacles spreading all over the world. And while those of us in the West may derive some degree of comfort because the phenomenon appears relegated to half a world away, there is actually no place of refuge. No safe rooms, if you will.

When he took office as head of Hamas, the late Abdel Aziz

Rantisi joined Osama bin Laden and other terror kingpins in declaring war on the United States and its citizens. Judging by what happened to the Zagha family, the kind of war Hamas wants to wage is in the living rooms of Americans and our Western allies.

The Zagha family in northern Samaria, Israel, lives 6,000 miles from America. But as things stand today, they are practically the people next door. On September 11, 2001, our neighbors died in the Twin Towers of the World Trade Center in New York, on the fields of Pennsylvania, and in the halls of the Pentagon in Washington, D.C. The war on terror is a real war—relentless, deadly, and personal. And the next time the enemy strikes, it may not be at a neighbor 6,000 miles away. It may be in your front yard or mine. Of course, there is no reason to believe the UN will do anything useful about that either.

In 2006 I listened to a Hamas terrorist being interviewed about an incident that took the lives of six Palestinian civilians. Israel was blamed because the deaths allegedly occurred when Israel responded to Arab rocket fire on Israeli towns from the Gaza Strip.

The man raved about the deliberate killing of innocent people and Israel's so-called determination to destroy the Palestinians, calling the incident a war crime. What he failed to mention was why the Israeli attack had taken place or why Palestinian terrorists have murdered more than 1,000 Israelis and injured thousands of others in a concerted, declared campaign to kill Israeli civilians.

And, of course, he further failed to mention that the Palestinians themselves probably killed the victims. In a June 16, 2006, column titled "Who Is to Blame for Grief on a Beach?" *Washington Post* columnist Charles Krauthammer exposed the entire fiasco: "Shrapnel taken from the victims (treated at *Israeli* hospitals—some "genocide") were not the ordnance used in Israeli artillery. . . . Aerial photography revealed no crater that could have been caused by Israeli artillery."

But the clincher was this Krauthammer observation:

> *Who is to blame if Palestinians are setting up rocket launchers to attack Israel—and placing them 400 yards from a beach crowded with Palestinian families on the Muslim Sabbath?*
>
> *Answer: This is another example of the Palestinians' classic and cowardly human-shield tactic—attacking innocent Israeli civilians while hiding behind innocent Palestinian civilians.*

And while Israeli officials immediately launch investigations into such incidents, Palestinians not only refuse to investigate their homicide bombings but celebrate Palestinian murderers as heroes of the "resistance."

Whatever one's political convictions, the core issue is the survival of a people who have a legitimate right to their place in the Promised Land.

How Long, Oh Lord?

There is little new about the current state of indifference toward atrocities committed against Jewish people. An overwrought prophet, Jeremiah, uttered the classic lament in mourning the destruction of Jerusalem by the Babylonians:

> *Is it nothing to you, all you who pass by? Behold and see if there is any sorrow like my sorrow, which has been brought on me, which the LORD has inflicted in the day of His fierce anger* (Lam. 1:12).

The Jewish captivity in Babylon was one of the low-water marks in the history of the Chosen People. Jeremiah and his companion prophets mourned for a city and a people who were forced to pass through the fire. But there is a word of hope and promise that is not found by a cursory examination of the inexpressibly terrible circumstances in which Israel and its people have been caught over the centuries. This word of comfort does not come from philosophers or the "wise" of this world. It comes from the Book of all books, the Bible. Ironically, in times of great stress, Jewish people, like many Gentiles, often turn *from* the faith of the fathers rather than *to* it.

Yet Jeremiah, the other prophets, and the writers of the psalms directed their laments and cries for explanations to the God who brought the nation and its people into existence. Not only did they receive answers for their frustrated minds, they also received evidence that, in spite of how bad things appeared, God was with them.

Isaiah, in reference to the Babylonian exile, was told,

> *When you pass through the waters, I will be with you; and through the rivers, they shall not overflow you. When you walk through the fire, you shall not be burned, nor shall the flame scorch you. . . . Fear not, for I am with you* (Isa. 43:2, 5).

Surpassingly marvelous words, these, because they bear two tremendous affirmations. First, God will never forsake the nation of Israel. Second, God guarantees its preservation by His own presence. The question, therefore, is never, "Where is God when we need Him?" Rather, it is, "Where are we in reference to Him and in obedience to what He is attempting to teach us?"

The psalmist asked the question during a time of prolonged distress:

> *How long O Lord? Will You forget me forever? How long will You hide Your face from me? . . . How long will my enemy be exalted over me?* (Ps. 13:1–2).

Although the writer did not, in the context of the psalm, receive an immediate answer, there was cause for hope and triumph to invade his soul. "But," he declared, "I have trusted in Your mercy; my heart shall rejoice in Your salvation. I will sing to the LORD, because He has dealt bountifully with me" (vv. 5–6).

This, in the end, is the answer to every inexplicable dilemma we face. As bombs continue to explode and the world continues to do nothing to help struggling little Israel, we would do well to remember Isaiah 43:1, where God promises,

> *Thus says the LORD, who created you, O Jacob, and He who formed you, O Israel: "Fear not, for I have redeemed you; I have called you by your name; you are Mine."*

In Psalm 13 He put it this way: "My heart shall rejoice in Your salvation" (v. 5). Circumstances fluctuate with the times and seasons of life; personal peace never does—if it rests in the Lord and His promised Redeemer.

The world is evil because the human heart is evil. As God said through the prophet Jeremiah, "The heart is deceitful above all things, and desperately wicked; who can know it?" (17:9). The answer is, "I, the LORD, search the heart, I test the mind, even to give every man according to his ways, according to the fruit of his doings" (v. 10). In the end, God Himself will mete out justice. After that, the bombs will stop forever; and Israel will be the victor.

> *Violence shall no longer be heard in your land, neither wasting nor destruction within your borders; but you shall call your walls Salvation, and your gates Praise. Also your people shall all be righteous; they shall inherit the land forever, the branch of My planting, the work of My hands, that I may be glorified* (Isa. 60:18, 21).

Meanwhile, the God of Israel stands ready to provide individual peace during suffering. We who have found that peace in Jesus commend it, along with our fervent prayers to all who suffer through tribulation too great for the mind to grasp or too mighty for our little strength to overcome.

ENDNOTES

[1] "Har Homa" <jewishvirtuallibrary.org/jsource/Peace/har_homa.html>.

[2] "Target: Israeli Children" <education.gov.il/children/page_42_b.htm>.

[2] "Yaakov (Kobi) Zagha," Israel Ministry of Foreign Affairs, April 3, 2004 <israel.org/MFA/Terrorism-+Obstacle+to+Peace/Memorial/2004/Yaakov+(Kobi)+Zaga.htm>.

CHAPTER 3

⟨∞⟩

A NEW CLASH OF CIVILIZATIONS

In the 1930s the Jewish people faced a different enemy. And by the 1940s, that enemy ended up engulfing the civilized world in a gigantic struggle for survival. The Nazi menace threatened all democracies in Europe and North America. In effect, World War II represented a clash of religious, political, and social ideas that could not coexist on this planet. The world was divided into Axis and Allied forces locked in a life-and-death fight to the finish.

Adolf Hitler and his brownshirts came to power when Germany, in the aftermath of World War I, was gripped by poverty, humiliation, and a deep-seated hatred for the forces that destroyed its dream of subjugating Europe. Hitler, who despised both Jews and Christians and saw himself as a messiah to rescue the German people, ascended to power with grand promises to improve the lot of the impoverished nation and create a *Reich* (German for "empire") that would endure for a thousand years—a millennium devoid of any god but himself and his kingdom.

Unfortunately, Hitler had admirers and apologists in the very countries he intended to destroy. Their catastrophic miscalculation cost 50 million people their lives and consigned millions more to the horror of memories they could never be rid of.

Ironically, the same thing is happening today. After decades of trying to build a better world and create a more benevolent global society, we find ourselves again in the throes of a struggle similar to the scourge of the Fuehrer and his minions. It is a battle of enormous magnitude.

Ostensibly, this is a war against terrorism and is aimed at men whose reason to exist is to take the lives of innocent men, women, and children—particularly Jewish and Christian—and to destroy societies with which they disagree.

For years, people in America and the West have been aware, if barely so, that terrorism threatens the existence of freedom and democracy in the Middle East. We read the newspapers with our morning coffee and watched the evening news after dinner, somewhat cognizant of the fight between the Israelis and Palestinians.

But on the morning of September 11, 2001, Americans awakened to the horrible realization that our country and our people are marked for destruction. As the president called the nation to arms and unity for the long struggle ahead, and citizens everywhere unfurled American flags in an unprecedented show of patriotism, the United States was plunged headlong into a state of war. But what kind of war? And against whom?

As we learned that the terrorists were Muslims from the Middle East, government officials embarked on a campaign to assure us that these men were but a radical sliver of fanatics, wholly outside the mainstream of Islam. "We don't want to turn this into a religious war," was the oft-repeated refrain. Their fear of a backlash against Arab Americans and Muslims was understandable. Immediately statements that Islam is a loving religion and that the Qur'an in no way condones or encourages such belligerent conduct filled news media reports. Anyone who dared to differ was regarded as a politically incorrect bigot worthy of shunning.

Admittedly, most Muslims probably are not bent on killing their neighbors and creating mayhem in their communities. And people who attack Arabs or Muslims because of their nationality or religious beliefs should be punished. But does this conflict truly have nothing to do with religion? Bin Laden and other voices within the Islamic world itself beg to differ.

"Yes, This Is About Islam"

Salman Rushdie, a Muslim who lived for years under a death sentence issued by Muslim clerics for allegedly blaspheming Islam in his 1988 book, *The Satanic Verses*, wrote the following in an article titled "Yes, This Is About Islam":

> *"This isn't about Islam." The world's leaders have been repeating this mantra for weeks, partly in the virtuous hope of deterring reprisal attacks on innocent Muslims living in the West, partly because if the United States is to maintain its coalition against terror it can't afford to suggest that Islam and terrorism are in any way related.*
>
> *The trouble with this necessary disclaimer is that it isn't true. If this isn't about Islam, why the world-wide Muslim demonstrations in support of Osama bin Laden and Al Qaeda?*
>
> *Highly motivated organizations of Muslim men (oh, for the voices of Muslim women to be heard!) have been engaged for the past 30 years or so growing radical political movements. . . . Poverty is their great helper, and the fruit of their efforts is paranoia. This paranoid Islam, which blames outsiders, "infidels," for all the ills of Muslim societies, and whose proposed remedy is the closing of those societies to the rival project of modernity, is* **presently the fastest growing version of Islam in the world** *[emphasis ours].*[1]

Osama bin Laden himself confirmed Rushdie's views in a

speech, the entire text of which was made available by the BBC. Here is a portion of it:

> *This war is fundamentally religious. The people of the East are Muslims. They sympathized with Muslims against the people of the West, who are the crusaders. Those who try to cover this crystal clear fact, which the entire world has admitted, are deceiving the Islamic nation. . . . Under no circumstances should we forget this enmity between us and the infidels. For, the enmity is based on creed.*[2]

Bin Laden also condemned Arab leaders who turn to the United Nations for peace negotiations, saying that this amounts to a renunciation of Islam:

> *Those who claim that they are the leaders of the Arabs and continue to appeal to the United Nations have disavowed what was revealed to Prophet Muhammad. . . . Those who refer things to the international legitimacy have disavowed the legitimacy of the Holy Book and the tradition of Prophet Muhammad. . . . Under no circumstances should any Muslim or sane person resort to the United Nations. The United Nations is nothing but a tool of crime.*[3]

Muslims, he said, "must understand the nature and truth of this conflict so that it will be easy for them to determine where they stand."[4]

Samuel P. Huntington, in his book *The Clash of Civilizations and the Remaking of World Order*, predicted years ago the colossal clash we are now witnessing.

Among the prominent Muslim journalists whom Huntington quoted is Egyptian journalist Mohammed

Sid-Ahmed, who commented on the core of the conflict in writing "of a growing clash between the Judeo-Christian Western ethic and the Islamic revival movement, which is now stretching from the Atlantic in the west to China in the east." A leading Tunisian lawyer stated, "There is a conflict between civilizations."

In summary, Huntington wrote:

> *The underlying problem for the West is not Islamic fundamentalism. It is Islam, a different civilization whose people are convinced of the superiority of their culture and are obsessed with the inferiority of their power. The problem for Islam is not the CIA or the U.S. Department of Defense. It is the West, a different civilization whose people are convinced of the universality of their culture and believe that their superior, if declining power, imposes on them the obligation to extend that culture throughout the world. These are the basic ingredients that fuel the conflict between Islam and the West.*[5]

It's Not About America and Israel

This information about the true essence of the war on terror emphatically answers some important questions: Is U.S. support of Israel the cause of America's woes? If America sold out Israel and backed the Palestinians, would it become safe from terrorism? And if you believe the answer to those questions is yes, why then are Muslims slaughtering non-American Christians?

If Israel did not exist, the situation would be the same. Israel represents a small bastion of Western values, freedoms, democratic ideals, and religious tolerance that threatens militant Muslims and their intimidating control over their people. To them, the Jewish presence is a humiliating intrusion into a speck of land they consider sacred to Allah and Islam. In a culture where religion drives both the political and military machinery, this factor is immense.

Interestingly, a huge influx of Muslim immigrants has been welcomed into the Western world; but Muslims have no such tolerance for Jewish immigrants who are not even invading Muslim countries but, rather, are moving to the Jewish state, which is a legitimate nation and member of the international community. In addition, Muslims are equally hostile toward Christians—American or otherwise—who immigrate to Islamic lands.

Responding to a statement by former U.S. Secretary of State Colin Powell concerning his vision "of a region [the Middle East] where all people worship God in a spirit of tolerance and understanding," journalist Cal Thomas wrote: "He [Powell] cannot point to a single Islamic state where tolerance and understanding are extended to non-Muslims. What makes him think," concluded Thomas, "a Palestinian state would exhibit anything but hostility toward anyone who does not toe its political and theological line?"[6]

This is a battle of civilizations. And it brings to the surface another situation that most public officials and virtually all of the secular media have concealed for much too long: militant Muslims are slaughtering Christians by the thousands in a host of countries. If the only issue between Islam and America is the U.S. alliance with Israel—if Islam is a loving, tolerant religion—then why are roving bands of terrorists and killers making war on Christians in the name of jihad, the Qur'an, and Allah?

Nigerians, Sudanese, Egyptians, Lebanese, Indonesians, Pakistanis, and others who follow Jesus are not Americans, nor are they Jews. They are marked for annihilation, however, because they are Christians and refuse to bow the knee to Allah.

The reality of the conflict is easy to see. It is global in scope and unremitting in intensity. And in Muslim lands, there abides a determination to drive out any and all people who represent Judeo-Christian commitment, Western ideas, and the stench of the "infidel."

No one said it better than bin Laden himself. He has neatly divided most of the world into two camps: Crusader and Muslim. He believes he is fighting a continuation of the war that Muslims fought in the 13th century when they recaptured Jerusalem from the Crusaders. He has accused President George W. Bush of conducting a "Crusade campaign against Islam." It does not matter to bin Laden if you vote Republican or Democrat, are a covenant theologian or a dispensationalist, or if you don't even understand the meaning of those terms. To bin Laden and radical Islam, Christians are Crusaders, Westerners are Crusaders, Crusaders are infidels, and infidels must be killed. So, my dear reader, as long as you remain a non-Muslim, you are an enemy of Islam. These "battles," bin Laden said, are "part of a chain of the long, fierce, and ugly crusader war."[7] Israel is not the main issue. Islam is.

Hitler had a vision. He wanted to establish the Third Reich—the Third Empire. Radical Islamists have a vision. They want to establish a global Islamic empire. Israel is in their way. And so is America. When President Bush and Western leaders said the war on terror is one we dare not lose, they stated a reality. The outcome of this struggle will shape the future of life on this earth. And regardless of the cost, we must see it through. There is no alternative to terrorism but to stop it.

ENDNOTES

[1] Salman Rushdie, "This Is About Islam," in "Israel News, Eye on Israel," National Unity Coalition for Israel, November 2, 2001 <israelunitycoalition.com>.

[2] "Bin Laden rails against Crusaders and UN," November 3, 2001 <news.bbc.co.uk/1/hi/world/monitoring/media_reports/1636782.stm>.

[3] Ibid.

[4] Ibid.

[5] Samuel P. Huntington, *The Clash of Civilizations and the Remaking of World Order* (New York: Simon and Schuster, 1996), 218.

[6] Cal Thomas, "Powell's 'Vision' Is a Mirage," November 25, 2001 <jpost.com/Editions/2001/11/25/Opinion/Opinion.38666.html.

[7] "Bin Laden rails against Crusaders and UN."

CHAPTER 4

✎✖✎

ISLAMIC IMPERIALISM IN THE REAL WORLD

When the majority of the secular news media laughs at the idea of Islamic imperialism, it closes its eyes to the bully that is moving in next door. U.S. Vice President Dick Cheney has warned that Islamists speak of a "seventh-century caliphate" to be "governed by Sharia law, the most rigid interpretation of the Koran." Defense Secretary Donald Rumsfeld elaborated: "Iraq would serve as the base of a new Islamic caliphate to extend throughout the Middle East, and which would threaten legitimate governments in Europe, Africa, and Asia."[1]

The New York Times quickly branded these views as balderdash. In an article titled *21st-Century Warnings of a Threat Rooted in the 7th*, Elisabeth Bumiller opined,

> *A number of scholars and former government officials take strong issue with the administration's warning about a new caliphate. . . . They say that although Al Qaeda's statements do indeed describe a caliphate as a goal, the administration is exaggerating the magnitude of the threat as it seeks to gain support for its policies in Iraq.*[2]

Oh really? Perhaps Ms. Bumiller should examine the evidence and the words of the late, Jordanian-born head of al-Qaida in Iraq, Abu Musab al-Zarqawi: "We will either achieve victory over the human race or we will pass to the eternal life."[3] Americans, he said, are "the most cowardly of God's creatures."[4]

In an October 2005 speech to the National Endowment for Democracy, President Bush accurately described today's most aggressive, carnivorous clan: Islamist imperialists. He said:

- They have a "murderous ideology" and pose the "great challenge of our new century."
- They intend to end Western influence in the Muslim world, overthrow all moderate Muslim governments, and establish a "radical Islamic empire that spans from Spain to Indonesia."
- They aspire to "develop weapons of mass destruction, to destroy Israel, to intimidate Europe, to assault the American people, and to blackmail our government into isolation."
- They want to "enslave whole nations and intimidate the world."[5]

Realistic journalist Daniel Pipes believes the president was still too restrictive in describing the dimensions of the Islamic vision:

> *His limiting the "radical Islamic empire" (or caliphate) to just the Spain-to-Indonesia region [is inadequate], for Islamists have a global vision that requires control over non-Muslim countries too— and specifically the United States. . . . Only when Americans realize that the Islamists intend to replace the U.S. Constitution with Shariah will they enter the fourth and final era of this war.*[6]

In his book *The Islamic Declaration*, published in 1970, the late Alija Izetbegovic, ex-president of Bosnia and leader of its Muslim Party of Democratic Action (SDA), argued for the "incompatibility of Islam with non-Islamic systems" and, in so doing, stated the case for all Islamic radicals: "There can be neither peace nor coexistence between the Islamic religion and non-Islamic social and political institutions."[7]

Samuel P. Huntington elaborated:

> *When the Islamic movement is strong enough it must take power and create an Islamic republic. In this new state, it is particularly important that education and the media [quoting Izetbegovic] "should be in the hands of people whose Islamic moral and intellectual authority is indisputable."*[8]

The fundamental problem is a clash of civilizations.

Islamists have made themselves clear: A caliphate—an Islamic global empire—is their vision. And in Pipes's words, "It requires monumental denial not to acknowledge it, but we Westerners have risen to the challenge."[9] Indeed. It seems that self-delusion is becoming a cottage industry in the Western world.

Tripping Over the Obvious

For starters, it is impossible to ignore radical Islam's military, religious, or terrorist campaigns in Iraq, Afghanistan, Israel, Sudan, Algeria, Nigeria, Kenya, Iran, Pakistan, Yemen, Ethiopia, Armenia, Albania, Chechnya, Daghestan, Tajikistan, Uzbekistan, Indonesia, Egypt, Jordan, the Philippines, United States, Great Britain, France, Germany, the Netherlands, Russia, Spain, Argentina, and the list goes on.

But the most telling evidence in this clash of civilizations is found where most Westerners have chosen not to go, that is, the relentless war against Christians in countries where they are most vulnerable. There, where believers have virtually no defenders, Islamists prey on Christians as carnivorous animals prey on their victims. Christians of all persuasions are fleeing Muslim countries. And the "single greatest cause of this emigration is pressure from radical Islam," wrote Jonathan Adelman and Agota Kuperman:

> *To be sure, there have been other reasons for the exodus. Educated Middle Eastern Christians sometimes emigrate for economic reasons. Some have left to avoid the endless procession of violent conflicts. . . . But an entire group does not cavalierly abandon a homeland in which its ancestors have lived for nearly 2,000 years simply because of the allures of a more prosperous society. Such people have to be pushed out, too. And that is precisely what radical Islamists are managing to do.*[10]

Moving Out, Moving In

In the past 20 years an estimated 2 million Christians have opted to exit the Middle East. And if the trend continues, some experts believe that in the next 50 years, there will be no significant Christian presence in the region.

The area controlled by the Palestinians and slated for Palestinian statehood exemplifies the phenomenon. In 1950 Christians there constituted 15 percent of the Arab population. That figure has reportedly fallen to only 2 percent today.

According to Adelman and Kuperman, "Today three-fourths of all Bethlehem Christians live abroad, and more Jerusalem Christians live in Sydney, Australia, than in the place of their birth. Indeed, Christians now comprise just 2.5 percent of Jerusalem."[11]

During a live broadcast from a mosque in Gaza, Dr. Ahmad Abu Halabiya, a member of the Palestinian Authority–appointed Fatwa Council and former acting rector of the Islamic University of Gaza, stated:

> *From here, Allah the almighty has called upon us not to ally with the Jews or the Christians, not to like them, not to become their partners, not to support them, and not to sign agreements with them . . . as Allah said: "O you who believe, do not take the Jews and the Christians as allies, for they are allies one of another. Who from among you takes them as allies will indeed be of them"* (Middle East Research Institute 2000).[12]

In street-level terms, Halabiya's message translates into discrimination and violence against, and even death for, Christian Palestinians. They live in fear. Christian girls are particular targets of public harassment and rape. A 23-year-old Christian Palestinian teacher from Beit Sahour said the discrimination began after Arafat came to power in 1993. "Before, [there were] no things like this. We could go to everyplace we wanted; we could walk in streets," she said. But now, "I don't walk alone on the street because of this bad thing."[13]

Another woman commented, "They spit at us, try to force us to wear headscarves, and in the [Islamic] fasting month of Ramadan . . . the Palestinian police even arrest us for smoking or eating on the streets. . . . The Muslims want to get rid of us, they want us to live like them."[14]

Land confiscation, extortion from Christian businesses, rape of Christian women, and murder have been reported but largely ignored by Palestinian authorities and the outside world. When an 18-year-old Palestinian Muslim stabbed to death the 14-year-old nephew of a convert to Christianity as a teacher watched, police were never contacted; and members of the victim's family were told to come and pick up the body.

And while Christians are being driven out of the Middle East, Muslims by the thousands are moving West and bringing with them their commitment to Sharia Muslim law and Islamic exclusivism.

Oriana Fallaci, the late outspoken adversary of Islamo-fascism, sounded an alarm in a speech while receiving an award in New York for her unwavering commitment to human rights: "I do not see Islamic terrorism as the main weapon of the war that the sons of Allah have unleashed upon us. It is the bloodiest, but not the most pernicious or catastrophic aspect of this war." Far more dangerous, she said, is the massive, unrestricted Muslim immigration that has flooded Europe with at least 25 million Islamics, a number expected to double in 10 years and create a Muslim Europe by 2100.[15]

The impact of the Islamic invasion of Europe, along with its consequences, has already been experienced through riots and bombings in European Union countries. Contemplating the problems in the Netherlands after a Muslim there viciously stabbed to death filmmaker Theo Van Gogh in 2004 because a Van Gogh film criticized Islam's treatment of women, Arnaud de Borchgrave wrote:

> *Could the Netherlands be a curtain-raiser for a wider clash of civilizations in the old Continent? Hundreds of thousands of young Muslims in Europe are potential jihadis, according to European intelligence chiefs speaking not for publication. They have been warning their political masters about the tinderboxes that many Muslim communities have become.*[16]

The global scale of the Islamic dream of a caliphate is demonstrated in the ongoing war in places like Indonesia, where militant Islamists are gaining ground at an alarming rate and saturating the earth with the blood of thousands of Christian victims. Wrote Jamie Glazov for FrontPage Magazine.com:

> *This development is of crisis proportions, since Indonesia plays a crucial role in guaranteeing security in Asia. This year's second Bali terror attack was only the symbol of Islamism's skyrocketing war on the country. Indeed, jihadists are intensely concentrating on annihilating any non-Muslim presence in Indonesia.*[17]

Why Then the Silence?

If, as is so thoroughly documented, such egregious genocide and widespread human rights transgressions are taking place, why the silence? Why is there so little international outrage, especially in Western democracies that should oppose such atrocities and take action to halt the Islamic dream of a new caliphate and global empire?

Actually, it's more of the same old story that undervalues human life in favor of "national interest." While nuclear and large-scale military aggression occupy the international roundtable, the jihad-driven murder and mutilation of individuals and destruction of religious (particularly Christian) communities attract little but lip service and promises. The U.S. Congress has repeatedly passed legislation condemning human rights violations in countries doing business with America. The International Religious Freedom Act passed by the House and Senate and signed into law by President Bill Clinton in October 1998 is specific. Violations of religious freedom include "arbitrary prohibitions on, restrictions of, or punishment for":

> *(i) Assembling for peaceful religious activities such as worship, preaching, and prayer, including*

arbitrary registration requirements; (ii) speaking freely about one's religious beliefs; (iii) changing one's religious beliefs and affiliation; (iv) possession and distribution of religious literature, including Bibles; or (v) raising one's children in the religious teachings and practices of one's choice.[18]

But there's a catch. Wrote Justus Reid Weiner:

However, the caveats written into the International Religious Freedom Act allow the President to subordinate actions taken against violating states to the national interest of the United States. . . . Combined with the waiver clause, this clause renders the International Religious Freedom Act virtually useless, unable to accomplish its intended goals.[19]

Clinton had opposed a prior bill on the grounds that it would make it impossible for America to put *national security and trade concerns* ahead of fighting religious persecution.

When Palestinian Christians persecuted by the Palestinian Authority complained to a State Department official, "the official's recommendation was for the Christians to keep a low profile or to seek asylum in another country," reported Weiner.[20]

The Moderate Muslim Majority

British Prime Minister Tony Blair has said, "The best defense of the Muslim community in this country is for the mainstream Muslim community to take on the extremists within their midst." Mr. Blair is correct. The problem, however, is locating the Muslim "mainstream." There are, indeed, rivulets of courageous Muslims who speak out, many under the threat of death from the bin Ladens and others who, we are repeatedly told, "hijacked a peaceful and loving religion" and are little more than a bloody aberration.

But where is the tangible evidence that there is a "peaceful and loving" Muslim mainstream? Some speculate that there is no such thing—it simply does not exist.

Figures for the Muslim population in the United States vary widely from approximately 2 million to as many as 7 million. Whatever the population, the important factor is the heavy Saudi Arabian influence. Haviv Rettig reported in *The Jerusalem Post* that terrorism expert Yehudit Barsky said, "Extremist organizations continue to claim the mantle of leadership" over American Islam:

> *The power of the extremist Wahhabi form of Islam in the United States was created with generous Saudi financing of American Muslim communities over the past few decades. Over 80 percent of the mosques in the United States "have been radicalized by Saudi money and influence," Barsky said.*[21]

And with the Saudi-sponsored mosques come Saudi clerics who indoctrinate adherents in the Saudi brand of Wahhabi ideology that promotes Sharia plus hatred of America, Jews, and Israel. Rettig continued:

> *This Saudi strategy was being carried out [in Barsky's words] "all over the world, from America to Bangladesh," with Saudis investing $70–80 billion in the endeavor over three decades.*[22]

Because imams who are less than friendly to their host countries wield heavy influence over their brethren, it follows that it would be difficult for Muslim moderates, who may either share the same global aspirations or are intimidated into silence, to mount a serious counterattack against Islamic terrorists.

Freedom House, an organization committed to democracy and freedom, sent Muslim volunteers into 15 prominent mosques from New York to San Diego. Daniel Pipes reported that they collected 200 books "and other publications disseminated by Saudi Arabia (some 90% in Arabic) in mosque libraries, publication racks, and bookstores. What they found can only be described as horrifying. These writings—each and every one of them sponsored by the kingdom—espouse an anti-Christian, anti-Semitic, misogynist, jihadist, and supremacist outlook."[23] Pipes said they all do the following:

- *"Reject Christianity as a valid faith:* Any Muslim who believes 'that churches are houses of God and that God is worshiped therein is an infidel.'
- *"Insist that Islamic law be applied:* On a range of issues, from women (who must be veiled) to apostates from Islam ('should be killed'), the Saudi publications insist on full enforcement of sharia in America.
- *"See non-Muslims as the enemy:* 'Be dissociated from the infidels, hate them for their religion, leave them, never rely on them for support, do not admire them, and always oppose them in every way according to Islamic law.'
- *"See America as hostile territory:* 'It is forbidden for a Muslim to become a citizen of a country governed by infidels because this is a means of acquiescing to their infidelity and accepting all their erroneous ways.'
- *"Prepare for war against America:* 'To be true Muslims, we must prepare and be ready for jihad in Allah's way. It is the duty of the citizen and the government.'"

COMING TO AMERICA

The Wahhabi presence in the United States is a foreboding one that has potentially harmful and far-reaching consequences for our nation's mosques,

schools, prisons and even our military. My fear is, if
we don't wake up and take action now, those influ-
enced by Wahhabism's extremist ideology will harm
us in as of yet unimaginable ways.
—U.S. Sen. Charles Schumer (D-NY)

An important fact to understand about Israel is that it is fighting the same forces that are gunning for America. These forces are not to be trifled with, and they are not confining themselves to the Middle East and other faraway parts of the world. In fact, they may have moved in adjacent to your own backyard.

In February 2003 a University of South Florida professor and six others were charged with aiding Islamic Jihad, a global terrorist organization.

In July 2004 a federal grand jury in Dallas, Texas, in a 42-count indictment, arrested leaders of the Holy Land Foundation for Relief and Development, charging its officials with raising more than $12 million to funnel to the terrorist organization Hamas.

Also in July two New York Muslim clerics were arrested for alleged connections to al-Qaida and for attempting to purchase a shoulder-fired grenade launcher.

These incidents raise the question of how deeply radical Islamic elements have become embedded in the United States. Among the prime suspects under investigation are groups financed by Saudi Arabian interests known to be making huge investments in the spread of the extremist Wahhabi Muslim doctrine in America. Larry Medford, assistant director of the FBI's Counterterrorism Division in 2003, reported to a Senate subcommittee that year that the FBI had launched an initiative to uncover such sleeper cells in 40 states.

Law enforcement officials believe dozens of Islamic extremists have been routed into the United States through

Europe and resettled into Muslim communities. An article by Jerry Seper in the February 10, 2004, *Washington Times* described how terrorists are increasing their efforts to infiltrate America: "Islamic radicals are being trained at terrorist camps in Pakistan and Kashmir as part of a conspiracy to send hundreds of operatives to 'sleeper cells' in the United States, according to U.S. and foreign officials." At least 400 terrorists had been trained by 2004. Seper called the network of camps "clandestine but aggressive," and said a high-ranking foreign intelligence chief told him the network "represents a serious threat to the United States, one that cannot be ignored."[24]

What are these terrorist operatives doing? "Awaiting orders and funding for new attacks in the United States. Financed in part by millions of dollars solicited by an extensive network of bogus charities and foundations, the cells use Muslim communities as cover and places to raise cash and recruit sympathizers," wrote Seper.[25]

State Department statistics show Islam is one of the fastest growing religions in the United States. One survey counted 1,209 mosques in America, with well over half founded since 1980. Between 17 and 30 percent of American Muslims are converts to the faith.

Whatever the population, non-Wahhabi Muslim leaders say approximately 80 percent of all U.S. mosques are controlled by Wahhabi imams and subsidized by Saudi Arabia. In addition to funding mosque construction and subsidizing programs, the Saudis are said to be pouring millions into creating a system of schools teaching militant Wahhabi doctrines.

Given the 80 percent figure, and considering that mosques are operating in every state in America, Wahhabis are becoming a formidable influence. For example, the U.S. State Department lists 327 mosques in California, 67 in Texas, 57 in Florida, and 140 in New York.

An example of anti-American Muslim rhetoric was documented in terrorist expert Steven Emerson's 1994 PBS documentary, *Jihad in America:*

> *If the Americans are placing their forces in the Persian Gulf, we should be creating another war front for the Americans in the Muslim world—and specifically where American interests are concentrated.*
> —Mohammad Al-Asi,
> leader of the Washington Mosque and head
> of the Islamic Educational Center in Washington, D.C.

What sets the Wahhabi segment of Islam apart as a danger to America and the West?

For starters, Wahhabism has been described as an Islamist totalitarian system. Its strictures include suppressing women and invoking the death penalty for alcohol consumption, sexual transgressions, and conversion to another religion. Western influence and close interaction with non-Muslims are seen with a mixture of disdain; contempt; and, at times, aggression that is believed to be sanctioned by the Qur'an.

Prime targets for Wahhabi animosity are Israel, of course, and the United States. Practitioners of the Wahhabi brand of Islam are committed to spreading the religion around the world by peaceful or coercive means.

The Muslim Student Association, with solid Wahhabi commitments, operates chapters on virtually every major campus in America. In league with militant left-wing organizations, it has been at the forefront of organizing and executing anti-Israel, anti-Semitic hate campaigns on campuses.

A student publication at Rutgers University in New Jersey published a cartoon depicting a Jewish man suspended over a burning oven. The caption read, "Knock a Jew in the oven." At Wooster College in Ohio, a guest lecturer spoke about the infamous *Protocols of the Elders of Zion* as if they were true. At

Northwestern University in Illinois, swastikas were painted throughout the campus nine times in a single year.

The Wahhabis' brand of religious militancy is not simply a matter of being out of step with the American values and Judeo-Christian traditions of their adopted home; it is a potential menace to other Muslims who do not embrace the excesses of Wahhabism. As has been demonstrated by the Muslim-on-Muslim war in Darfur, Sudan, Wahhabis are not above attacking other Muslims whom they consider not Muslim enough for their taste.

Emerson, an investigative reporter, produced the one-hour documentary that featured never-before-seen terrorist conferences and the operation of a terrorist network in the United States. He used footage shot by the terrorists themselves, often in meetings where Islamic leaders exhorted their followers to commit violence against Jewish people, Christians, and moderate Muslims.

All of which brings us to the question of how much the average American knows, or even cares to know, about such potentially deadly activity going on right under his nose. According to columnist Cal Thomas, not much. In a piece titled "The Threat Among Us," Thomas wrote:

> One of the advantages the United States has had over its enemies is that they openly state their goals. One of the advantages our enemies have over the United States is that too many Americans don't take them seriously. We prefer the short-term comfort that denial brings. We fear being labeled "bigots" more than we fear the intentions of those who hate us, and so we are reluctant to speak ill of another person's faith, unless it is the majority faith.[26]

We watch events in the Middle East from a distance and the comfort of our living rooms. It is a violent and bloody region of the world. And we must realize that the worst perpetrators of violence are on a global quest. Israel and other freedom-loving people on the other side of the planet are not the last intended victims. Europe and North America are engaged, like it or not, in a conflict that will surface with fury if the denizens of the "sleeper cells" have their way.

A Bully in the Schoolyard

The grammar school I attended had its resident bully. His mission was to scare and rough up other kids, always sizably smaller than himself. When a message came down the pipeline that you were his chosen source of entertainment for the afternoon, there was never a doubt that he intended to do exactly what he promised: roll you in the dirt and do what he could to rearrange the contours of your face. Denying the reality of his threat didn't help. You got punched out anyway.

The principle in the real world of grown-up aggressors is the same. You can ignore radical Islam's declaration of intent, as the secular media loves to do, but it won't keep the bully from rearranging the contours of your world.

And for those who find comfort in denial or in believing that an ocean or desert safely separates them from the bad guys, listen to someone who is living a nightmare he probably never believed possible.

Reverend Murtala Marti Dangora lives in Kano, West Africa. Christians there are afraid to send their children to public schools for fear they will be forced to convert to Islam. Students are compelled to study Arabic and Islam and to say Islamic prayers. Moreover, the government refuses to grant churches permission to establish schools in rural areas. "The strategy," said Rev. Dangora, "is to force Christians to send their children to public schools so they can be converted to Muslims." Another Christian leader said Christians in Kano have lost their religious liberty and are second-class citizens. Some were forced to flee their villages because of Muslim antagonism. So it goes in the land of the caliphs.

Their lives may not be yours today. But if you close your eyes to the bully moving in next door and Islamic imperialists achieve their dream, Rev. Dangora's today could be your tomorrow.

The lesson from 9/11 is that we probably didn't learn much from that terrible episode.

Thus far, understanding the full extent of our problems has escaped most Americans. Many of them are jumping on the anti-Israel bandwagon thinking that siding with the Palestinians will make all their troubles disappear. But in the words of Saudi Arabian-born terrorist Osama bin Laden, "Those who distinguish between America and Israel are the real enemies of the [Islamic] nation. . . . Every Muslim must stand under the banner of There is no God but Allah and Muhammad is God's Prophet. . . . Fear God, O Muslims and rise to support your religion. Islam is calling on you: O Muslims, O Muslims, O Muslims."[27]

ENDNOTES

[1] Elisabeth Bumiller, *21st Century Warnings of a Threat Rooted in the 7th*, December 12, 2005 <nytimes.com/2005/12/12/politics/12letter.html?ex=1136696400&en=8217c69f9f0f4a82&ei=5070>.

[2] Ibid.

[3] "President Commemorates Veteran's Day, Discusses War on Terror," November 11, 2005 <whitehouse.gov/news/releases/2005/11/print/20051111-1.html>.

[4] "President Discusses War on Terror at National Endowment for Democracy," October 6, 2005 <whitehouse.gov/news/releases/2005/10/20051006-3.html>.

[5] Ibid.

[6] Daniel Pipes, "Bush Declares War on Radical Islam," October 11, 2005 <danielpipes.org/pf.php?id=3026>.

[7] Quoted in Samuel P. Huntington, *The Clash of Civilizations and the Remaking of World Order* (New York: Touchstone, 1996), 269.

[8] Ibid.

[9] Daniel Pipes, "What Do the Terrorists Want? [A Caliphate]," July 26, 2005 <danielpipes.org/pf.php?id=2798>.

[10] Jonathan Adelman and Agota Kuperman, "The Christian Exodus From the Middle East" <jewishvirtuallibrary.org/jsource/arabs/christianme.html>.

[11] Ibid.

[12] Quoted in Justus Reid Weiner, *Human Rights of Christians in Palestinian Society* (Jerusalem: Jerusalem Center for Public Affairs, 2005), 17.

[13] Ibid., 14.

[14] Ibid., 10.

[15] Robert Spencer, "Fallaci Warrior in the Cause of Human Freedom," November 30, 2005 <frontpagemag.com/Articles/ReadArticle.asp?ID=20359>.

[16] Arnaud de Borchgrave, "Mini clash of civilizations," November 15, 2004 <washingtontimes.com/commentary/20041114-103944-4700r.htm>.

[17] Jamie Glazov, "Symposium: Indonesian Jihad," January 2, 2006 <frontpagemag.com/Articles/ReadArticle.asp?ID=20728>.

[18] International Religious Freedom Act of 1998, 105th Cong., 2d sess. (27 January, 1998) <http://usinfo.state.gov/usa/infousa/laws/majorlaw/intlrel.htm>.

[19] Weiner, 33–34.

[20] Ibid., 27.

[21] Haviv Rettig, "Expert: Saudis Have Radicalized 80% of US Mosques," December 5, 2005 <jpost.com/servlet/Satellite?cid=1132475689987&pagename=JPost%2FJPArticle%2Fprinter>.

[22] Ibid.

[23] Daniel Pipes, "Saudi Venom in U.S. Mosques," February 1, 2005 <danielpipes.org/article/2384>.

[24] Jerry Seper, "Islamic Extremists Invade U.S., Join Sleeper Cells," February 10, 2004 <washtimes.com/national/20040209-115406-6221r.htm>.

[25] Ibid.

[26] Cal Thomas, "The Threat Among Us," May 21, 2003 <washtimes.com/commentary/20030520-102255-8107r.htm>.

[27] "Bin Laden rails against Crusaders and UN, November, 3, 2001 <news.bbc.co.uk/1/hi/world/monitoring/media_reports/1636782.stm>.

CHAPTER 5

⸎

LET'S CALL A SPADE A SPADE

Upon entering the ancient city of Jaffa in Israel, you will see a weathered bronze statue of a whale. Immediately the story of Jonah, God's recalcitrant prophet, comes to mind.

We all know the story. Jonah was commissioned by God to go to pagan, Gentile Nineveh with a message of impending doom. Rather than obey, he said no to God and hopped a ship in the opposite direction. The result of his folly is well documented in the account of the prophet and the great fish in the book of Jonah.

Over the years, I've watched the United Nations deliberate the issue of how to curtail the activities of tyrants every bit as godless and tyrannical as were the Ninevites. And I think of Jonah and his excruciating excursion into the belly of his dilemma, which hinged on how to face the facts of his position and accept the responsibility committed to him.

We have a duty today to face the facts and accept our responsibilities to proclaim the truth. It's not a popular thing to do because men, as always, prefer darkness rather than light. The evidence is everywhere. Despite the fact that Muslims like bin Laden shout from the rooftops that they are fighting a holy war against the infidel "Crusaders," politicians constantly bombard us with statements that the war on terror has nothing whatever to do with religion. Ever careful not to offend Muslim world leaders, they tell us the enemy is a misguided, extremist liberation movement led by an overzealous few who are attempting to free Palestinians and other Arabs from the impaling injustices of Israel and the Western democracies.

Some have gone so far as to remove the stigma of identifying these people as the terrorists they truly are. Arafat was a marvel of news media sanitation. Suddenly he was alchemized into a "fighter" rather than the murderer we all knew him as for decades. In like fashion, Islamists are now dignified as "freedom fighters," "militiamen," "insurgents," and members of "liberation movements." It amazes me that any thinking American would swallow this swill. But swallow it they do.

Painting these false faces on terrorists is a despicable deception and outrageous breach of responsibility. And it wrongfully anoints them with a designation they do not place on themselves. By their own declarations, they self-righteously slaughter the innocent in the name of their religion, to honor Allah. And our saying so does not constitute intolerance or bigotry. It merely restates what they themselves proudly proclaim.

America's apparent failure to recognize the true nature of the conflict is not because militant Muslims have deceived us. It is because Western leaders and media moguls have failed to face the facts and to transmit them responsibly to Americans and others in the democratic Western world. It is extreme malfeasance—and it is often fatal.

Why, for example, do politicians and journalists give such scant attention to the thousands of Christians who are being killed, starved, tortured, enslaved, and driven from their churches and homes, all in the name of jihad, the Qur'an, and Islam? Horrendous atrocities are perpetrated in many countries while the vast majority of people in the world, including "moderate" Muslims, ignore the growing catastrophe.

Why? Because those responsible for exposing such cruelty are reluctant to call it what it is—an Islamic holy war against Christians, Jews, and Western democracies. The rationale is that we cannot afford to stigmatize peace-loving Muslims by mentioning religion in the same breath with terrorism. Apparently it doesn't seem to matter that, while Christians and Jewish people are being viciously slaughtered in the name of Islam, one can cut the silence with a knife.

Several years ago I was asked to speak to the National Press Club in Washington, D.C. My subject related to the Middle East struggle. I stated that the basic issue is religion and that the Islamic claim to the land lies in the belief that all territory ever ruled by Muslims is sacred to Allah. Consequently, if infidels—namely, Christians or Jews—ever gain control of such land, Muslims can never rest in their beds until Allah's honor is restored and the infidels annihilated, subjugated, or driven out.

After the meeting, a member of the mainstream media told me he had never before heard that side of the issue discussed. Frankly, I was astonished. He had attended numerous press conferences where major political figures had spoken on the Middle East. None, however, apparently addressed this element, which formulates the essence of the controversy.

The Shuttle Disaster Speaks

On January 16, 2003, the United States launched the space shuttle Columbia from Cape Canaveral, Florida. It was a landmark event for NASA and the global community. For Israelis, it was a euphoric occasion that saw the first Israeli astronaut, Col. Ilan Ramon, embark on a mission into outer space. Ramon was already a national hero and had participated in the 1981 raid on the nuclear reactor in Iraq, setting the former Iraqi dictator's plans to build an atomic bomb back for decades.

Tragically, the space vehicle disintegrated on reentry, and all aboard, including Col. Ilan Ramon, were killed. For the vast majority in the civilized world, it was a horrible loss.

Memorial services were held around the world, lamenting the catastrophe that took the lives not only of Americans but also of astronauts of other nationalities. For some in the Islamic world, however, it was a time to celebrate.

In England, a firebrand Muslim cleric, Abu Hamza al-Masri, gloated over the shuttle disaster and rejoiced over the astronauts' deaths. He referred to the Columbia crew as a band of "thugs in space who deserved to die" and further claimed that the disaster was a sign from Allah because debris rained down on a Texas town named Palestine. While more rational Muslim officials rightly denounced these fanatical rantings, others in the Islamic world agreed when al-Masri said,

> The target of this event was the trinity of evil, as the shuttle carried Americans, an Israeli, and a Hindu, the trinity of evil against Islam. This is a message to the American people that Bush's term is nothing but a string of curses cast upon them, and that it will lead to the exhaustion of their resources and the elimination of the false American dream. . . . This is a divine message to the Israelis, saying that they are not welcome in space.[1]

Were these but isolated incidents, they could be written off as the meanderings of demented minds. The problem for us all is that such anti-Israel, anti-America venom flows freely from the pulpits of mosques throughout the Middle East, America, and the Western world—and it is not something we can afford to whisk aside in the interests of ecumenical harmony.

Stumping for a Palestinian State

The vaunted Road Map for peace in the Middle East was designed to impose a settlement on Israel and the Palestinians. With Hamas now in control of the Palestinian legislature, it seems that *Jerusalem Post* columnist Caroline Glick's description of the plan as the "road map to perdition" grows more accurate every day.

Consider these factors. The proposed constitution for the new State of Palestine will incorporate Islamic Sharia law as the legal basis for the nation. This is the same Sharia law that Sudan has forced on Christians and animists, resulting in their torture and death. Under Sharia law, tens of thousands of non-Muslim Sudanese women and children alone have been brutally force-marched, beaten, mutilated, enslaved, and forced to convert to Islam. Despite all of the noble rhetoric about establishing a "democratic" Palestinian state alongside a "secure" Israel, under current circumstances such a thing cannot happen. There is no democracy under Sharia law. A "Sharia democracy" is an irreconcilable contradiction in terms and practice.

In addition, the proposed constitution calls for the conscription of Palestinian youth for the defense of the country. This feature comes in spite of the fantasy that a State of Palestine will be a demilitarized entity. With an army dedicated to the principles of radical Islam and Sharia law, democracy is only a gossamer-winged dream—one that may live in the minds of wishful thinkers in the West but is almost certain to disintegrate after the state becomes a dreadful reality.

This being the case, what will happen when Islamic law becomes an official fact of life and the official doors of state slam shut to the scrutiny of the outside world? You can be sure Palestinian Christians will be no more welcome there than any of their Israeli neighbors. It can be said unequivocally that, in addition to the Israelis, the biggest losers in the plan for peace will be Arab Christians.

A Muslim-Christian Alliance?

Coexistence with the West used to be a high-agenda item in the world of Islam. Some Muslims still believe there is much to be gained in the Middle East and among Western nations through infusive relationships that will eventually win the day for Allah and his people. Islamic strategists believe that time is on their side—time and the incredible naiveté of Europeans and Americans who, in Islam's view, are ripe to be plucked by the persistent disciples of Muhammad.

A Muslim booklet, *Muslim-Christian Alliance*, published in Istanbul, Turkey, makes a case for the necessity of an alliance between Christians and Muslims:

> *Moreover, the Saying of the Prophet Muhammad further states that in the end of time, true pious, devout Christians will unite with Muslims and put a great fight together against the common threat Atheism. For the time being, true devout Muslims must unite not only with their coreligionists, colleagues and fellow brothers, but with true Christian believers by skipping any dispute, since they have to unite urgently against the common enemy, aggressive, dreadful Atheism.*

"In the past," the booklet reads, "the Christian States were not supporting and were not in favor of the Islamic Alliance. But, now both U.S.A. and European countries have to support the unity of Islam and holy Qur'an due to rising powers of anarchism."

Although the booklet attempts to draw favorable comparisons between Islam and Christianity, the smoke screen evaporates when the objective becomes clear:

> *Eventually, Christianity will be purified and get rid of all superstitions and misbeliefs and will unite with the true Islamic Religion, thereby Christianity will be in a way transformed into Islam, and by adopting guidance to Qur'an, the Christian*

community will become a follower of Islam and Islam Religion will be the leader position. The true Religion of Islam will gain a great power as a result of that unification.

The above statements reflect rather well Islam's agenda for the conquest of the Western (Christian) community: friendly alliances eventuating in final victory—an Islamic world.

Islam divides the world into two segments: the world of peace and the world of the sword. The world of peace is cradled in the Islamic nations. The world of the sword is the world yet to be conquered.

The International Muslim Brotherhood, headquartered in the Sudan, is pursuing a plan for the conquest of the Western world. It boasts that, in the Orient, Islam rules from Indonesia to Malaysia. Islam is supreme in Pakistan, Afghanistan, Iran, the Arabian Peninsula, and the whole of North Africa to the Atlantic Ocean. Its sights are now set on Europe and the United States.

How does Islam intend to accomplish its objective? The plan in the Middle East is obvious: destroy Israel, the bastion of democracy and Jewish values. The strategy involves weakening it, first with debilitating peace agreements and terrorism, and finishing it off with wars of eradication. By now we should be well versed in Islam's glorification of the sword as a holy instrument of conquest.

In the world of Islam, however, the sword is not reserved for the infidel alone. From 1948 to 1985, the Arab world witnessed 54 successful revolutions; 65 more were unsuccessful. During the same period, 30 heads of state or prime ministers were assassinated. The Syrian minister of education wrote in 1968, "The hatred which we indoctrinate into the minds of our children from birth is sacred."[2]

In the West, some Muslims use another tactic. They call

for interfaith cooperation and tolerance. In fact, infiltration is the key to submerging the West in a sea of Islamic domination. In Brussels, Belgium, the world center for the European Economic Community, there are more mosques than churches. Of the 6 million Muslims in France, 600,000 are eligible to vote. Judging by the Muslim riots that tore up France in 2005, Islam is making its presence strongly felt there, and it could conceivably wield pivotal influence in French elections in the future.

In Holland, with its population of approximately 10 million, Muslims already number 1 million. And given average Muslim birthrates, that number is certain to climb and become a significant force for the country to deal with. Other European countries echo the same story. Even North America is caught in the rising wave of Islamic determination to "have it all."

Perhaps the simple formula articulated by the Muslims themselves is the best way to view their strategy. In their holy war against the infidels of the Judeo-Christian faiths, they declare that they will first reckon with *Saturday* (that is, conquer the Jews). Then *Sunday* will succumb to the conquering hordes of the prophet and his god, Allah. Islam will triumph over the "Christian" world.

The most chilling, immediate prospect for us all is the fact that Islamic fundamentalists have mounted Herculean efforts to obtain nuclear technology and weaponry. Iran has become the latest and possibly biggest threat to peace with its nuclear capability. This is the country whose president declared in 2005 that Israel "must be wiped out from the map of the world."

Then he added, "And God willing, with the force of God behind it, we shall soon experience a world without the United States and Zionism."[3] First the Saturday people, then the Sunday people. And there you have it. The battle begins with Israel. But it will end with the United States and the world. Are you willing to participate in an alliance that eventually will end in your destruction? I am not.

Neither is Nonie Darwish. She wrote the following column as an open letter titled "Shame on You" in response to a PBS television documentary aired on its program *Frontline*. She pretty much says it all. And what she says is well worth listening to.

I am a former Moslem, born and raised in the Middle East. I am very disappointed and almost scared after watching your presentation about Islam. One of the reasons I fled to the United States of America was to escape the oppressive regime of Islam in the Middle East. From a former Moslem, these people are in the U.S. to Islamize America and have a scary agenda. They audaciously buy churches and convert them into mosques!

I think your show was insensitive to the Judeo-Christian community of the United States. Islam is cruel, anti-women, anti-religious freedom and anti-personal freedom in general. How could you sympathize with a religion that kills adulterers, homosexuals and people who convert out of Islam? How could you present Islam with such affection? I am sorry that PBS failed to represent the oppression, fear and the straight jacket I had to endure when I lived under that crazy regime.

In the show, you stressed how the West should understand Islam. Why is America responsible for understanding every little and big culture and religion around the world, failing which we are branded bigots and racists? How about asking the Moslems if they could open their minds and hearts and understand the West? Perhaps they will slow down their terrorism, burning our flags and hijacking airplanes. Unfortunately, the Middle East has no clue about the American culture and they only judge us by Hollywood! How about U.S. media educating Moslems about U.S. culture and the virtues of our Constitution? Did that ever occur to you?

When I married a Christian man in my home country twenty-five years ago, I could have been killed by Moslems for daring to do so. I was questioned about my husband's religion even by Moslem workers at the U.S. embassy, who asked me point blank if he converted to Islam, implicitly threatening to report me to Moslem authorities! I personally know Moslem women who were circumcised against their will! How could you defend a religion that declares a fatwa, or death sentence, to anyone who is critical of the religion? How could you defend a religion that inspired 9/11? Of course not all Moslems are terrorists, but unfortunately, the majority of "moderate" Moslems respect the fundamentalists as "true" Moslems and even feel guilty toward them. If this were not true we should be seeing massive displays of support for the U.S., strong denouncements of radical Islam by the moderates. This has not happened. Instead, the most vocal Islamic groups in the West are taking a confrontational stance, complaining of discriminatory treatment, taking their cue from liberal civil-rights groups.

The liberal media is only too eager to egg them on.

I now write articles critical of Islam and speak to many groups about the Middle East but have to use a pseudonym so I do not get killed by some of your Moslem friends in the U.S. mosques you were interviewing! They have no shame to be complaining of discrimination after 9/11, thanks to media outlets like you who gave them a voice. The U.S. goes out of its way to protect them. What discrimination? Are you kidding? These mosques in the U.S. are financed by Saudi money and have an agenda and they scare people like me who want to write and speak freely. Scared and oppressed former Moslems like me could be killed by these Moslem extremists in U.S. mosques. There are many moderate Moslems and former Moslems like me who feel intimidated by some U.S. Moslem extremists. Former Moslems have to be given a voice on why they escaped Islam. People like me and oppressed Christians and Jews in the Moslem World had no say on your show. That is very sad. I wish you had defended my right to choose or reject Islam without getting killed.

Is Islam now the "in" thing to defend to sabotage America, or did Saudi money corrupt you?!

Is it any wonder Nonie Darwish started a Web site called arabsforisrael.com? The site is filled with letters from Arabs who agree with her and who love Israel. One letter, posted January 1, 2006, said this:

> *They say Israel is our first enemy and never stop to think for a moment without their blind prejudice. If they do they would discover that terrorists are all Muslims only, Bin Laden, Zawaheri, Zarkawi etc. What has Israel done to you fools? Considering Israel as an enemy is the wrong assumption because we all know we have a more dangerous enemy hiding within our nations. Their imagination is far from reality. . . . I love Israel. I love USA.*

Deep within the prisons of Islam are Muslims who want the freedom to think for themselves and to choose which paths to follow. Such is not the way of radical Islam. As Nonie Darwish so concisely put it, the radicals want to "Islamize America." They have a specific agenda, a defined strategy, and a determination to win. It is the perfect trifecta for the naïve and gullible West.

Here's the test. Jonah had a clear mandate to act responsibly. Instead, he chose to run in the other direction—and paid the price. Will we be rejectionists like Jonah or face the unpleasant task of being branded "bad guys" while doing a good work for our people and the world? It's time we called a spade a spade and acted accordingly. Time is fast running out.

ENDNOTES

[1] *Al-Sharq Al-Awsat*, London, February 4, 2003, in "Arab Media Reactions to the Columbia Space Shuttle Disaster: Part II," Inquiry and Analysis Series No. 123, February 7, 2003 <memri.org/bin/articles.cgi?Area=ia&ID=IA12303>.

[2] From a letter sent to M. Rene Mheu, director general of UNESCO, and reproduced in *Al-Thawra*, May 3, 1968. Cited in Mitchell G. Bard, *Myths and Facts Online* <jewishvirtuallibrary.org/jsource/myths/mf15.html>.

[3] "Iranian Leader: Wipe Out Israel," October 27, 2005 <cnn.com/2005/WORLD/meast/10/26/ahmadinejad/>.

CHAPTER 6

⟨∞⟩

EMERGING SHADOWS
OF THE HAMMER AND SICKLE

*What do you fellows intend to preach about Ezekiel
38, since Communism is dead and the Soviet Union
is no longer a threat to anyone? It doesn't even exist.
You've got a lot of explaining to do.*

The question was put to me after I had finished bringing
a prophetic message at a conference in the spring of 1992. The
Soviet Union had disintegrated the previous year and was
supposedly on the road to freedom and democracy. The new
Russia, we were told, would be more an ally than an enemy.

My answer to my inquisitor was, "It isn't over yet."

That was 1992. In February 2005, 13 years later, Russian
Foreign Minister Sergei Lavrov announced that the
Palestinian Authority wants to buy Russian "hardware,
including armored personnel carriers." And he praised PA
leader Mahmoud Abbas for supposedly keeping the wraps
on terrorism and ably coordinating "the activities of all
Palestinian organizations, including those who hold tough
positions toward the Israelis." In April 2006 Abbas was
barely heard from, the terrorist organization Hamas had
taken over the Palestinian Authority, and Russia had agreed
to give the Hamas PA "urgent financial aid."

According to BBC News, "A Russian foreign ministry
statement said, 'Mahmoud Abbas stated his high appreciation of Russia's intent, confirmed by Sergei Lavrov, to grant

71

the Palestinian Authority an urgent financial aid in the nearest future.'"[1]

Have we heard the last from Russia? Hardly.

I confess that I answered the question in 1992 with confidence. First, a last-days attack on Israel from "out of the far north" (Ezek. 38:15), a region clearly associated with Russia, is an integral part of the last-days scenario portrayed in God's Word. Articulating that fact as biblical, prophetic revelation was neither sermonizing from the newspaper nor building eschatology from a current-events manual.

Yet there was also another, quite compelling reason for my confidence: Russia is imperialistic. Imperialism is the driving force behind Russia's political, social, and religious regional and global considerations. And though this hunger for power may lie dormant from time to time, inevitably it will surface.

It was folly to believe that, although bankrupt and dispirited after the Soviet breakup, Russia would be content to ride in the backseat of the global political limousine and exist on the largesse of the West. What is taking place is bearing this fact out.

Heady Days and Hopeful Hearts

On June 8, 1982, President Ronald Reagan delivered his famous "evil empire" speech before the British House of Commons. He said in part,

> *If history teaches anything, it teaches self-delusion in the face of unpleasant facts is folly. We see around us today the marks of our terrible dilemma— predictions of doomsday, antinuclear demonstrations, an arms race in which the West must, for its own protection, be an unwilling participant. At the same time we see totalitarian forces in the world who seek subversion and conflict around the globe to further their barbarous assault on the human spirit. What,*

then, is our course? Must civilization perish in a hail of fiery atoms? Must freedom wither in a quiet, deadening accommodation with totalitarian evil?

The president understood much better than most the issues and potentially painful alternatives we must employ in the interests of international stability or, for that matter, survival.

Five years later, on June 12, 1987, Mr. Reagan stood before the Brandenburg Gate in what was then West Berlin and issued a challenge bordering on an ultimatum to then Soviet leader Mikhail Gorbachev:

General Secretary Gorbachev: if you seek peace, if you seek prosperity for the Soviet Union and Eastern Europe, if you seek liberalization: Come here to this gate! Mr. Gorbachev, open this gate! Mr. Gorbachev, tear down this wall!

On June 13, 1990, hammers began to pound away at the infamous Berlin Wall that had held East Germans captive since its construction in 1961. Opening the gates and destroying the wall, a symbol of the Cold War between the Soviet Union and the West, caused optimism to soar. And as families embraced and the barrier collapsed, optimism seemed well justified. Two words characterized the benefits of the breakup of the Communist Soviet empire: *egress* and *access*.

For millions of Jewish people long oppressed behind what Winston Churchill dubbed the "Iron Curtain," the dissolution of the Soviet Union brought a golden opportunity to leave it. Thus in the 1990s, a mass exodus got under way. Hundreds of thousands of Jewish people immigrated to Israel and other Western nations. The Jewish people's massive exit brought ancient images to mind of Israelites fleeing from Egypt under Moses. This modern exodus, however, was led by men like Siberian gulag survivor and Soviet dissident Natan Sharansky.

For Westerners, the Soviet collapse provided access to a people no longer under the cloak of secrecy woven by Karl Marx, Vladimir Lenin, and facilitated by Joseph Stalin and his despotic successors. The new Russia was destitute, bankrupted by 70 years of corrupt Communist, socialist delusion. Consequently, no options existed for those picking up the pieces other than to put their hands out to the democracies in order to fend off anarchy and chaos.

Perhaps the greatest of all doors that swung open during this time was for Christians, particularly evangelicals. Finally they were free to enter the region and minister to a spiritually starving population. For decades the Soviets deliberately excluded God as they passionately pursued their socialist, secular excursion into an atheistic nirvana, a state Webster's Dictionary rightly defines as "a goal hoped for but apparently unattainable."

What the Communist commissars failed to account for was the human heart's inherent instinct to worship, to experience some link to the eternal. Predictably, when the opportunity to hear divine truth became available, floodgates of desire opened; and opportunities abounded. The fields were ripe, and the harvest was abundant.

Shadows of the Past

But in all of this, there remained an unsettling political, social, and religious reality that would eventually have to be reckoned with. To remain a client state for the long haul was never something Russia saw as a viable option. After all, the Soviet empire had been a major player on the world stage. Power, prestige, massive territories, and fearsome military power caused continual international apprehension, as nations tried to ascertain what the Russian "bear" would do next.

The Soviets hated everything democracy stood for. They despised evangelical Christianity. They had evicted the God of the Judeo-Christian world. And anti-Israel/anti-Semitic militancy ranked high on their list of preferred national pastimes. At one critical juncture in the Soviet-Israel standoff, Moshe Dayan, the famous Israeli general and political leader, was quoted as saying, "The key to war in the Middle East is in the hands of the Soviets, while the key to peace is held by the United States." Those words succinctly articulated the essence of the major issues during the not so Cold War.

A few facts about arms agreements with Israel's archenemies exhibit Arab and Soviet intentions in the Middle East extremely well.

Soviet Arms Agreements
1955—Egypt—Soviets the main supplier.
1955—Syria—Soviets the main supplier.
1958—Iraq—Soviets the main supplier.
1962—Algeria—Soviets the main supplier.
1967—Sudan—Soviets the main supplier.
1967—Iran—(terrorists) Soviets a partial supplier.
1970—Libya—Soviets a partial supplier.

Today it seems Moshe Dayan's cryptic words may be emerging from the shadows.

The 'Bear' Begins to Stir

In 2005 Russia began a serious Middle East venture designed to reassert its influence. In a deal with the besieged outlaw Syrian government, the Russians cancelled most of Syria's $10 billion debt and, in a formal declaration, jump-started their once intimate relationship. That cozy alliance began in the Cold War days of the mid-1950s and came to a halt only with the collapse of the Soviet Union a decade ago.

The move was a big win for Bashar Assad and Syria. Assad regained an ally that will presumably protect it from the United States and patronize it in the international arena.

What's in it for Russia? Orly Halpern of *The Jerusalem Post* tells us:

> *Russia's ambitions are growing to Soviet-era size. It wants to be involved in the international games that are now the recreation of the European Union and the United States. But the US is not letting it get involved in the Arab-Israeli conflict, and it has little to say in the Iraq issue because it refused to make war on a country that owed it so much money.*
>
> *By renewing political and military relations with countries the US has blackballed, the downsized former superpower aims to bring back the glory of its Soviet-era days when it played countries like chess pieces.*[2]

To add to Israeli and American concerns, the Russians were contemplating selling advanced missiles to Syria. Russian President Vladimir Putin eventually halted the sale of Iskander-E tactical missiles but still sells Syria surface-to-air missiles. Former Israeli Prime Minister Ariel Sharon protested to Moscow that such missiles could fall into the hands of terrorists and gravely endanger Israel. Given Syria's track record, one can virtually be assured this will be the case.

Furthermore, in April 2006 Rosoroboroneksport, the state arms exporter, announced that it had finalized weapons contracts worth $18 billion, a 61 percent jump over 2005.[3] And 2005 wasn't a bad year either:

> *In December 2005, Moscow also agreed to sell 30 Tor M-1 air-defense missile systems to Tehran. In addition to Syria and Iran, Moscow has negotiated sales agreements with Sudan. Also, Moscow continues to sell small arms and helicopters to the Hamas administration in the Palestinian Authority, which*

is boycotted both by Washington and Jerusalem. All in all, Russia should sell weapons worth $4 billion to Iran, worth $2 billion to Syria, and worth $400 million to Sudan.[4]

Russia also has agreed to help the Iranians to further develop their nuclear program. Although the Russians claim they will only help Iran achieve the ability to produce nuclear generating power, the West knows better. We now know Iran is well advanced in uranium enrichment and is well on the way to having nuclear weapons, which it probably would not hesitate to use.

In 2005 Mahmoud Abbas made every effort to make sure his first trip abroad was to Moscow. He did so, he said, to demonstrate the respect the Palestinian people feel toward the Russians and their role as major players on the world scene, particularly in the Middle East.

Russia and Religion

On January 13, 2005, 20 members of Russia's Duma (lower house of parliament) sent a letter to the prosecutor general asking him to investigate their allegations and, if confirmed, to initiate proceedings prohibiting all religious and ethnic Jewish organizations in Russia, branding them as "extremist." They argued that the Jewish people are the cause of the anti-Semitism that has reemerged in the country in recent years. The charge is hauntingly reminiscent of the threadbare, but too often effective, lies that instigated the vicious "blood libels" and *Protocols of the Elders of Zion*, which have served Russian anti-Semites so well in the past.

Evangelical Christians in Russia and some of the commonwealth states also felt the heat. It is no secret the Russian Orthodox hierarchy is in a huff over the giant inroads Bible-believing Christians are making among a spiritually emaciated people long stifled by the sterile formalism of the Orthodox system. Consequently, the Russian Orthodox have forged alliances with some of Russia's most radical political groups, branding evangelicals as cultists who prey on unsuspecting citizens. Of most concern is that evangelical churches, once unregistered and "underground" during Communism, are now in the open and are exposed targets for the anti-Christian establishment, should the hammer of hate fall once again.

Perilous Times, Desperate Measures

We have long been warned that in the last days, perilous times would come upon the face of the planet. For all but those who persist in maintaining a debilitating state of spiritual hibernation in order to avoid the facts, that time is upon us. The great powers are moving inexorably toward the final convulsions prewritten in the Scriptures. What we have described as developing in the North in the prophetic scenario is merely one piece of the puzzle.

And though some may argue that the words *desperate measures* should not be used to describe what Jesus' followers must take in response to the crisis, no one can argue the legitimacy of the desperate need to buy up the time and make a difference; *time* is most assuredly of the essence.

Muslim terrorist organizations have not been dismantled, disarmed, or dissuaded from their determination to destroy Israel. Suicide bombings continue; and writing them off as mutant, temporary manifestations is a devastating mistake. Whatever promises of *hudna* (cease-fire) the Palestinians make are only temporary. In their minds, the issue has not been settled. And whatever concessions the Israelis, starved for peace, are willing to offer, will never be enough. There is not enough land that Israel can give away in any land-for-peace scheme that will both allow the Jewish nation to survive and the Islamists and Palestinians to declare victory.

Take a long look. Syria, Iran, and remnants of Saddam

Hussein's decimated Iraqi regime still carry on the fight against freedom and democracy. Unfortunately, many people have dignified these murderers and thugs by calling them insurgents. They are not insurgents; they are terrorists. By the same token, Hamas, Islamic Jihad, Popular Front for the Liberation of Palestine, Hezbollah, and al-Aqsa Martyrs Brigade and their bedfellows are not freedom fighters in quest of a noble cause. They are cold-blooded, ruthless killers of innocent men, women, and children.

These elements will not disappear. An insatiable passion to destroy or drive out the "infidel" consumes them. And they will surely continue their crusade to destabilize democracies and find rogue states from which to operate. For this reason, a sovereign Palestinian state cannot be allowed to fall prey to these forces of evil. Russia offering military materiel to the Palestinian Authority may seem of little consequence today. But it should be a wake up call for us all.

Someone once said, "The only juncture where time and eternity meet is at this moment." If that is true, it makes what we do for the cause of Christ at this moment the great imperative of our lives. Face it. Our moments to touch eternity are running out.

ENDNOTES

[1] "Palestinians to Get Russian Aid," April 15, 2006 <news.bbc.co.uk/1/hi/world/middle_east/4911310.stm>.

[2] Orly Halpern, "Analysis: Russia's ambitions growing," *The Jerusalem Post*, January 27, 2005 <jpost.com/servlet/Satellite?pagename=JPost/JPArticle/ShowFull&cid=1106796046758>.

[3] Victor Yasmann, "Russia: Putin Pushes Greater Arms Exports," Radio Free Europe, April 4, 2006 <rferl.org/featuresarticle/2006/04/4a183e57-5ac6-4e4b-ab6e-f9ce326e0a90.html>.

[4] Ibid.

CHAPTER 7

⟨∞⟩

THE DISINVESTMENT CRUSADE

The wisdom and courage to discern the truth elude many these days. Despite the fact that the land of Israel belongs to the Jewish people because (a) they received it from God, (b) they received it from the UN in 1947, and (c) they won it fighting wars of self-defense, many Christian denominations refuse to support it. They turn their backs on the truth of the situation and buy into the big lie that tiny little Israel is the oppressive aggressor and the Arab behemoth is the helpless victim. So "helpless" are the Muslims, in fact, that they must resort to blowing themselves up and pumping bullets into Israeli women and children in order to redress the "evil" they suffer under Israeli "occupation."

Joan Peters called this propaganda *turnspeak*—the inverting of facts. She defined the word as "the cynical inverting or distorting of facts, which, for example, makes the victim appear as culprit."[1] The Jewish people in the land, she said, have always been the true victims, just as they are today.

But the Presbyterian Church (USA), for example, does not think so. It finally came out of the closet regarding Israel at its 216th General Assembly in 2004. Not that the denomination has been soft on the Jewish state, its leadership, or its citizenry in the past. But what made this occasion interesting was the decision to cast its animosity in an official document so no one would miss the point.

The Reverend Victor Makari, the church's liaison to the Middle East, made the denomination's intentions clear by stating that, because Israel had not changed its policy toward the Palestinians, the church was compelled to "send a clear and strong message." If such was the intent, the Presbyterians achieved their purpose.

The Presbyterian Church (USA) is the largest of the Presbyterian denominations, with approximately 2.5 million members, 11,200 congregations, and 21,000 ordained ministers. It lays claim to an illustrious history dating back to the 16th century and the Protestant Reformation.

The implication, therefore, is that when PCUSA speaks, the church has spoken—which, of course, is not the case. There are obviously many thousands of Presbyterians, in and out of the PCUSA, with more amicable attitudes toward Israel and the rights of the Jewish people to live in peace and security in the land of their fathers.

So what's the beef about the decision to speak out? And what did the Presbyterian General Assembly, by a vote of 431 to 62, approve?

1. Gathering data to support selective divestment of holdings in multinational corporations doing business in Israel/Palestine.

This divestiture involves its nearly $8 billion portfolio, excluding those companies profiting from sale of products and services that cause harm to Palestinians or Israelis or both. Fact: Israel is the target, and the only country tagged for divestment.

2. Condemning Israel's security fence, which, in the view of the delegates, annexes land without negotiation.

Never mind that, since the Palestinian war on Israel began, thousands of Israelis, Americans, and others have died from suicide attacks. These have been largely thwarted in areas where the fence now exists. Never mind the reason why the fence was built or that the Palestinians have resolutely rejected opportunities to negotiate with Israel.

3. Identifying Israel as espousing policies comparable to those of South Africa under the former apartheid regime.

This position conveniently overlooks the fact that more than 1 million Arabs hold full Israeli citizenship plus representation in Israel's ruling body, the Knesset. It also conveniently overlooks the fact that many of the world's countries are 100 percent Muslim and do not allow Jews to live there—Saudi Arabia being one of them. But we don't see the PCUSA condemning Saudi Arabia for its anti-Jewish policy, do we?

4. Disavowing Christian Zionism as a legitimate theological stance.

It is ironic that the very week the PCUSA was passing its resolutions, the Roman Catholic Church signed a document equating anti-Zionism with anti-Semitism. And what is the definition of *Zionism*? Basically, it is the belief that the Jewish people have a right to a secure homeland in *Eretz Yisrael*, sanctioned under international law. For Zionist Christians, that right is, without reservation, a God-ordained possession consistent with irrevocable biblical promises. In addition, though some seem to forget it, Israel is a legitimate state recognized under international law. The missing element at this juncture is secure, recognized boundaries.

5. Insisting on the Palestinians' right of return to Israel proper.

Implementing this position would effectively dismantle the Jewish nation by turning it into another state with a Palestinian majority, such as Jordan.

Planking for the Anti-Israel Platform

Those five points represent the essence of the Presbyterians' Middle East Manifesto. Details can be found in works of liberal Presbyterian Middle East "experts," such as Wheaton Professor Gary Burge who, in lockstep with his denomination, has taken it on himself to make the case for the

Palestinians and condemn the Israeli "Goliath" in a revision of his 1993 book on the subject, now titled *Whose Land? Whose Promise?*

Burge terms Christian Zionism a "territorial religion" focusing on land rights: "But it [the land] no longer has an intrinsic part to play in God's program for the world."[2] This statement is the crux of the issue between Zionist evangelical Christians and the proponents of Replacement Theology. In his book, Burge charges Israel with discrimination, stealing land, stealing water, destroying villages, genocide, and an innumerable host of human rights violations against the Palestinians. With regard to the flight of Palestinians from Bethlehem, he made this observation:

> *The same is true of traditionally Christian Arab cities such as Bethlehem and Ramallah. . . . Frustration with the devastated Palestinian economy, anger with the lack of freedom, and hopelessness about the future have led many to simply leave.*[3]

The villain, predictably, is Israel. But what is not said is that the Arab-Christian exodus began following Yasser Arafat's takeover of Bethlehem. Before then, local Christian Arabs and Christians from abroad had always enjoyed cordial and economically profitable relationships. But, as we said earlier, after Arafat took over, the city became a prime center for exporting terrorism and suicide attacks against innocent Israelis, not to mention militant Muslim thugs who terrorize Arab Christians and businessmen, causing them to leave.

In his book, Burge gave Arafat and homicide bombers and their ilk a virtual pass in favor of vilifying Israelis and their Christian supporters who happen to hold eschatological views contrary to his. One might say that the capstone of this mindset is the lionization of several dubious characters for no explicable reason. Consider this:

> *Moreover today a new leadership is just over the horizon. Two young men in their thirties now rule in Damascus and Amman. In Iraq, Saddam Hussein's eldest son, Odai Hussein, won a seat in the Iraqi Parliament (March 28, 2000), will likely become the speaker of the house, and is the heir apparent.*[4]

Allied forces killed Odai in a shootout in July 2003. A villainous and depraved murderer, rapist, and torturer, he was called the most reviled man in Iraq. He had no compunctions about grabbing women off the street to rape them, or about murdering or torturing people who failed to yield to his car in traffic.[5] When he headed Iraq's Olympic committee, he mercilessly tortured athletes who did not meet his expectations.

You might say Burge could be charged with flawed judgment. But this is the core of the issue between Zionist Christians and liberals who make their case based on reckless abandon more given to castigating their opponents than to supporting the balance and tolerance they claim to cherish.

Setting the Record Straight

A consistent strain among detractors of Christian Zionists is that our motivation for a relationship with Israel and the Jewish people is self-serving; manipulative; and, above all, fanatically misguided. Those accusations can be answered emphatically, without guile or apology.

Do we believe that the Bible—Old Testament and New—holds irrevocable and unrescinded promises to Abraham and his posterity?

Yes, we do.

But while our detractors claim that prophetic revelation regarding the Messiah's First Coming must be taken as literal and historical, they find it acceptable to then disregard God's promises for Israel's future, morphing those portions of Scripture into a spiritualized, Gentile church. We do not.

This is the great divide between Dispensationalism and Replacement Theology. We believe that what God promised to Israel, He most certainly will deliver.

Do Zionist Christians believe in a Jewish end-times return to Israel and a later period called the Time of Jacob's Trouble?

Yes, we do.

And the reason is that this is precisely what the Scriptures clearly teach in both Testaments (Jer. 30:7; Mt. 24:21). It is not the invention of glowering evangelicals who have an ax to grind with the Jewish people and want Israel destroyed so the church can triumph and cause a Messianic advent. God will act according to His timetable, not ours. And there will, indeed, be a national reconciliation between Israel and her Lord, in preparation for a future Kingdom (Zech. 14:9; Rom. 11:26–27).

As a matter of fact, on this subject there is little difference between the positions of Orthodox Jewry and Zionist Christianity—except, of course, the big one: the identity of the Messiah. And do we believe we're right? You bet we do. But what does that issue change regarding our concern for Israel and her people according to our biblical marching orders? Absolutely nothing.

Do Zionist Christians detest Palestinians?

Certainly not.

This accusation is deeply offensive and atrociously unfair to believers who recognize Israel's rights and our obligation to comfort His Chosen People yet feel no less compassion for suffering Palestinians. Let's face the facts honestly. The pathway of such compassion for suffering Palestinians did not run through the offices of Yasser Arafat in Ramallah or the terrorist enclaves on the West Bank or in the Gaza Strip.

Good-faith negotiations between Israel and the Palestinian people could have taken place long ago. But the facts tell us two things: (1) In their quest for a Jewless Palestine, Arafat and his terrorist comrades walked away from numerous peace tables to pick up guns. In the process, they enriched themselves through systematic corruption at the expense of their brethren. (2) Their determination to pursue terror led to the necessity of the security fence, the closures, searches, and subsequent deprivation of their people.

Has Israel always been right?

No. Israelis are human, the same as people in seats of authority in Washington or Europe or the councils of the PCUSA. But it must be understood that Israel's struggle is, first and foremost, for national survival. Consequently, the issues of peace must be settled and Israel's survival assured.

We weep for and reach out to our fellow Christians who are Arab Palestinians. They are members of the family. But we do not accept our vilification by those who differ with our eschatology; nor are we willing to aid and comfort radicals, terrorists, and thugs who are as quick to kill their own kin who disagree with them as they are to kill innocent Israelis and Americans. Compassion is not the exclusive province of those who choose to assign it to themselves. Compassion is a binding obligation placed on all of us. And we would do well to concentrate our energies where it will do some good.

Do Christian Zionists believe that the Jewish people, after 2,000 years of dispersion, humiliation, and suffering, have a moral as well as legal right to a homeland where they can pursue normal lives free from the constant fear of annihilation?

Certainly.

And the commitment to respect the human rights and dignity of this small nation and its people should not be ridiculed as the misguided zealotry of right-wing extremists. Rather, it should be the shared commitment of all who enjoy the freedoms and values of civilized societies.

The fit of Presbyterian passion to "send a clear and strong message" should indeed serve as a strong wake-up call. And that call blares in two directions.

First, it should alert the parishioners who, as people of faith, occupy the pews of PCUSA churches. Many probably have little understanding of what some of their leaders actually believe and where their theological hearts reside. The Scriptures reiterate over and over again that the old "I didn't know" excuse will not cut it with the Lord—particularly after the case has been laid out for public viewing. These Presbyterian leaders have done that for their people, which may be an unintended blessing in disguise.

Second, it should be a signal to the American Jewish community, which for so many years has labored under the illusion that liberal Protestantism was where to find friends and common values. Well, the 216th General Assembly of the Presbyterian Church (USA) has put that opinion to rest. Its stand should also cause Jewish leaders to reevaluate their estimate of Zionist evangelical Christians and find out what we're really made of.

Jewish journalist Dennis Prager has an appropriate word:

> *It is time now for good people, Presbyterians specifically, Christians generally, to distance themselves vigorously and publicly from this morally sick church. And it is time, once again, for Jews to realize that the enemies of the Jews in our day are to be found on the Christian Left while their friends are far more often on the Christian Right.*[6]

A Partial Retreat

The divestiture language of the PCUSA General Assembly resolution of 2004 caused such a firestorm of opposition that the issue was revisited at the 2006 meeting in Birmingham, Alabama. The heat generated by the controversy was acknowledged, and Presbyterian James Woolsey (former CIA director) prompted the decision. Said Woolsey:

We have, I'm afraid, moved into a posture . . . that unless what we did two years ago is rejected, we are clearly on the side of theocratic, totalitarian, anti-Semitic, genocidal beliefs, and nothing less.[7]

Consequently, the divestiture resolution was, in a manner of speaking, altered. At a press conference, Moderator Joan Gray acknowledged the "hurt and misunderstanding among many members of the Jewish community and within our Presbyterian communion."[8]

By a vote of 483 to 28, the General Assembly set as policy that "financial investments of the Presbyterian Church (USA) as they pertain to Israel, Gaza, East Jerusalem, and the West Bank, be invested in only peaceful pursuits."[9] However, Assembly Clerk Clifton Kirkpatrick stated that the new resolution did not overturn the 2004 action. Therefore, other odious features of the 216th General Assembly resolution still stand as stated, except that no consideration of divestiture could take place before 2008 and then only with the permission of the General Assembly—which means that the much ado over the 2006 revision was more shadow than substance. As one member described it, this changes nothing about what the leaders believe, only that they were backed into a corner by an unexpected rebellion from the pews.

The central observation one can make is that, for whatever it's worth, the damage done by the PCUSA leadership in 2004 and modified in 2006 continues to set the tone for the actions of the liberal, leftist denigration of Israel's right to self-protection in the interest of survival.

Playing The Blame Game

No country on Earth wants peace more than Israel. It has made innumerable concessions to that end, all to no avail. Yet the world blames Israel for the problems in the Middle East rather than blaming the real culprit: the Arab/Islamic leadership that refuses to settle for anything less than Israel's destruction.

The blame game is not a new phenomenon in the arsenal of human defense. It is as old as the first pair that inhabited the planet and is being played in many arenas besides the Middle East. The blame game is a tactic we would do well to recognize because its consequences are as nefarious as that of turnspeak.

Although the story of Adam and Eve is well known, in view of what is to follow, a reminder wouldn't hurt:

> *Then the LORD God called to Adam and said to him, "Where are you?"*
>
> *So he said, "I heard Your voice in the garden, and I was afraid because I was naked; and I hid myself."*
>
> *And He said, "Who told you that you were naked? Have you eaten from the tree of which I commanded you that you should not eat?"*
>
> *Then the man said, "The woman whom You gave to be with me, she gave me of the tree, and I ate."*
>
> *And the LORD God said to the woman, "What is this you have done?"*
>
> *The woman said, "The serpent deceived me, and I ate"* (Gen. 3:9–13).

The environment of this biblical account is known as the Fall—the time when innocence died and the sin nature became a fact of life for Adam, Eve, and all their posterity. Adam blamed Eve, Eve blamed the serpent, and the first link was forged. Thus a premier negative attribute woven into the pattern of fallen humanity is the prolific capacity to prevaricate—the ability to lie, deceive, pass the buck, and blame the other guy. And after many millennia of practicing the art of blame deferral, the situation has not improved or become less apt to create serious problems for the innocent.

This fact could be a severe blow to proponents of both secular and theistic evolution and the "every day in every way I'm getting better and better" crowd, if it weren't for their refusal to admit that in the moral and spiritual spheres, nothing has really evolved. King David said it for all of us: "Behold, I was brought forth in iniquity, and in sin my mother conceived me" (Ps. 51:5).

Biblically, we find evidence of this truth at practically every turn in the road. Historically, we encounter it on every page. So we should not be surprised to experience it in these days of decadence and moral bankruptcy.

Fury From the Left

The vilification of Christian believers continues unabated and with an added measure of venom. The liberal left still compares "fundamentalist" Christians to Osama bin Laden's al-Qaida and Hitler's brown-shirted Nazis.

When evangelicals go to the polls, as is their right, and vote their convictions, it is not a happy circumstance in the eyes of the far left. These self-appointed moral liberators become infuriated that their rampaging, radical minority agenda to establish a brave, new, godless world becomes stalled by a majority of Americans. When this happens (as it did in 2004 when President George W. Bush won reelection), their response to this unwelcome phenomenon is predictable: Play the blame game. Ignore the fact that a majority of Americans want traditional values and point the finger at "bigoted, intolerant," conservative Christians who oppose social "progress."

What is lost on these merchants of change is the fact that other issues existed besides the broad-based revulsion at their attempts to rewrite the republic's essential commitment to Judeo-Christian values. Christians, along with thousands of others, demonstrated their concern that America was being taken down the wrong road. So they decided to act as responsible citizens, go to the polls, and vote in favor of what they believe is right for the country.

A prominent radio personality, who by no means claims to be a Christian, voiced the feeling many acted on. "It was a simple matter," he said. "People asked themselves whom they would choose to have as a role model for their lives: Jesus Christ or Michael Moore." Moore, you will recall, trashed President Bush in his film *Fahrenheit 9/11*.

For Bible-believing Christians the answer was easy. We had been watching the debilitating factors described in Romans 1 unfold before our eyes, and we didn't like what we saw. What God calls moral and spiritual disintegration, radical social revolutionaries hail as progress and liberation. Therefore, as Israel's Old Testament history so aptly demonstrated, national degeneracy was turning the civilized world upside down. On the descent into the pit, right becomes wrong, justice becomes injustice, righteousness becomes unrighteousness, victims become villains, and every conceivable vice is sanctified as desirable. The Lord puts it this way:

> [They] exchanged the truth of God for the lie, and worshiped and served the creature rather than the Creator, who is blessed forever. Amen. For this reason God gave them up to vile passions. And even as they did not like to retain God in their knowledge, God gave them over to a debased mind, to do those things which are not fitting (Rom. 1:25–26, 28).

Christians came down on the side of biblical rationality. For so doing, we will not be forgiven; and the struggle for the nation's soul will continue. We must remember that for well over a generation, the mainstream centers of secular higher learning, as well as liberal religious institutions, have nurtured students on situation ethics: There are no moral absolutes and no valid biblical mandates; every situation demands a personal evaluation, and individuals can do whatever seems right in their eyes. Those who criticize are labeled self-righteous, intolerant bigots and misfits.

The late Dr. Francis A. Schaeffer, among others, foresaw the course of future events decades ago:

> *Does the church have a future in our generation?... I believe the church is in real danger. It is in for a rough day. We are facing present pressures and a present and future manipulation which will be so overwhelming in the days to come that they will make the battles of the last forty years look like child's play.*[10]

How insightful he was.

The Somerville Experience

There are few better examples of playing the blame game than what took place in the fall of 2004 in a suburb of Boston. Somerville is a community of about 80,000 and bears the distinction of being the first municipality in the United States to consider a resolution to join the cadre attempting to strip Israel of financial investments. The campaign was also designed to boycott companies supplying Israel with equipment deemed militarily usable in its struggle for survival.

The Somerville experience was an arm of the disinvestment crusade the Presbyterian Church (USA) had initiated earlier in the year. Although the debacle in Somerville mirrored what the PCUSA and others have done, it had some distinguishing features. It was spearheaded by a group calling itself the Somerville Divestment Project (SDP), a soul mate of such anti-Israel organizations as the Palestine Solidarity Movement that unsuccessfully lobbied the city of Seattle, Washington, to drop investments in Israel.

After drafting a divestment resolution, the SDP obtained

1,200 signatures on a petition and took it to the city's 11 aldermen. Eight signed on, and the proposal came close to passing without debate when introduced before the Board of Aldermen. Fortunately, red flags began to flutter. The mayor threatened to veto the move, and the board had second thoughts, deciding it might not be a bad idea to let the public have a say before passing a resolution recommending divestment.

One alderman later told *The Jerusalem Post*, "My intentions were just to make a statement about human rights, and unfortunately I hadn't taken into consideration what kind of division it would cause in the city, and the arguments in the rest of the community that were quite strong." It would not have taken an Einstein to predict the ensuing uproar.

Under the guise of a human rights declaration, the SDP resolution accused Israel of virtually every crime possible against humanity. As is the case with such things, almost without exception, no mention is made of Arab and Palestinian atrocities, like suicide bombings, institutionalized hatred of all Jews and everything Jewish, incitement to violence, and determination to destroy the State of Israel.

Which raises the question, one with potentially serious consequences, of how eight of 11 civic leaders in an American city could be so abysmally ignorant of the basic issues in the Israeli-Palestinian conflict that they would sign such an inflammatory, divisive proposal without objective examination. And in so doing, they put the blame for the conflict on the people and leaders of a nation attempting to survive in a sea of Islamic hostility. It goes without saying that a legitimate, democratic state in the Middle East is America's staunchest ally in the region.

Are most U.S. citizens paying attention to this kind of subversive manipulation? Probably not, but you can be certain that radical elements in the Muslim community take such events very seriously. A letter circulated to the Islamic

Society of Boston, reported on the Dhimmi Watch Web site (www.jihadwatch.org/dhimmiwatch), states in part,

> *It is in such a perilous hour that we live today, when we have no choice but to stand up against the raging Beast consuming all that is beautiful and holy on this earth. . . . The State of Israel is the primary threat to World Peace today, especially in that it controls American politics. The American people have a duty to break the neck of the State of Israel by cutting off its supply of funding. We must kill the stranglehold that the supporters of Israel have placed upon our throats.*

So, in effect, the aldermen of Somerville unwittingly played into the hands of Islamic militants and their naïve—or not so naïve—American fellow travelers whose interests are not in justifiable human rights but in the eventual annihilation of Israel.

If we view as tolerable and benign this capitulation to militant radicals posing as do-gooders, then we need to take a long look at what is taking place in the Netherlands, Germany, and France. For years these countries have turned a blind eye to the enemies within their borders and allowed the malignancy of hatred and terror to fester until it erupted in hate campaigns against Israel and the Jewish people. Such hatred was capped in 2004 by the vicious murder and mutilation of 47-year-old Dutch filmmaker Theo Van Gogh because a film he produced exposing Muslim discrimination and suppression of women reportedly offended the Muslims.

In Germany, the Muslim imams' malicious diatribes against Germany and its citizens prompted the president to tell Islamic people to "learn German, fit in, and commit to democratic rules." He even proposed that Muslim clerics be forced to preach in German.

So while some on the left may believe it fashionable to endorse the blame game, they are falling into lockstep with forces that mask more sinister intentions; and they are acting against themselves, their fellow countrymen, Israel, and that segment of the Muslim population wishing to live in peace. Although the blame game originated in the Garden of Eden, it is no less deadly today. It plays into the hands of those who call good evil and evil good and prompts Americans to support disinvesting from a free and democratic country in favor of people who use murder and terror to get what they want.

ENDNOTES

[1] Joan Peters, *From Time Immemorial* (1984; Chicago: JKAP Publications, 1993), 173.

[2] Gary M. Burge, Ph.D., "Christian Zionism, Evangelicals and Israel," The Holy Land Christian Ecumenical Foundation [www.hcef.org/hcef/index.cfm/ID/159].

[3] Gary M. Burge, *Whose Land? Whose Promise?* (Cleveland, OH: The Pilgrim Press, 2003), 200.

[4] Burge, *Whose Land? Whose Promise?* 31.

[5] Scott Calvert, "Inside the private prison of Odai Hussein: Evidence of torture, death at behest of dictator's son," April 28, 2003 <baltimoresun.com/news/nationworld/iraq/bal-te.jail28apr28,0,3741580.story?coll=bal-home-headlines>.

[6] Dennis Prager, *Presbyterian Church USA Defames Christianity* <jewish ledger.com/articles/2004/07/28/editorial/edit05.prt>.

[7] Mike Ferguson, "Harsh words: Former CIA chief Woolsey sharply criticizes 2004 GA decision," 217th General Assembly News, June 16, 2006 <pcusa.org/ga217/newsandphotos/ga06031.htm>.

[8] Toya Richards Hill, "GA overwhelmingly approves Israel/Palestine recommendation," 217th General Assembly News, June 21, 2006 <pcusa.org/ga217/newsandphotos/ga06124.htm>.

[9] Ibid.

[10] Francis A. Schaeffer, *The Church at the End of the 20th Century* (Wheaton, IL: Crossway Books, 1994), 5.

CHAPTER 8

⬦⬥⬦

ANTI-ZIONISM OR ANTI-SEMITISM— BY ANY NAME, THE GAME'S THE SAME

The Muslim world, in league with some intellectual, European bedfellows, is floating a new message these days. It, too, is part of an overall, yet subtler, strategy to destroy Israel then move on to more fertile fields. Since outright anti-Semitism might not play well in the West, Islam has invented something else: It is not, say some Muslims, that they are anti-Semitic; they merely oppose Zionism. The implication is that, if the political State of Israel were dismantled, Palestinians and Jewish people could live in peace and harmony in Palestine. No country should be distinctively Jewish, they say. Yet there are at least 46 distinctively Muslim countries in the world, several of which (including Saudi Arabia, Libya, Qatar, and United Arab Emirates) are 100 percent Muslim. But for some reason it is unreasonable to allow even one country that is 80 percent Jewish!

There are Muslims, of course, like the leaders of Hamas and Hezbollah, who vow to destroy Israel and never to live in peace with it. But that hard line has limited appeal in the West. So Muslim politicians have introduced a softer line—the anti-Zionism approach—that attracts a broader spectrum. But as we say, if it looks like a duck, quacks like a duck, and walks like a duck, it's probably a duck. Anti-Zionism and anti-Semitism look, "quack," and "walk" exactly the same.

Some Muslims in Great Britain have even gone so far as to

demand the British apologize for the Balfour Declaration and repudiate the very notion of the document as soon as possible. Arthur James Balfour conveyed the Balfour Declaration to Baron Lord Rothschild and the Zionist Federation in a letter on November 2, 1917. It affirmed, "His Majesty's Government view with favor the establishment in Palestine of a national home for the Jewish people, and will use their best endeavors to facilitate the achievement of this object."

The Zionist Movement

Such recognition by Western governments represented the consummation of nearly 2,000 years of pent-up Jewish desire to return to the land of the forefathers—*Eretz Yisrael*. This undying hope is memorialized today in the Israeli national anthem, "Hatikvah":

> *So long as still within our breasts*
> *The Jewish heart beats true,*
> *So long as still towards the east*
> *To Zion looks the Jew,*

> *So long our hopes are not yet lost—*
> *Two thousand years we cherished them—*
> *To live in freedom in the land of*
> *Zion and Jerusalem.*

A Jewish writer expressed it his way: "Upheld and fortified in the dispersion by the Messianic vision of an ultimate return, the Jews never forgot or forsook their ties with the Homeland. This imperishable hope of redemption gave them fortitude to endure discrimination and persecution."[1]

In 1897 in Basel, Switzerland, the First Zionist Congress met under the auspices of Theodor Herzl and several other groups, such as *Hovevei Zion* ("lovers of Zion"). There was no central direction or political program driving the Congress. It was simply the formal outgrowth of a mass movement toward Zionism within the Jewish and Christian communities. The definition of *Zionism* resulted from the deliberations of a committee headed by Max Nordau, a Hungarian-born doctor who had drifted from Judaism but returned due to anti-Semitism. He wrote:

> *The aim of Zionism is to create for the Jewish people a home in Eretz-Israel [the land of Israel] secured by international law.*

That dream was realized following the near annihilation of Europe's Jews during the Holocaust of the Hitler era. As men like Herzl had discerned half a century earlier, Europe was no longer a place Jewish people could comfortably call home. So they pursued emigration to Palestine in earnest.

On November 29, 1947, the UN General Assembly adopted Resolution 181 (Partition Plan). The vote was 33 in favor, 13 against, and 10 abstentions. With that historic vote, Israel became a sovereign state under international law. Theodor Herzl had written in his diary after the 1897 Congress, "At Basel, I founded the Jewish state . . . if not in five years, then certainly in fifty, everyone will realize it." In 1947 his dream came true.

Arab Rejectionism

Arab and Muslim reaction to the reality of modern Israel was swift and violent. It rejected the Partition Plan and began a war of annihilation immediately after the official launching of the state on May 14, 1948. Five Arab armies unsuccessfully fought to make the State of Israel a stillbirth. Over the next 50 years they continued their battle through military adventurism, only to come up empty time after time.

Realizing they could not wipe out the state by military means, they turned to terrorism and international campaigning to discredit what they chose to attack as "political Zionism." Political Zionism was deemed odious, illegitimate, and the basis upon which the nation existed.

As with the revisionist crusade now under way that denies all of Jewry's historic associations with the Temple Mount, the strategy is to convince the world that the Jewish people have no right to an exclusive, national entity in the Middle East. It treats Israel as though it did not exist as a legitimate, legal national reality in the international community, but as a mutation dubbed "Zionism"—a plague to be snuffed out.

One Arab source claims that anti-Zionism does not mean Jewish people have no right to immigrate to the region . . . only that there should not be a racially exclusive state built on "ethnic cleansing" and maintained through an "apartheid" system.

Such accusations blatantly ignore the fact that 20 percent of Israel's citizens are Palestinian Arabs (Muslim and Christian), Druze, and other ethnicities.

And though the Muslim public relations campaign declares "political Zionism," not anti-Semitism, the issue at hand, the facts speak for themselves.

Itamar Marcus, director of the Palestinian Media Watch, reported the following:

> *PA [Palestinian Authority] academic and religious leaders teach that Islam is at war against Jews. They cite Islamic sources to demand Jews be hated and killed. Tens of times in recent years they have taught the Hadith [Islamic tradition attributed to Muhammad] demanding Muslims kill Jews is a current obligation, in order to bring "the Hour"— the Resurrection. Two examples are Dr. Hassan Khader, founder Al Quds Encyclopedia on PA TV on July 13, 2003 and Dr. Ibrahim Mad, on PA TV on April 12, 2002.*[2]

Peddling the 'Big Lie'

One way to convince people of the "evils" of "political Zionism" is, of course, to libel the Jews themselves. It is the tactic Hitler used so efficiently. And the same poisonous, anti-Semitic material is not only still around but available at your neighborhood bookstore.

The infamous *Protocols of the Elders of Zion* is a libelous document that will not go away. Peddling the venomous fabrications of the *Protocols* has been the stock-in-trade of anti-Semitic hate merchants since it was produced by agents of the czarist intelligence service in Russia more than a century ago. Hundreds of studies have been produced over the years that authoritatively expose the *Protocols* for the hoax that it is. A credible example is found in a report prepared by a subcommittee of the U.S. Senate Judiciary Committee in 1964. Partial quotations from the committee's findings shed light on the preposterous fallacies represented in *Protocols:*

> *Every age and country has had its share of fabricated "historic" documents which have been foisted on an unsuspecting public for some malign purpose. One of the most notorious and most durable is the Protocols of the Elders of Zion.*

It claims that international Communism is simply a manifestation of a world Jewish conspiracy that seeks to subjugate all the non-Jewish peoples of the world. *Protocols* made the enemy "international Jewry" rather than Communism. It speaks of clandestine Jewish meetings among Jewish power-brokers and a Jewish plot to take over the world. By 1926 it had been translated into Arabic and was being widely circulated in Muslim countries.

Ironically, there are 1.3 billion Muslims in the world and a paltry 15 million Jews. The Jewish people constitute a mere 2.5 tenths of 1 percent of the world population. More people live in the state of Florida than there are Jews in the entire world. And the Muslims think the Jewish people are going to take over the globe? I doubt it. They fear no such thing. However, they conveniently use the smear campaign as part of their strategy to do precisely what they claim the Jewish people are doing.

Unfortunately, *Protocols* is a runaway best seller in the Muslim world. In Saudi Arabia schools teach it to children as fact. In the March/April 2006 issue of *Israel My Glory* magazine, Steve Herzig cited three of the *Protocols'* major themes:

1. Jewish people control the news media worldwide. (In truth, the majority of the secular press is hostile to the Jews and favors the Palestinians.)
2. Zionism is the root of the world's system today. (In truth, Zionism pertains only to the desire for a Jewish national home in the tiny land of Israel. It is Islam that overtly seeks world domination and currently controls more than 25 percent of the world's countries.)
3. Jewish people seek to eliminate nationalities and religions, especially the Christian nations. (In truth, it is the Muslims who use torture, jihad, and terrorism to force worldwide conversion to Islam.)[3]

The Arab press skillfully and frequently refers to the *Protocols*, plying its people with lies of a "Jewish conspiracy" that wants to convert people, "spread corruption among all human societies," and control "Hollywood, the press, economics, and world resources."[4]

Steven Stalinsky, in a September 30, 2005, article in Frontpagemag.com, said the Palestinian Authority routinely cites these vicious lies as fact:

Leading Palestinian Authority religious figures often cite the "Protocols." Saudi Al-Majd TV aired an interview on February 20 [2005] with Palestinian Arab Mufti Ikrima Sabri on the assassination of Lebanese leader Rafiq Al-Hariri: "'The Protocols of the Elders of Zion' and specifically the Talmud will discover that one of the goals of these protocols is to cause confusion in the world and to undermine security throughout the world." Another example includes a Palestinian Authority TV Friday sermon by Sheik Ibrahim Mudeiris on April 16, 2004: "Our battle with our enemy is great . . . We face a battle against the Crusaders and against World Zionism" [5]

Although *Protocols* has been repeatedly and authoritatively exposed as a vicious hoax, it continues to be circulated by the unscrupulous and accepted by the unthinking. The Subcommittee on Internal Security not only receives inquiries about the book from time to time from sincere but misguided people, but on occasion is even exhorted to advert to this "document" as a source of information.

Its continued circulation cannot be explained on the basis of its contents, which is obviously rubbish, but rather on the techniques employed by its peddlers. They use the Hitler technique of the "big lie."

On June 2, 1961, Richard Helms, then assistant director of the Central Intelligence Agency, testified before a Senate subcommittee on "Communist Forgeries." Speaking of the *Protocols,* he declared, "The Russians have a long tradition in the art of forgery. More than 60 years ago the czarist intelligence service concocted and peddled a confection called *The Protocols of the Elders of Zion.*"

But Hitler used *Protocols* most effectively, as did anti-Semites before him. Even though it has been called "the fictional product of a warped mind," the Arabs use the book successfully to generate an everlasting hatred among their people. Wrote Judge Hadassa Ben-Itto:

> *To this day excerpts from the* Protocols *are printed periodically in the Arab press, occasionally accompanied by cartoons copied from the Nazi* Stuermer, *and appear not only in Iran, but even in a country like Egypt which has made peace with Israel and in the Palestinian press. The* Protocols *are specially mentioned in the 1988 Covenant of the Hamas, and they are known to be an incentive for suicide bombers, used to convince them that by saving the world from these dangerous Jews they secure their place in Paradise.*
>
> *Over time the use of the* Protocols *has become increasingly bold: it is not enough that the* Protocols *are published and sold in bookstores, they are taught in schools, serialized in official newspapers accompanied by* Stuermer-*style cartoons, quoted on numerous sites on the Internet, and as a special feature they are now aired on television during the month of Ramadan, presented as the main theme of a 41 episode television series* Knight Without A Horse *created in Egypt and shown in most Moslem countries.*
>
> *Millions of viewers are now exposed to this lie, and past experience shows that such damage is irreversible. History teaches us that, in the words of Norman Cohn, this is a "Warrant for Genocide," first used in Czarist Russia to incite pogroms, and then again in Nazi Germany to legitimize the extermination of the Jews.*[6]

Throughout the Middle East, Europe, and unfortunately,

on many campuses in the United States, Jewish people have become the victims of verbal and physical assaults. By any standard, these attacks are anti-Semitic and cannot be written off as venting on "political Zionism."

Therefore, by any name, the game is the same: Anti-Zionism equals anti-Semitism.

Ironically, the Palestinian rush toward statehood is a declaration of intent and purpose to establish a Muslim state. In January 2006, the terrorist organization Hamas won 76 of the 123 seats in the Palestinian parliament. Islamic Sharia law will rule, the military will be led by Palestinians, and Palestinian citizens will be subject to the dictates of a purely Palestinian state . . . all of which begs the obvious. How can a Palestinian state be more legal and legitimate than one that happens to be legitimately Jewish?

It cannot, of course. But the drive to devalue and extermi-nate Zionism is a glaring exhibition of the "final solution" envisioned by Hitler and now articulated by Palestinians, Muslims, and the majority of Arab leaders. The ruse of "political Zionism" is nothing more than a device to expel the Jewish people from the Middle East in a modern dispersion and plant the Palestinian flag on the whole of the land God gave to the physical descendants of Abraham, Isaac, and Jacob.

Christian Zionism

For all of the talk about "political Zionism," the concept of Zionism reaches far beyond the confines of secular legisla-tures or UN corridors.

First and foremost, Zionism is an integral element in the biblical mandate and record handed down by God Himself. Therefore, it is not surprising that evangelical Christians were vitally involved in the establishment of the modern Jewish state. And what was their reasoning? It was as simple as this: Because the Bible says so.

An outstanding illustration of this stance is seen in the involvement of the venerable Englishman William H. Hechler, who shared Herzl's dream of a return of the Jewish people to Zion.

Hechler had an enormous circle of contacts among religious leaders and in the royal courts of Europe. Thus he was able to introduce the father of modern Zionism to individuals who would become invaluable resources to the cause.

Herzl, a Jewish journalist, said of Hechler, a Christian clergyman,

> *He counsels me superbly, and with unmistakably genuine good will. He is at once shrewd and mystical, cunning and naïve. So far, with respect to myself, he has backed me up in quite a wonderful way . . . I would wish the Jews to show him a full measure of gratitude.*[7]

For those of us who identify with the aspirations of men like William Hechler and other early Christian Zionists, our mandate is grounded in the Scriptures. And we are unabashedly committed to the fact that the promises God made to Abraham and his posterity are irrevocable.

God's Irrevocable Promises to Abraham—

> *Now the LORD had said unto Abram: "Get out of your country, from your family and from your father's house, to a land that I will show you. I will make you a great nation; I will bless you and make your name great; and you shall be a blessing. I will bless those who bless you, and I will curse him who curses you; and in you all families of the earth shall be blessed" (Gen. 12:1–3).*
>
> *And I will establish My covenant between Me*

and you and your descendants after you in their generations, for an everlasting covenant, to be God to you and your descendants after you. Also I give to you and your descendants after you the land in which you are a stranger, all the land of Canaan, as an everlasting possession; and I will be their God (17:7–8).

God's Promise to Preserve the Jewish People—

Yet for all that, when they are in the land of their enemies, I will not cast them away, nor shall I abhor them, to utterly destroy them and break My covenant with them; for I am the LORD *their God. But for their sake I will remember the covenant of their ancestors, whom I brought out of the land of Egypt in the sight of the nations, that I might be their God: I am the* LORD (Lev. 26:44–45).

Therefore know that the LORD *your God, He is God, the faithful God who keeps covenant and mercy for a thousand generations with those who love Him and keep His commandments* (Dt. 7:9).

God's Promise of a Return to the Land—

Then He said to me, "Son of man, these bones are the whole house of Israel. They indeed say, 'Our bones are dry, and our hope is lost, we ourselves are cut off!' Therefore prophesy and say to them, 'Thus says the Lord GOD: *"Behold, O My people, I will open your graves and cause you to come up from your graves, and bring you into the land of Israel"'"* (Ezek. 37:11–12).

Yes, I will cause men to walk on you [the land], My people Israel; they shall take possession of you, and you shall be their inheritance; no more shall you bereave them of children. For I will take you from

*among the nations, gather you out of all countries,
and bring you into your own land* (36:12, 24).

New Testament Assumptions and Assertions—

The New Testament everywhere assumes that the Jewish
people will be in *Eretz Israel* during the final phase of the current dispensation. Speaking of the Jewish people during a
future time of seven years, called the Tribulation, Jesus said:

> *Therefore when you see the 'abomination of desola-
> tion,' spoken of by Daniel the prophet, standing in
> the holy place . . . then let those who are in Judea flee
> to the mountains. For then there will be great
> tribulation, such as has not been since the beginning
> of the world until this time, no, nor ever shall
> be. See, I have told you beforehand* (Mt. 24:15–16,
> 21, 25).
>
> *For I do not desire, brethren, that you should be
> ignorant of this mystery, lest you should be wise in
> your own opinion, that blindness in part is happened
> to Israel until the fullness of the Gentiles has come
> in. And so all Israel will be saved, as it is written:
> "The Deliverer will come out of Zion, and He will
> turn away ungodliness from Jacob"* (Rom.
> 11:25–26).

God's Promise of a Millennial Kingdom Under the Messiah—

> *And in that day His feet will stand on the Mount of
> Olives, which faces Jerusalem on the east. And the
> Mount of Olives shall be split in two, from east to
> west, making a very large valley; Half of the moun-
> tain shall move toward the north and half of it
> toward the south. And the LORD shall be King over
> all the earth. In that day it shall be—"The LORD is
> one," and His name one* (Zech 14:4, 9).

To these great and irrefutable promises we can only say, "Even so, Come, Lord Jesus."

ENDNOTES

[1] *Anti-Semitism,* Israel Pocket Library (Jerusalem: Keter Publishing House Jerusalem, 1972), 13.

[2] TV Archives—Video Library: Encouraging Genocide, Incitement to terrorism, and anti-Semitism, "Muhammad Demands Muslims Kill Jews" <pmw.org.il/tv%20part6.html>.

[3] Steve Herzig, "The Protocols of the Elders of Zion," *Israel My Glory* 64, no. 2 (2006), 31.

[4] Steven Stalinsky, "HBO Weighs in on 'Protocols,'" September 30, 2005 <frontpagemag.com/Articles/ReadArticle.asp?ID=19661>.

[5] Ibid.

[6] Judge Hadassa Ben-Itto, "President's Message," *Justice* 34, (winter 2002) <intjewishlawyers.org/docenter/viewDocument.asp?id=9281>, 3.

[7] Claude Duvernoy, *The Prince and the Prophet* (Jerusalem: Christian Action for Israel, 1966), 43.

CHAPTER 9

c✖️᠀

THE CHRISTIAN THING TO DO

Many of us are becoming increasingly weary with the fatuous harping of the World Council of Churches. We can always depend on the WCC to oppose conservative Christian and traditional Judeo-Christian positions.

A current example is the volley fired in May 2006 by the WCC's ultraliberal executive council at a meeting in Geneva, Switzerland. The council declared that Israel's actions toward the Palestinians cannot be justified morally, legally, or politically. Furthermore, the WCC top brass called for relaxation of sanctions against the Palestinians' genocidal, terrorist Hamas government; and it railed against the security fence being constructed to protect Israeli civilians from terrorist attacks.

Time was when mainline denominations and secular forces largely accepted the WCC as the voice of worldwide Christianity. Today it claims to speak for 340 member churches, denominations, and fellowships numbering 550 million adherents in more than 100 countries.[1] But it does not speak for us all, as certified by its exposure as the handmaid of extremist radicalism that targets, among others, evangelical Christians who continue to accept biblical authority, cherish the democratic norms upon which Western society has been constructed, and support the rights of the Jewish people to a secure homeland in the Middle East.

Matter of fact, someone has suggested (and I agree) that the majority of WCC leaders would do well to acknowledge their repudiation of the faith of our fathers and declare their own cult. Such will not be the case, of course, largely because these people control the funds and fortunes of adherents who remain unaware of the truths of spiritual life and the moral bankruptcy of their leaders.

Christian Concern for Israel and the Jewish People

Holocaust heroine Corrie ten Boom once answered a question as to why she and her Christian family willingly risked their lives to protect Jewish people from the Nazis. Her answer was simple and thoroughly Christ-like: Because her father told her, "It was the Christian thing to do." It was, and so it remains.

Also in May 2006, Elbert Colenbrander and his now deceased parents were officially recognized as "Righteous Among the Nations" at a ceremony at Yad Vashem, the memorial in Jerusalem to the Holocaust. The honor was bestowed because of the Colenbrander family's heroism in risking their lives by sheltering Jewish families at their farm in Holland during World War II.

Elbert Colenbrander, then 79, was surprised when contacted, because he felt it was a "big honor he did not deserve." *The Jerusalem Post* reported that his daughter Wilma said her father "never talked much about the war with his children, and only discussed it when asked. . . . Over the years, he always said that he was taught that as a Christian, you do these things for other people."[2]

The Colenbranders and Corrie ten Boom are among the 13,000 Gentiles, including three Americans, currently honored in the Garden of the Righteous at Yad Vashem. Many of them were essentially humanitarians moved by the horrifying plight of the Jewish people. Thousands of others, however, were Christians. They were motivated, despite the risks, by a biblically instilled compassion concerning "the Christian thing to do."

Calling Israel apartheid, expansionist, illegal, and predatory is a perverse, bigoted, and unwarranted transgression of the truth. At its base, it is a heinous assault that extends far beyond the borders of aggression against a legitimate nation. It is, in fact, a violation of the viability of the Jewish people's struggle to survive in the world's most hostile environment. Every day Israelis face heavily armed enemies determined to destroy them.

What is often swept under the proverbial rug by those attacking Zionism—Christian or otherwise—is the fact that more than 5 million Jewish people live in the State of Israel. They approximate in number the Jewish people exterminated in the Holocaust. To side with those trumpeting their intention to annihilate these people is anything but biblical or Christian; it is, in actuality, a crime against humanity.

On the other hand, the survival of the Palestinian Arabs has never been in jeopardy. I remember a conversation I had in the 1970s with Gen. Uzi Narkiss who led the Israel Defense Forces that captured Jerusalem in 1967. One of his major concerns was for an equitable settlement with the Palestinians and a genuine peace between Jews and Arabs. The claptrap that Palestinian militants consistently spew about Israeli and American intentions to destroy the Palestinian people is utter propaganda and absolute rubbish.

It Is About People

It is a fact that millions of evangelical Christians have no compunction about being identified as Christian Zionists, and this commitment spills over into the realm of international politics. But the bottom line for Christian Zionists is an unfathomable love for the Jewish people and their land—a love that is biblically instilled and so profoundly personal it cannot be explained. It can only be expressed by the lives and actions of Christians who prove their affection for Israel and the Jewish people in quite extraordinary ways.

I remember speaking at a church in Michigan some years ago where I recounted an interview I had had with a Jewish senator about his personal experiences with prejudice and anti-Semitism. Near the end of the interview, he rather pensively confessed that, from time to time, he would scan his circle of friends and ask himself a question he felt most Jewish people ask themselves: If an Adolf Hitler were to rise to power in America, who among these people would give me a place to hide?

A year later I returned to the church for another speaking engagement. As I entered the building, I was met by a young woman who immediately asked if I remembered my comments about the interview. "Of course," I said.

She replied that her employer was Jewish and that, for some time, she had wanted to explain her faith to him and why she cared deeply for Jewish people and Israel. So she decided to speak to him at her earliest opportunity. The next morning, as she walked to her desk, she met him in the aisle. He seemed to sense that she had something on her mind.

"Is there something I can do for you?" he asked.

Because of the suddenness of the encounter, she found herself speechless. Suddenly, she burst out with the only thing that came to mind. "I just want you to know," she said, "that if an Adolf Hitler ever comes to America, I'll give you a place to hide."

Her employer was so moved that he wept.

This is not merely a story. It is the genuine reflection of the hearts of many, many thousands of Christians. Some of them don't know quite how to say what they feel, but they feel it nonetheless.

The late Will H. Houghton, president of the Moody Bible Institute in Chicago, Illinois, from 1934 to 1947, put it in a few rather simple but immensely expressive lines of poetry:

Say not a Christian e'er would
    persecute a Jew;
A Gentile might, but not a Christian true.
    Pilate and Roman guard that folly tried.
And with that great Jew's death an empire died!

When Christians gather in cathedral,
    church or hall,
Hearts turn toward One—the name of Jesus call.
    You cannot persecute—whatever else you do—
The race who gave Him—Jesus was a Jew!

Or hear the words from the intrepid Poet of the Sierras, Joaquin Miller, in his "To Russia":

Who taught you tender Bible tales
Of honey-lands, of milk and wine?
Of happy, peaceful Palestine?
Of Jordan's holy harvest vales?
Who gave the patient Christ? I say,
Who gave the Christian creed? Yea, Yea,
Who gave your very God to you?
Your Jew! Your Jew! Your hated Jew![3]

The Christian-Zionist phenomenon is not a monolithic, political strategy brewed by right-wing conservatives with an agenda to attain or an ax to grind. It is the totality of many millions of individual believers who have arrived at their conclusions about Israel and its Jewish heritage because of two things: (1) a personal relationship with Jesus Christ and (2) interaction with the Scriptures—Old and New Testaments —that inevitably direct intellects and hearts to an affinity for the land and the people of the Book.

I have been asked repeatedly over my decades of association with Jewish people in and outside of Israel why, as a

Gentile, I've chosen to invest my life in this fashion. My answer is not unique but, rather, what you will hear in one way or another from virtually every Christian with a serious commitment to the mandates of God's Word: "One day I met a Jew who changed my life, assured my eternal destiny, and set my life's course in another direction. That Jew is Jesus Christ, and I owe Him everything."

And the testimonies of myriads of other Bible-believing Christians are on record. Blanche Dugdale, niece of Lord Arthur James Balfour, said of her uncle,

> "He always talked eagerly on this ["the Jew in the modern world"] and I remember in childhood imbibing from him the idea that Christian religion and civilization owes to Judaism an immeasurable debt, shamefully ill repaid."[4]

And where did the primary instigator of the British decision to create a mandate for a Jewish state in Palestine find his inspiration?

> Balfour liked to read from the Old Testament prophets, particularly Isaiah. He loved to read aloud, and did so . . . 'beautifully and reverently.' [Because of his biblical insight] he was one of those devout Christians who was able to view the Jews with insight and simple, down-to-earth understanding.[5]

As with other early supporters of a Jewish homeland, Bible knowledge was the key to Balfour's commitment.

Of more recent vintage was Ed McAteer, now with the Lord, whose love for Israel and the Jewish people made him a modern pioneer in Jewish-Christian relations. It was Ed who, in 1981, launched the groundbreaking annual National Prayer Breakfast in honor of Israel in Washington, D.C. His journey as an ardent Christian Zionist began with a challenge from his wife, Faye. In a book published about Ed in 2004 titled *The Power of One: The Ed McAteer Story*, Thomas and Jonathan Lindberg and Daniel E. Johnson wrote:

> [McAteer said,] "Her grandfather told her to be good to the Jews, citing Genesis 12:1, where God promises to bless those who bless Abraham and his family." Over the years, as a result of disciplined study of the Word of God, he had become a "Christian Zionist."

A New Way of Thinking

What saddens many evangelicals is that, for so very long, we were viewed as no better than the pseudo-Christians who tormented the Jewish people and opposed a Jewish homeland. Fueling this misconception is Replacement Theology, the erroneous idea that the church has replaced Jewry as the true Israel of God.

In like vein, there has been a chasm of misunderstanding separating Jewish people and evangelicals, propagated by the fallacy that the driving force in Christian support is the motivation to proselytize unwary Jews and facilitate their return to the land merely to bring about apocalyptic convulsions and hasten the return of Jesus.

To be fair, evangelicals need make no apology for desiring to communicate their faith to Jewish people. Many years ago in New York City, I spoke about this issue with a prominent national Jewish leader. He said he had no trouble with Christian evangelism. The nature of evangelicalism is to evangelize, he said. To do less would violate the commission Jesus gave the church.

His problem was when Christians evangelized in the guise of some form of Judaism or worked like undercover agents for Jesus, representing themselves as something they are not in order to seduce Jews into converting.

I have no problem with his observation. We have an obligation to make Christ and the gospel known to all people, Jewish and Gentile. In the words of Scripture, "There is no difference" (Rom. 3:22). And the gospel is to be proclaimed to all (Mt. 28:19–20).

Ironically, the desire of Christians to communicate their faith is actually more unifying than divisive. I know of no Christians today who think less of their Jewish friends who fail to believe in Jesus. Their friendships are strong, demonstrating unequivocally an unconditional love. And they will remain friends—unvarnished and irrevocable, no apologies necessary—as far as Christian Zionists are concerned.

It's the Christian thing to do.

ENDNOTES

[1] "What Is the World Council of Churches?" <wcc-coe.org/wcc/who/index-e.html>.

[2] Etgar Lefkovits, "A righteous family is honored after 60 years," May 31, 2006, <jpost.com/servlet/Satellite?cid=1148482084949&pagename=JPost% 2FJPArticle%2FshowFull>.

[3] Joaquin Miller, "To Russia," *An American Anthology, 1787–1900,* ed. Edmond Clarence Stedman (1900; New York: Greenwood Press, 1968), 429.

[4] Cited in Michael Pragai, *Faith and Fulfilment* (London: Vallentine, Mitchell and Company Limited, 1985), 84.

[5] Ibid.

CHAPTER 10

❧

CHILDREN IN THE FIRE

To the west and south of the Old City of Jerusalem is a deep gash in the landscape. It is identified as the Hinnom Valley. Today it is a lush area lending itself to picnics, outdoor concerts, and public events. However, to ancients, it was known as the valley of the sons of Hinnom and later the Valley of Tophet. In the seventh century B.C. it became Gehenna, a designation synonymous with hell, the place of burning.

Most notorious in the history of Hinnom is the practice of child sacrifice—placing infants and children in the fire to appease the ancient pagan god Molech. Talmudic tradition asserts that the image of Molech bore a brass calf's head adorned with a royal crown. He was represented as sitting on a brazen throne, arms extended to receive his youthful victims.

When, in the reign of King Josiah, the book of the Law was rediscovered in the Temple in Jerusalem, the young king initiated a program to purge the land from idolatrous worship. Among his sweeping reforms was the defiling of "Topheth, which is in the Valley of the Son of Hinnom, that no man might make his son or his daughter to pass through the fire to Molech" (2 Ki. 23:10). The power of God's Word in His covenant with the Jewish people was revolutionary:

Then the king stood by a pillar and made a covenant before the LORD, to follow the LORD and to keep His commandments

and His testimonies and His statutes, with all his heart and
all his soul, to perform the words of this covenant that were
written in this book. And all the people took a stand for the
covenant (v. 3).

King Josiah's commitment to reject pagan practices revived a divine standard reflective not only of Judaism but also of Christianity, which came later, and all civilized societies on the face of the earth. The willful sacrifice of innocent children in the name of pagan gods remains a vile abomination that goes against everything true religion holds sacred.

Yet the Palestinians have no qualms about murdering Israeli children. They kill them wantonly and rejoice over their deaths. It is one of the more despicable aspects associated with serving a "god" who withholds love and forgiveness but supposedly dispenses heaven based on killing and dying "for Allah." Deadly as this situation is for Israelis, it is deadly for Palestinians also. In the name of religion, Palestinian children are pawns in the game of politics.

In March 2004 a terrified 14-year-old Palestinian boy, Hasam Abdu, stood with his hands up at the Hawara checkpoint near Nablus. Quick-thinking Israeli paratroopers at the checkpoint discovered the lethal device strapped to his body. The child's mission was to get as close as he could to Israeli soldiers and detonate his bomb. His reward: a hundred Israeli shekels—about $20—and (so Islam claims) 72 virgin brides when he arrived in Paradise to celebrate his martyrdom in the presence of Allah.

A few days earlier, another boy, only 11 years of age, was asked to carry a bag through the checkpoint and deliver it to a woman waiting on the other side. He was given no explanation about the bag's contents. He, too, was discovered; and while the people who dispatched him frantically tried to detonate the device, wanting desperately to kill him and everyone around him, Israeli sappers were able to defuse it and save the boy's life. Abdullah Quran was promised five shekels (approximately one dollar).

These episodes are not random acts of spontaneous terror. They are part of a calculated, cold-blooded plan by ruthless Palestinian leaders who, to get what they want, are quite willing to send their children into the fires—all in the name of their god.

In a speech to the UN General Assembly in December 1988, then Palestinian Authority Chairman Yasser Arafat brought greetings "from the children of the stones who are challenging occupation forces armed with warplanes, tanks and weapons—an unarmed Palestinian David facing a heavily armed Israeli Goliath."

In a January 2002 interview on PA TV, Arafat was asked what message he would like to send to the Palestinian children. His reply was reported by the Palestinian Media Watch: "The child who is grasping the stone, facing the tank; is this not the greatest message to the world when that hero becomes a *shahid* [martyr for Allah]? We are proud of them."

This is what the "children of the stones" is all about. Youngsters are being fed into the fires for consumption by the world media and a susceptible international community. These acts are not laudable expressions of pent-up anger and frustration. They are an intolerable, figurative return to Hinnom and the furnace of Molech. Children sacrificed in the name of their god.

One of the best ways to view the differences between Judeo-Christian values and those of Islam is to examine the ethics regarding children.

On September 1, 2004, Chechen terrorists attacked a school in the Russian town of Beslan in North Ossetia. They held the faculty and students hostage and withstood Russian security forces for almost three days until a shootout erupted, leaving 344 dead—186 of them children. A Russian pastor said the terrorists were affiliated with al-Qaida and that the operation was "one part" of the global Islamic war. It is no secret that al-Qaida and its cohorts intend to kill as many children as they can. The operation in Beslan was planned over many months, with explosives and weapons planted at the school while the building was undergoing repairs for the fall term.

It is also well documented that international terrorists believe there are no noncombatants in their war with Israel, America, and the West. Every person is seen a target; no one is a civilian. When Iraq's former leader, Saddam Hussein, decided in 1988 to test his chemical weapons, he chose the Kurdish village of Halabja. The dictator was pleased to learn that his poison gas had killed more than 5,000 people, among them hundreds of small children, many still clutched in their mothers' arms.

In the war between Iran and Iraq (1980–88), thousands of Iranian children were used in wave after wave of assaults on the Iraqis. Few of them survived the war, which was best described as a monument to futility and barbarism.

If "moderate" Islam is more than merely a wish of the West, where are the voices of the majority of moderate Muslim clerics who claim love, peace, and compassion as hallmarks of their faith? Why are they not speaking out against Islam's treatment of children? Their compassion evidently does not extend in that direction—particularly when it comes to the world of the brainwashed children of the suicide belts and sack bombs.

All Are Victims

A friend of mine who lives in Jerusalem was on his way to work on the morning of January 29, 2004. He was suffering the usual heavy morning traffic, three cars behind an Israeli bus loaded with schoolchildren and commuters. Suddenly a huge explosion and ball of fire tore through the rear of the bus, ripping it to shreds and flinging bodies and body parts high into the air.

A young suicide bomber had boarded the bus a few stops earlier. He had left his Bethlehem home at four o'clock in the morning to carry out his deadly attack. His mentors and suppliers of the lethal device laden with metal balls, nails, and bolts were members of Arafat's Fatah-linked al-Aqsa Martyrs Brigades.

As rescuers rushed to the scene, they saw 10 bodies and more than 50 wounded scattered amid the wreckage. Both counts rose over the next few days. Sanitized news reports spoke of political frustration and offered reasons why Arabs consider genocide a legitimate enterprise. Then there were the protestations, sincere or insincere, condemning the acts, often coming even from those behind the deadly bombings. In the West, these horrific atrocities are seen only in short clips that provide glimpses of the scene after the victims' remains have been removed. These images are far from what my friend witnessed from the windshield of his car.

What reporters tend to obscure is the human side of the issue. Virtually nothing is mentioned about the young Palestinian victim who carried his backpack onto a bus and flipped the switch on the detonator. Yes, he is a victim too—a victim of years of brainwashing and incitement in class-rooms, summer camps, and vehemently anti-Israel mosques by unscrupulous leaders who promise paradise, a martyr's welcome by Allah, and money that will enrich his family after he "sacrifices" himself.

Before his fall, Saddam Hussein and our "allies," the Saudis, sent thousands of dollars to the families of suicide bombers. Through notes and prerecorded videotapes left behind, to be exploited by those who feed these victims into the jaws of certain death, the bombers urge their families to celebrate their "heroism" and send candy to the people of their towns and villages.

The pathetic episodes are an inexpressible horror that should bring the wrath of civilized nations down on the purveyors of this newest weapon of war. But they don't. Instead, there is silence or a sort of justification and placing of blame on the victims themselves. In this case, victims who were just trying to get to school.

But what brings these unspeakable atrocities into sharp focus is the immediate aftermath of such attacks. Everywhere are charred bodies, body parts, bits and pieces of human remains in the streets, on the storefronts, and on the faces of those who stood nearby. Innocent lives were cruelly snuffed out because they were Jewish and unfortunate enough to get on a bus at the wrong time and on the wrong day.

The other lives snuffed out are those of Palestinian children, who are exploited as human bombs after being fed lies about the joys of martyrdom and the paradise that awaits after they commit suicide and murder.

For one observer, the January 29, 2004, attack seemed different. As he ran to the scene to offer whatever assistance he could render, he heard the sound of dozens of cell phones scattered among the carnage, ringing endlessly.

"The cell phones," he said, "wouldn't stop ringing."

On one end of the relentless ringing were frantic parents, friends, or family members hoping to confirm that their child or loved one was all right. On the other end, lying in the bloodied street, were phones that would never be picked up. On one end life; on the other, death.

Sadly, that is only the beginning of the story. The next day come the funerals. The faces and lists of the dead appear in newspapers and on television. But the hardest blow of all is the finality of the event, starkly depicted in the echoes of the unanswered cell phones. That loss will stalk every day and night for all of the years to come.

You see, the story isn't told by the remains of bombed-out buses—vehicles that can be replaced and service restored the next day. It is told by human casualties, who cannot be replaced. And if the mania and hysteria of war subside before the Lord brings it to an end, the casualty count will still be the same. And tears will continue to stain the faces of the innocent survivors.

God's Word and the Sanctity of Children

A comparison of the Islamic extremist attitude with what the Bible says about God's love for children and His mandate regarding how we must nurture them constitutes a litmus test of whether Judaism, Christianity, and Islam serve the same God. Clearly, they do not.

> *Behold, children are a heritage [gift] from the* LORD,
> *the fruit of the womb is a reward* (Ps. 127:3).

A gift from the Most High can never be accepted lightly. Nor can it be regarded as something to be used, abused, or cast aside based on individual whims or self-indulgent preferences. Consider this statement in relation to the gift of salvation:

> *For by grace you have been saved through faith, and that not of yourselves; it is the gift of God, not of works, lest anyone should boast* (Eph. 2:8–9).

The God-given gift referred to in Ephesians is no less than the creation of new life—spiritual life. Such life revolutionizes an individual and raises one to an entirely new lifestyle. We recognize it as the "new birth." Each new birth is a spectacular creation effected by God through faith in Jesus Christ: "If anyone is in Christ, he is a new creation" (2 Cor. 5:17). This new creation is cherished and nurtured until it matures into a radiant manifestation of God's singular ability to create. The same is true of a child, "a heritage [gift] from the Lord."

We should not be surprised, therefore, to hear Jesus say,

> *Let the little children come to Me, and do not forbid them; for of such is the kingdom of God. And He took them up in His arms, laid His hands on them, and blessed them* (Mk. 10:14, 16).

And again,

> *Then Jesus called a little child to Him, set him in the midst of them, and said, "Assuredly, I say to you, unless you are converted and become as little children, you will by no means enter the kingdom of heaven. Whoever receives one little child like this in My name receives Me. Whoever causes one of these little ones who believe in Me to sin, it would better for him if a millstone were hung around his neck, and he were drowned in the depth of the sea* (Mt. 18:2–3, 5–6).

And in a mysteriously compelling statement, Jesus declared,

> *Take heed that you do not despise one of these little ones, for I say to you that in heaven their angels always see the face of My Father who is in heaven* (v. 10).

These passages emphasize the intimacy of God's relationship with His crowning creation. From the instant of conception, a child is, in the eyes of the Lord, a treasure attended by angels, loved by the Savior, and committed to us through an unbreakable trust.

The Old Testament and Godly Instruction

The same pristinely lofty standard is conveyed in biblical Judaism. In a portion familiar to many of us, the Hebrew

Scriptures give specific instructions on how to teach children biblical and spiritual truths. In the immediate context of God's instruction to love Him with the whole heart, soul, and might, we find these words:

> *And these words which I command you today shall be in your heart. You shall teach them diligently to your children, and shall talk of them when you sit in your house, when you walk by the way, when you lie down, and when you rise up* (Dt. 6:6–7).

In addition to teaching the actual biblical text, the Israelites could clearly infer from Scripture that they were to communicate through the example of their lives. The apostle Paul said as much in his appraisal of young Timothy:

> *I remember you in my prayers night and day. When I call to remembrance the genuine faith that is in you, which dwelt first in your grandmother Lois and your mother Eunice, and I am persuaded is in you also* (2 Tim. 1:3, 5).

We do well to remember that the faith of Timothy's mother and grandmother was unwavering belief in the God of Abraham, Isaac, and Jacob. It was a pre-New Testament faith. Equally important is the fact that the apostle brought to this family the fulfillment of what had been promised and anticipated through the millennia—that is, faith in the Messiah, who finished the work.

Lois and Eunice had the same relationship with Jehovah as the "heroes" of the faith, mentioned in the eleventh chapter of the Epistle to the Hebrews. That faith never varied in its quality. What differed was how the individuals manifested the reality of such a faith. Yet, in whatever fleshly form that faith resided, it showed. Consequently, believers, regardless of station in life, gender, age, or color, embodied the faith articulated in the precepts of Scripture. Ephesians

2:10 says it well:

> *For we are His workmanship, created in Christ Jesus for good works, which God prepared beforehand that we should walk in them.*

Lois and Eunice lived their testimonies before young Timothy, not because they were trying to make a favorable impression, but because they were being who they were. Simply put, they did what they did because they were who they were—women of faith.

The Irrevocable Standard

If we understand what Scripture faithfully communicates to us, we can never, for any reason, sanction violating God's trust regarding the responsibility He has given us for children. That any group, individual, or religion would justify using children as sacrificial pawns for its self-instituted brand of political hell is an unspeakable outrage. Yes, hell—the "New Gehenna" of prostrate, pagan infidels chanting to drown the screams of innocent children being consumed in the fiery hands of their Molech delusion.

Justification of, or indifference to, this monstrous atrocity is evidence of the biblical illiteracy strangling even our Western societies. And marching in lockstep with this terrible malignancy is the affliction of compassionless lives devoid of faith and lacking the capacity to care about the devastating consequences of turning their backs upon God, His Word, and His children.

The prophet Isaiah spoke of a coming day when "the wolf also shall dwell with the lamb, the leopard shall lie down with the young goat, the calf and the young lion and the fatling together; and a little child shall lead them" (Isa. 11:6).

A child shall lead them, indeed. But to green pastures, not into the New Gehenna.

CHAPTER 11

⟨∞⟩

RACHEL IS STILL WEEPING

A voice was heard in Ramah, lamentation, weeping, and great mourning, Rachel weeping for her children, refusing to be comforted, because they are no more (Mt. 2:18).

Just outside the entrance to the town of Bethlehem stands a tomb. It is the tomb of the patriarch Jacob's beloved Rachel. Two thousand years ago, the writer of Matthew's Gospel selected this quotation from the prophet Jeremiah to describe events of his day. Herod the Great had dispatched Roman legionnaires to the village to slaughter all children two years old and under. They were the calculated victims of his fiendish paranoia. To Herod's demented mind, these babies threatened his authority and unmitigated lust for power. Therefore, they were dispensable.

But brutality was nothing new to this petty tyrant. There came a time when he felt it expedient to murder his own sons, Alexander and Aristobulous, and his professed favorite wife, Mariamne. Crazy? Not to his demented mind. It made perfect sense to Herod to secure his position at the expense of the innocent. Whether they were children or adults made no difference. It was Herod alone who mattered—a fact of history that is quite incomprehensible to people in Western democracies who are spoon fed from childhood on the notion that innocent people should be protected.

Fast Forward

One might conclude that these facts are ancient history, and civilized people in the 21st century no longer operate on such callous principles. Don't believe it. Although Rachel has been in her tomb for millennia, we still hear the echo of the prophet Jeremiah. And as her tomb grows freshly pock-marked with the bullet holes put there by a new generation of Herodian kindred spirits, Rachel still weeps for her children. And the little town of Bethlehem has been anything but peaceful.

In an attempt to evade an Israel Defense Forces (IDF) incursion that was mounted to stem suicide-bombing activity, Palestinian terrorists decided to storm the Church of the Nativity in Bethlehem on April 2, 2002. They took more than 200 nuns and priests, plus other civilians, as hostages to be used as shields that would spare them the retribution they had brought down on their own heads. For 38 days they held out in the church, ransacking and vandalizing it, while Israelis refused to fire on the Christian holy site.

This ploy, of course, was nothing new. Arab terrorists have a long history of using innocent people as shields to protect their own lives. Yet these are the same types of individuals who convince their children to become "heroic" suicide bombers, while they themselves cower behind the skirts of nuns and priests for protection.

While the church was being occupied, *The Jerusalem Post*'s Arieh O'Sullivan donned military garb and ventured into Jesus' birthplace, now an enclave for Muslim terrorism. Here is some of what she found:

Water from a broken main gushes into the streets, now filled with plastic bags of garbage that the residents have thrown out and which, of course, have not been picked up. Tanks and armored personnel carriers are packed in most of the main streets circling the town center. . . . We reach the massive walls of the Armenian monastery. Its tiny but thick, solid wooden door, hundreds of years old, has been blasted off its hinges. What is left of it is leaning precariously in place.[1]

Ironically, while his 200 henchmen holed up in the Church of the Nativity were desecrating the site, PA Chairman Arafat was declaring his commitment to be the protector of Christian sanctuaries within the PA's jurisdiction. Events in Bethlehem, Jerusalem, and elsewhere, however, tell a different story. And though the situation may seem at first glance to be localized and parochial, it is crucial we understand that what happened in Bethlehem casts a critically long shadow over what is transpiring on a vastly larger scale. In fact, it typifies Islamic relations with groups that Islam views as infidels. And when the occupation of the church in Bethlehem is all but forgotten, the larger issues will remain.

Islamic Absolutists

For years many Christians have been led to believe that Islam is a benign religion promoting love, peace, and harmony with other faiths. This tone surfaced in 1992 when the Anglican bishop of Jerusalem decided to join a world Islamic organization in cosponsoring a conference on the situation of Christians in Israel. The bishop's decision mirrored the sentiments of other mainline Christian leaders in Israel who were increasingly championing not only an alliance with Muslims but also the drive for a Palestinian state. The intervening years have seen this naïve pandering go up in the smoke of the scattered remains of suicide bombers and their helpless victims.

On the other hand, some politicians were more insightful when it came to the burgeoning threat of radical Islam. Israel's late Prime Minister Yitzhak Rabin had this to say in 1993:

This [radical Islam] is a real and serious danger that threatens world peace in future years. And just as Israel was the first to perceive the Iraqi nuclear threat, so today we stand on the line of fire against the danger of fundamentalist Islam.[2]

Unfortunately, Islamists had a far more precise view of what a Muslim-Christian alliance would accomplish than Christians did. And while some liberal Christians dreamed of a utopian era of ecumenical harmony, their Muslim counterparts were—and still are—visualizing Islamic imperialism. Islam's program for Christianity differs little from its plan to liquidate Israel. The only variance is in the degree of violence.

With Islam's increasingly violent campaigns against Israel, the Jewish people, and Christians over the last decade in particular, we have come to understand that volatile Muslim threats are not merely rhetoric. They announce, with no attempt at subtlety, the Islamic commitment to global domination.

When Huntington's book *The Clash of Civilizations and the Remaking of World Order* was published in 1997, some critics scoffed at the idea of a cataclysmic confrontation between absolutist Islam and the Western "Christian" democracies. With the advent of Osama bin Laden; September 11, 2001; the advancing crusade against Israel; and the purging from the Islamic world of any vestiges of Christianity and its people, some intellectual muddy water has become pristinely clear. The lines have been drawn and the battle joined.

What has been done in the Palestinian Authority is a microcosm of what has been identified by a number of expert observers. The Palestinian educational system has been reduced to the systematic brainwashing of innocent children to commit acts of unspeakable horror. The Palestinian and Arab media have been reduced to a mechanism for spewing the most vicious, anti-Semitic diatribes imaginable. Bethlehem, a citadel of Christian devotion, has been turned into a haven for murderers and terrorists. A struggle is being waged in Nazareth to establish Islamic dominance over traditionally Christian sites involving the annunciation of Jesus' birth.

In Nablus, the traditional tomb of Joseph has been destroyed and converted into a Muslim shrine. The Temple Mount, revered by both Jews and Christians, is now claimed as the exclusive province of Muslims. There also has been a concerted effort by the Muslim Waqf (Muslim Trust) to destroy all artifacts testifying to the Jewish people's ancient presence on the sacred Mount. All of these components confirm that there is only one page in the Islamic game plan, and it calls for total Muslim dominance over the "infidel" Judeo-Christian world, which Islamists believe must be destroyed or subjugated.

When Israel pulled out of Bethlehem in 1995 and turned the city over to Yasser Arafat, it became a difficult place to be for Christians, many of whom fled. Islam does not have a history of making life easier for people. It makes life infinitely more difficult. A case in point is when the Good Fence disappeared.

Turning Back the Clock

On May 24, 2000, the border between Israel and South Lebanon known as The Good Fence became another bad place to be. Israeli troops pulled out, and as soon as they left the South Lebanon security zone, hostile forces set up shop just meters away from Jewish towns, eerily reminiscent of life prior to the 1967 Six-Day War. Before Israel cleared the Syrians out in 1967, nearby Israeli farmers suffered daily harassment and intimidation of the kind now being carried out by their Hezbollah terrorist neighbors north of the Lebanese border. The clock essentially was turned back, and life became miserable for people on both sides of the border who want peace.

The Good Fence was a blessing to many South Lebanese, particularly Christians and Druze, who came through the border crossing into Israel at Metulla to receive food, shelter, and medical attention while Arafat's Palestine Liberation Organization (PLO) helped wage a civil war that focused heavily on slaughtering Christians. More than 75,000 people were killed. As a humanitarian gesture, Israel opened its northern border in June 1976 to permit the Lebanese to cross into Israel, where more than 11,000 wounded Lebanese received medical treatment.

After the war in Lebanon ended and the southern security zone was established in 1978, Muslim Arabs, the United Nations, and Western leaders all contended that Israel was occupying the territory of a sovereign country, and they demanded that the Jewish nation implement UN resolution 425, calling for the IDF to evacuate the area. Yet, while Israel maintained the security zone, there was not one successful infiltration into northern Israel by terrorists. The terrorist organization Hezbollah had to lob its Katyusha rockets into Kiryat Shmona and other Israeli towns from the other side of the zone.

Furthermore, after Israel evacuated the area in May 2000, more than 6,500 Lebanese fled into Israel through the Good Fence, clearly indicating they would rather be under Israeli authority than under Muslim domination.

When Is Enough, Enough?

Understandably, the Israelis wanted out of the quagmire that many had called Israel's Vietnam. They had hoped that giving the Lebanese, Syrians, and Western politicians what they demanded would open a window for peace. Israelis are always searching for that illusive window. *Perhaps,* they thought, *sacrificing another slice of security might be enough.* But the Jewish people should know by now that enough is never enough for anti-Semites—be they Muslims, Nazis, or the like. Such people have but one goal—a world with no Jews and no Israel. And these days, that goal has been expanded to read, "a world with no America." The immediate aftermath of the IDF pullout in 2000 made the point.

More Land—

The moment Israel announced it would return to the international border, Hezbollah declared that the border actually was much farther south. Furthermore, Hezbollah declared that it would keep up the fight for the Shaba farms near Mount Dov, which have never been a part of Lebanon.

Prisoner Release—

Another demand was that Israel release imprisoned terrorists. The UN, of course, supports putting some of Israel's worst enemies back on the street. The gesture, according to UN sources, would demonstrate Israeli good-will. To no one's surprise, pulling out of Lebanon evidently did not indicate sufficient Israeli goodwill.

Resettling Refugees—

When interviewed on television, Lebanese President Emile Lahoud had few words of appreciation for the IDF's withdrawal. His own failure to immediately dispatch Lebanese forces south to control Hezbollah was not a major topic of discussion. What he did want to talk about was disposing of the 300,000 "refugees" housed in Lebanon who wanted to return to Israel. The refugee issue became another excuse for terrorists to keep up the armed attacks in hopes of further decimating Israel.

What everyone conveniently seemed to have forgotten is that the Arab world has carefully nurtured the entire refugee issue for more than half a century. Israel has agreed to pay reparations to all former landowners having legitimate claims. But returning land forfeited by Palestinians who fled the country in 1948 at the behest of their Arab leaders should be out of the question.

One might ask why the Arab world has allowed its brethren to languish in such squalid circumstances for so many decades. These "refugees" could easily have been resettled in Arab countries. But not allowing resettlement and retaining the refugee camps keeps alive the issue of taking back the entire land of Israel.

The argument that Israel is culpable for the displacement of Palestinian Arabs and dispassionate toward their plight is gaining momentum among some sincere but uninformed people in the West. Why, they reason, shouldn't Israel be responsible for resettling the refugees or at least paying a heavy penalty for appropriating their properties? Some contend that Germany's reparations to Jewish families from the Holocaust era should serve as a model for Israel's treatment of the Palestinians.

But at least two salient facts stand out here: (1) Israel has said it will pay all legitimate claims registered with the state; (2) Germany has paid some reparations but has made no move to restore land or properties owned by Jews before World War II. Nor, we might add, has the UN or any other nation pressured Germany to do so.

Finally, there is one question almost no one raises. What about Arab reparations to Jews who became refugees because of the Arab wars against Israel? Some 800,000 Jewish people fled Arab countries—approximately the same number as Arabs who fled Israel. Those Jewish refugees left with little more than the clothes on their backs. Yet upon arriving in Israel they were quickly assimilated at great expense into the tiny state—with little notice from those decrying the Palestinian plight. Certainly, no Arab country is amenable to doing for displaced Jews what it demands for displaced Arabs.

Syrian Intransigence—

A key component in Israel's continuing struggle for survival is Syria. Why the late Syrian President Hafez Assad was ever regarded as a legitimate, potential peace partner by Israel, the United States, or the UN remains a mystery. His intentions were never a secret. He demanded no less than the return of every inch of the Golan he lost as a result of his aggression against Israel. Since his death, Syrian demands have remained unaltered.

Furthermore, Syria maintained a military occupation force of some 35,000 troops in Lebanon for more than two decades; and few, except Israel, seemed to mind. One reason Syria wanted to stay in Lebanon was the rich harvest of heroin it reaped from the Bekaa Valley and sent to the West at enormous profit. How ironic that while America fights a desperate battle against drugs, American and Western diplomats court one of the world's biggest suppliers of heroin to addicts in the United States and Europe.

Add the fact that Syria plays host to the world's most notorious terrorist groups who maintain offices in Damascus. In spite of promises to do so, President Bashar Assad did not expel terrorist leaders and allowed them to continue to direct attacks on Israel from his country. Add to this his blatant collaboration with Saddam Hussein, the Iranians, and his connivance in allowing terrorists to use his border with Iraq as a conduit on their way to kill coalition troops and innocent Iraqi civilians, and you begin to get the picture.

Syria also continues to receive missiles from North Korea and Iran, and has made a deal with the Russians to purchase air defense missiles.

Peace With Security

Many political factions lambasted former Israeli Prime Minister Benjamin Netanyahu, calling him an intransigent obstructionist because he insisted on a negotiating policy based on security and reciprocity. But these principles are not difficult to understand. Negotiation demands that each party be responsible to respond in kind, quality, and spirit to every concession made by its opponent. When the Palestinians refused to uphold their end and abide by their promises, the negotiations were halted. This move so incensed those who sought peace through one-sided concessions that they demanded Netanyahu's demise as prime minister. Furthermore, the administration of American President Bill Clinton dispatched its top political operatives to Israel to help insure his defeat.

Liberal thinkers who are attempting to manipulate the peace process harbor at least two major misconceptions. First is the matter of the nature of man. In their view, humanity is inherently good. They believe that if Israel's adversaries are shown enough goodwill, forbearance, and prosperity, they will embrace social and political civility and become neighbors with warm hearts and helping hands. However, this view is at odds with all that Scripture teaches and history certifies about man's capacity for evil. Jeremiah the prophet knew something about the human proclivity toward unseemly conduct when he called man's heart "deceitful above all things, and desperately wicked" (Jer. 17:9). That statement sums up the substance of the Hitlers, Sadaam Husseins, and all like-minded tyrants who walk among us.

The next misconception—one widespread in the West—is that religion is incidental to the basic conflict. The Qur'an sanctions the right to kill in the name of Allah. While millions of Muslims may not be disposed to killing those who disagree with them, the radical Islamic elements operating in the Middle East and places like the Sudan are driven by jihad. Palestinian leaders articulate this commitment to subjugate or eradicate the "infidels" many times daily. The late Palestinian leader Abu Ali Mustafa said it in the immediate aftermath of Israel's pullout from South Lebanon. In an interview published on the Web site of the Middle East Media and Research Institute (Memri), Mustafa said,

> *We do not view the Palestinian State that may be established now, and that we are told will have the June 4 [1967] borders as the final goal of the Palestinian people. This is a more forward point on our way to . . . the Palestinian and Arab unified democratic state.*[3]

He merely echoed what Arafat and others have consistently declared, namely, that the fight will continue until the Palestinian flag flies over Jerusalem and, indeed, the whole of Israel.

Back to Bethlehem

Today the Palestinian flag flies unfettered over Bethlehem. Consequently, Christians are leaving in droves, as they left Lebanon through the Good Fence.

Before his death, Arafat effectively completed the Islamization of Bethlehem and the adjacent Arab-Christian villages of Beit Jalla and Beth Sakhur, which once were Christian enclaves in Judea and Samaria. He changed the area demographically, cleverly flooding it with Muslims by (1) redrawing boundaries to encompass 30,000 Muslims from three refugee camps, (2) encouraging Muslim immigration to Bethlehem from Hebron, and (3) persecuting Christians so that they would leave. Ironically, more Arab Christians from Beit Jalla reside in Belize, Central America, today than in Beit Jalla itself.[4] Aaron Klein, of WorldNetDaily.com, reported the following:

> *Bethlehem's Christian population has declined drastically after the Palestinian Authority took control in December, 1995. Once 90 percent of the city, Christians now compose less than 25 percent. . .*

*One religious novelty-store owner cited examples of
Muslim gangs defacing Christian property, the PA
replacing Christian leaders on public councils with
Muslims, and armed Palestinian factions stirring
tensions. One such incident was last week's storm-
ing of Bethlehem's City Hall, across the street from
the Church of the Nativity, believed to be the birthplace of Jesus, by gunmen from the Al Aqsa Martyrs
Brigades terror group.*[5]

A consequence of the de-Christianizing of Bethlehem was
the terrorist occupation of the Church of the Nativity. Rather
than urge the terrorists to surrender, Arafat charged the
Israelis with committing an "atrocious crime" that "cannot be
forgiven." In the end, most of the terrorists received safe
passage to Europe. Twenty-six of them, guilty of serious
crimes, were taken to Gaza for trial. On their arrival they
were greeted with a celebration and hailed as heroes. It was
left to the IDF and outraged church clerics to clean up the
debris.

Among the items the terrorists left behind were 40 explo-
sive devices, garbage, and human excrement. One of the
monks complained that the Palestinians ransacked the rooms
one by one and stole everything of value, including crosses
and prayer books. Several monks reported being beaten.

Ralph Peters, a retired U.S. military officer, wrote in the
May 3, 2002, edition of the *New York Post*, "The war crime—
committed brazenly before a global audience—is the occupation of the Church of the Nativity, in Bethlehem, by
Palestinian terrorists. . . . The immediate and well-organized
occupation of one of Christianity's holiest shrines was an
illegal, cynical gambit."[6]

Not only was the occupation of a holy place a clear
violation of the Geneva Convention, but the fact that the
perpetrators got away with it without provoking international

condemnation and outrage provides a tacit license for more of the same. Wherever Islam is in control, Muslim mosques are destined for predominance. That fact was evident during the heated 5-year dispute over the construction of a mosque near the Church of the Annunciation in Nazareth. Muslims seized the property where a tourist plaza was to be built to celebrate 2,000 years of Christianity in Nazareth. They then demanded the property be deeded to the Islamic authorities for a mosque. Opponents argued that the spires of the proposed mosque would tower over the church and demean the basilica. Israel, under pressure, decided in 2002 to withdraw approval to build on the site.

The Church of the Annunciation incident illustrates a fundamental point: A tenet of Islam is that no Christian, Jewish, or other religious building be taller than the Muslim sanctuaries. The issue is simple but revealing. Islam must dominate the landscape, indicating superiority over infidel religious pretenders.

How extreme can the situation become? Consider Saudi Arabia, where extreme Wahhabism rules the day. There are no churches or synagogues. As a matter of fact, Jewish people are not allowed in the country, and, among other things, Christians are not allowed any outward evidences of their faith. Here is what Daniel Pipes reported:

In November 1990, President George H. W. Bush went to the Persian Gulf region with his wife and top congressional leaders at Thanksgiving time to visit the 400,000 troops gathered in Saudi Arabia, whom he sent there to protect that country from an Iraqi invasion. When the Saudi authorities learned that the President intended to say grace before a festive Thanksgiving dinner, they remonstrated; Saudi Arabia knows only one religion, they said, and that is Islam. Bush acceded, and he and his entourage instead celebrated the holiday on the U.S.S. Durham, an amphibious cargo ship sitting in international waters.[7]

The Palestinians have lost much already and will continue to pay an exorbitantly high price because of their belligerent leaders who consistently create hysteria then manipulate it, driving these people and their children to the streets on rock-throwing escapades and terrorist campaigns against Israel. Christian Arabs will continue to pay a high price as long as Islam is allowed to murder and persecute them for following Jesus Christ. And Muslims who want peace and freedom will pay that price as well because radical Islam will brook no opposition—even from other Muslims—in its goal to suppress and dominate the world. The history of the conflict already has been written in blood, and we can be sure the future holds much more of the same.

If those who long for peace, as did Egypt's late President Anwar Sadat and Jordan's late King Hussein, will assert themselves and deal decisively with the radical elements in their midst, they can have a better day. Neither Israel nor America nor the UN can do this for them. As long as they choose to be intimidated by or sympathetic to terrorism, the conflict will continue.

We who are Christians continue to pray and labor earnestly for the peace of Jerusalem today and for the time when the entrance of the Messiah will ultimately turn the clock forward to a pristinely better time, when Rachel will no longer be weeping for her children—and there will be peace.

ENDNOTES

[1] Arieh O'Sullivan, "A Place Under the Gun," *The International Jerusalem Post*, April 19, 2002, 9–11.

[2] *Los Angeles Times*, "Warning to West: Beware of Militant Islamic Radicals," in *The News-Press* (Ft. Myers, Fla.), January 3, 1993.

[3] Special Dispatch Series, No. 94, May 15, 2000, The Middle East Media Research Institute <memri.org/bin/articles.cgi?Area=sd&ID=SP9400>.

[4] Yoram Ettinger, "The Islamization of Bethlehem by Arafat," *The Jerusalem Cloakroom* 117, December 25, 2001 <www.acpr.org.il/cloakrm/clk117.html>.

[5] Aaron Klein, "Muslim Grinches Steal Bethlehem Christmas," December 25, 2005 <worldnetdaily.com/news/article.asp?ARTICLE_ID=48064>.

[6] Ralph Peters, "The Real War Crime," New York Post, May 3, 2002 <aijac.org.au/updates/May-02/080502.html>.

[7] Daniel Pipes, "The Scandal of U.S.–Saudi Relations," *National Interest,* (Winter 2002/03) <danielpipes.org/article/995>.

CHAPTER 12

THE TEMPLE MOUNT CONTROVERSY

It was Jehovah, the God of Israel—not Allah—who said, "In this house [Temple] and in Jerusalem, which I have chosen out of all the tribes of Israel, I will put My name forever" (2 Chr. 33:7). The hue and cry these days is that the Jewish people have "stolen" Muslim land in order to create the State of Israel. The claim is absurd on many levels, not the least of which is the fact that there has been a continual Jewish presence in the land since the days of Joshua. Jerusalem has never been the capital of any Arab country, but it was made the Jewish capital by King David and has been the heartbeat of Judaism for more than 3,000 years.

The Israelites began conquering the land of Canaan around 1400 B.C., and from 1000 B.C. to A.D. 637 they formed what historian Martin Gilbert termed the "main settled population of Palestine."[1]

They built their first Temple—Solomon's Temple—when Solomon was king. It stood until 586 B.C., when the Babylonians destroyed it. They began building their second Temple on the same spot, Mount Moriah in Jerusalem, in 536 B.C. and completed it in 516 B.C. It was this Temple that Herod later enlarged, Jesus visited, and the Romans destroyed. Muhammad was not even born until A.D. 570. That was 500 years after the Romans destroyed the second Temple in A.D. 70. And the first Muslim presence in Jerusalem did not appear until A.D. 630—after the Jewish people had been the "main settled population" for 1,600 years.

It wasn't until 691 that the Dome of the Rock was built on the Temple Mount. Simple mathematics reveal the obvious truth that the Muslims must remain in the land for another 230 years merely to equal the number of years the Jews were the main population *prior* to the advent of Islam. They would have to live there even longer to account for the years the Jews have remained in the land *after* A.D. 637.

Since the facts clearly don't help their cause, Palestinians and many of their fellow Muslims now claim there has never been a Jewish Temple or presence on the Temple Mount in Jerusalem. Jewish people and evangelical Christians know this astonishing perversion of history is patently ridiculous. Nevertheless, it is gaining credence both in the Muslim world and with biblical and historical illiterates.

These are the people who buy the absurdity that the Holocaust never actually took place, even though the Third Reich meticulously and thoroughly recorded the details of its own atrocities during Hitler's infamous bloodbath of the 1940s.

Digging Up the Truth

To certify their claims, Muslim authorities involved with illegal excavations at the Mount have deliberately destroyed archaeological artifacts from the first and second Temple periods that would contradict their revisionist propaganda.

In 1996 the Muslim Waqf began digging into the subground in the southeastern corner of the Mount in an area called Solomon's Stables. It built a subterranean mosque so large that it can accommodate 10,000 worshipers. In 1998 it built yet another illegal mosque in a passageway of what was the second Jewish Temple. In doing so, Muslims removed 400 truckloads of dirt saturated with ancient archaeological treasures, which they unceremoniously dumped into the Kidron Valley and Jerusalem landfills.

In 2004 Israeli archaeologists, led by Dr. Gabriel Barkay of

Bar Ilan University in Tel Aviv, finally received permission to sift through the debris. What they found was spectacular. The treasures not only verify that they came from debris illegally excavated from under the Temple Mount, but they also verify the Jewish presence there all the way back to the time of Solomon's Temple and Jeremiah, who prophesied from 627 to 585 B.C. The most incredible artifact was a lump of clay baked in fire that contained textile fibers indicating it was a seal that had been pressed against the fabric. Contained in the clay was the script, "son of Immer." The Bible tells us,

> *Now Pashhur the son of Immer the priest who was also chief governor in the house of the LORD, heard that Jeremiah prophesied these things. Then Pashhur struck Jeremiah the prophet, and put him in the stocks that were in the high gate of Benjamin, which was by the house of the LORD* (Jer. 20:1–2).

Dr. Barkay's team found residue of Pashhur's official seal. Old Testament biblical records, written more than 2,000 years before Islam's Qur'an, verify that the great Temples of Israel stood on the Temple Mount where the Muslim Dome of the Rock and al-Aqsa mosques now stand. The archaeological finds all support the truth of the Scriptures. Scripture is full of references to the Jewish Temple:

> *Three times a year all your males shall appear before the LORD your God in the place which He chooses: at the Feast of Unleavened Bread, at the Feast of Weeks, and at the Feast of Tabernacles; and they shall not appear before the LORD empty-handed. Every man shall give as he is able, according to the blessing of the LORD your God which he has given you* (Dt. 16:16–17).

And where was that place "which he shall choose?" It was in Jerusalem on Mount Moriah, where Abraham had brought Isaac in Genesis 22—the threshing floor of Araunah the Jebusite, which David legally purchased:

> *Then the king [David] said unto Araunah, "No, but I will surely buy it from you for a price; nor will I offer burnt offerings to the LORD my God with that which costs me nothing." So David bought the threshing floor and the oxen for fifty shekels of silver* (2 Sam. 24:24).

It was at this very place, Mount Moriah in Jerusalem, where Solomon, son of David, was instructed to build Israel's first great Temple:

> *Now Solomon began to build the house of the LORD at Jerusalem on Mount Moriah, where the LORD had appeared to his father David, at the place that David had prepared on the threshing floor of Ornan [Araunah] the Jebusite. And he began to build on the second day of the second month in the fourth year of his reign* (2 Chr. 3:1–2).

At that sacred place, the great, festive occasions would be lived out in the national life of the Jewish people.

Later the eyewitness accounts of historians testified to the presence of the Jewish Temple and the glory of it. Josephus, in his book *Wars of the Jews*, left this description of the second Temple prior to its destruction by the Romans in A.D. 70:

> *It was covered all over with plates of gold of great weight, and, at the first rising of the sun, reflected back a very fiery splendour, and made those who forced themselves to look upon it to turn their eyes*

*away, just as they would have done at the sun's own
rays. But this temple appeared to strangers, when
they were at a distance, like a mountain covered with
snow; for, as to those parts of it that were not gilt,
they were exceedingly white.*[2]

The white stones Josephus spoke of can be seen today.
Some of them lie in a jumble, exactly where they fell during
the Roman destruction 2,000 years ago, on the excavated
Roman street that ran along the base of the Temple platform's
wall.

The evidence is conclusive. The Bible confirms it, eyewit-
nesses wrote about it, and irrefutable physical evidence exists
that anyone who visits Jerusalem can see. Nevertheless,
Muslims continue to declare that the Jewish people and their
Temples have no prior claim to the Temple Mount. In fact,
according to Islamists, they have no claim at all.

Why Muslims Deny Jewish Rights to Mount Moriah

During negotiations in July 2000 at Camp David near
Washington, D.C., during President Bill Clinton's administration, then Israeli Prime Minister Ehud Barak and American
intermediaries offered a plan to share sovereignty of the
Temple Mount or declare it under "divine sovereignty." PA
Chairman Arafat flatly refused the offer. In an article titled
"Power of the Myth," which appeared in the November 20,
2000, issue of *The New Republic,* author Gershom Gorenberg
wrote:

*Arafat's sole concession was to suggest "Islamic
sovereignty" under the Islamic Conference
Organization. . . . The Palestinians refused to
acknowledge any Jewish connection to the site, a
position that exasperated even left-wing Israelis. It
made the denial of Jews' historical roots in their*

homeland into the central Palestinian negotiating point. By dismissing the Jewish past, Arafat focused Israeli public attention on the Mount and invited Ariel Sharon to use the spot's symbolism for his own statement of ownership.[3]

Despite the facts, Muslims dedicated to the total supremacy of Islam over Judaism and Christianity worked on two fronts to discredit Jewish claims to the site. They contended the Jewish people have never had a serious or prolonged presence on the sacred mountain, and they renamed the site al-Haram al-Sharif. In the world of Islam, where rhetoric is more forceful than fact, the absurd is often a marketable product. Add to this situation the historical illiteracy afflicting much of a credulous Western society, and you have a world where lies, as in the Hitlerian era, become volatile and destructive commodities.

To establish an identity that is exclusively Arab for the area historically known as the Temple Mount, Arafat resorted to his old trick of name-changing. Not many years ago, he chose to call Arabs living in Palestine by a new name. Rather than being Arabs with homes in Palestine, he determined they would henceforth be called Palestinians. This move, he reasoned, would create a perception that the Arabs were the ancient inhabitants of the land, whereas the Jews were Hebrews-come-lately. In truth, however, the vast majority of Palestinian Arabs had been there no longer than their Jewish neighbors, who had always been known as Palestinian Jews. Joan Peters, in her book *From Time Immemorial,* documented that the Jewish people actually have been in the land longer than the Arabs. However, Arafat's ploy was swallowed completely by the Western news media, which has perpetuated the myth to the advantage of the Arab world ever since.

So Arafat invoked his old standby. After being known for 3,000 years as the site of Israel's Temples, the Temple Mount emerged in the news media in 2001 with a new name. The well-calculated change came at the very time Palestinian negotiators began to demand exclusive control of the Temple Mount and East Jerusalem.

It is easy to see that by digging under the Temple Mount and dumping the dirt containing artifacts testifying to thousands of years of Jewish history, the Muslims are blatantly attempting to destroy as much physical evidence as possible of the Jewish presence there.

When Arafat attempted to ingratiate himself and his cause to Christians, he once referred to Jesus walking the streets of East Jerusalem, implying that the Lord walked where the Palestinians will soon be directing the affairs of their future state. Ehud Olmert, formerly the mayor of Jerusalem, was ready with an answer. He stated, and accurately so, that when Jesus walked the streets of ancient Jerusalem, He would have seen no Dome of the Rock or al-Aqsa mosque on the Temple Mount. Nor would He have seen a mosque anywhere in all of Israel. He would have seen a Jewish Temple on Mount Moriah and scores of synagogues dotting the landscape. Islam would not come into existence for another 600 years.

Furthermore, Jerusalem is not mentioned even once in the Qur'an. In fact, Islam's claim to sovereignty over the Temple Mount is based solely on the tradition that Muhammad journeyed from Mecca to Jerusalem to paradise and back to Mecca all in one night. The legend says Muhammad's "winged" steed touched down in Jerusalem, where he met Abraham, Moses, Jesus, "and the other prophets" whom he led in prayer, before a ladder of golden light descended to take him into Allah's presence. Allah then gave him instructions, and he flew back to Mecca in Saudi Arabia. On the basis of this tale, Jerusalem became the third holiest site for Muslims. Islam's heart still beats for Mecca and Medina, but Jewry's heart longs only for Jerusalem, which is deeply enshrined both in archaeologically validated history and the Word of God. Scripture says it best:

> *If I forget you, O Jerusalem, let my right hand forget its skill! If I do not remember you, let my tongue cling to the roof of my mouth—if I do not exalt Jerusalem above my chief joy* (Ps. 137:5–6).

Whereas Judaism has no problem living in peaceful coexistence with other religions, the Islamic worldview is absolutist. Every shrine and scrap of land that Muhammad's followers laid claim to is to be controlled exclusively by Muslims. Sharing property rights or acknowledging another faith's legitimate interests in sacred places is out of the question. Non-Muslims may be allowed to visit as spectators—for a fee, of course. But Islam believes it holds the rights and title deed to all such land, along with the ability to dictate who will enter and when.

Rewriting the history of the sacred mountain has overwhelming spiritual implications. Islamic militants want to turn fact into myth for reasons that go far beyond ownership of a 33-acre platform on a small mountain in Jerusalem. Their obsessive motivation is to establish Islam as the only credible religion in the world and make the third-string Muslim holy place in Jerusalem a purged shrine, forging a trinity of purified sites for Muslim pilgrims: Mecca, Medina, and Jerusalem.

Implications for Christianity and Judaism are also significant. If the Muslims succeed, both the Old and New Testaments will be perceived as flagrant falsehoods because much of the material in both is set in and around occasions related to the Jewish Temple on the Mount. It would look as though biblical Judaism perpetrated a lie and, for thousands of years, practiced a most despicable deception. In addition, the revered records of the New Testament, transmitting the knowledge of Jesus' extended ministries at the grand Herodian Temple in Jerusalem, would appear to be a fabrication, and Christianity would have to join Judaism as a shameless purveyor of myth and spiritual skullduggery.

The conclusion is obvious. If Jews and Christians fabricated their tales of the Temples and the centrality of those edifices to legitimate relationships to God, then both religions would be discredited. And the only major religion left, of course, would be Islam. Since Muslims already regard Islam as the only true religion, this coup would seal the final phase of their centuries-long jihad against their rivals.

Beyond the arguments about rights to the Temple Mount lurks a more ominous, and actually more important, theme: Satan's plan to ultimately claim the Jerusalem Temple as his possession alone. Such contemporary events as the rush for international Gentile intervention to control Jerusalem, denial of Jewish rights on Moriah, the desire of Orthodox Jews to rebuild their Temple, the growing anti-Israel/anti-Semitic global outbursts, and the search for a world leader who can bring peace all converge to form a backdrop for climactic events that will come to the stage in the last days.

Temple Fervor

Consequently, the controversy over the Temple Mount is bound to intensify in the days ahead, particularly because of the determination some have to rebuild the Temple. Interest in rebuilding rose to a fever pitch in 1998 when a group called the Temple Mount Faithful attempted to lay a cornerstone for the Third Temple at the Western Wall plaza. Denied a place near the wall, Yehuda Cohen and his followers placed the stone at a nearby quarry, awaiting the day when it would be put "in its rightful place." Later, at a commemoration of the reunification of Jerusalem, the same group sounded the *shofar* and claimed the sacred Mount for the Messiah and His Temple.

Some religious and secular Israelis denounced the event as the work of "dangerous lunatics." Jerusalem's former mayor, Teddy Kolleck, said he was outraged; Rabbi Shlomo Goren called the ceremony "foolishness."

A primary concern, of course, was the potential effect on Arab-Israeli relations. Temple fervor, however, is not a new phenomenon. In fact, much more speculation about rebuilding is centered in Western Christianity than in Israel.

An example were the efforts of a man named Vendyl Jones, whose search for the ashes of the red heifer received wide publicity in the secular and religious media. Although Jones's quest at least was dignified by a smattering of reputable sources, others have made outlandish claims that have captured the fancy of credulous Christians. One such claim had Jewish people building a new Temple in a cavern secreted beneath the Dome of the Rock.

The search for stones for a new Temple has been going on longer than Jones's search for the ashes. Some say stones have been quarried and hidden in Israel, Indiana, Texas, and various other places. Searching for them has led to some bizarre situations.

While visiting author and geographer Zev Vilnay in his home in Jerusalem before his death in 1988, I asked him to give me his thoughts on theories about the Temple Mount. Vilnay, a Jewish authority who knew more about the physical attributes of the Holy City than perhaps anyone else, was quick to reply with a story about how extreme some people have become.

One evening he received a call from a man whose tone of voice was extremely serious. Without even telling his host his name, he requested to see Dr. Vilnay that very evening. "Yes, come," he was told.

When the man arrived, he stepped inside, looked at Vilnay, and asked, "Do you have a Bible in the house?"

"Yes, of course I have a Bible in the house," Vilnay replied.

"Then go get it," the guest insisted.

His host went to his study and produced a Bible. The man took the Bible, took Dr. Vilnay's hand in his, then placed it on the Bible. "Now swear to God."

"My friend," Vilnay countered, "do you mind if, before I swear to God, you tell me what I will be swearing about?"

"Swear," his guest stated earnestly, "you will take me to the secret cave where you Jews have hidden the stones for the new Temple."

"Stones—so you wish to see stones. Come out on my veranda, and I'll show you stones all over the hills of Jerusalem. Come with me tomorrow, and we can have a look at as many caves as you wish. But I can tell you now that we will find no stones cut out for the Temple; they do not exist."

Dr. Vilnay, of course, didn't think much of his visitor, who had placed his faith in stories fabricated on untruths. Such stories distract people who should be seriously pursuing productive spiritual matters, and they make even greater skeptics of people who would benefit from a credible Christian witness.

Fact or Fiction

The fact is that Jews, Christians, and Muslims are all interested in what happens on the Temple Mount. Some Jewish people believe that rebuilding the Temple is an essential element in the Messiah's coming—first or second, depending on whether the view is Jewish or Christian.

Jewish devotees of the concept are serious about such issues as the Temple's exact location and matters related to sanctuary worship. And there is research being conducted along these lines. For example, the Temple Institute in Jerusalem has done extensive research on the priestly garments, sacrificial ceremonies, and implements used in Temple worship. Many of these articles have been reconstructed and are ready for service. Reasons behind this meticulous preparation are stated clearly in the group's *Treasures of the Temple* booklet:

> *The dream of rebuilding the Temple spans 50 gener-*
> *ations of Jews, five continents and innumerable seas*
> *and oceans. The prayer for the rebuilding is recited*
> *in as many languages as are known to humanity . . .*
> *with the rebirth of a Jewish state and the creation of*
> *a Jewish army and the flowering of the desert and the*
> *scientific and social strides made by the nation*
> *Israel. This new dimension is a possibility . . . With*
> *G-d's help we will soon be able to rebuild the Temple*
> *on its holy mountain in Jerusalem, ushering in an*
> *era of peace and understanding love and kindness,*
> *when "G-d will be king over all the earth, in that day*
> *G-d will be one and his name will be one."*

In other words, Messiah's reign and the rebuilding of the Temple are inexorably linked. This contention is also widely promoted among Christians. One of the questions most frequently asked in prophecy conferences concerns the rebuilding of the Temple as a prerequisite to the return of Christ. The answer to this query makes a vital point. It is emphatically NO!

Will future Temples be built on Mount Moriah in Jerusalem? Yes. There will be a Tribulation Temple and a Millennial Temple. But the belief that the absence of the Temple is restraining the Lord's return is pure fiction, wholly unrelated to biblical fact. Nowhere is this even hinted at in Scripture.

Our Lord's return is imminent—the next event on the prophetic time line. No occurrence on the face of the earth acts as a restrainer or indicator. He may come for His church at any moment. All historic realities are incidentally related to this overwhelming event. He will schedule every other event in relationship to His coming.

Temple Teaching

Revelation related to the Temples, which have and will grace Moriah, is a central teaching in the Bible. Each of these Temples presents a unique aspect of God's light to a darkened world. In totality, they reveal how the Shekinah glory, fully manifested in the Messiah, will ultimately shine through in absolute triumph.

Solomon's Temple: The Light Descending (1 Ki. 8—9)

The priests could not continue ministering because of the cloud; for the glory of the LORD filled the house of the LORD (1 Ki. 8:11).

In Solomon's grand Temple, God dwelled among His people, and the light of the Lord's presence filled the place with His glory. It stood as Jehovah's declaration of intent— God was lighting the way home for sin-blinded humanity. More light was on the way.

Zerubbabel's Temple: The Light Dedicated (Ezra 3—6)

Then the children of Israel, the priests and the Levites and the rest of the descendants of the captivity, celebrated the dedication of this house of God with joy (Ezra 6:16).

Solomon's Temple was eventually besieged by the Babylonians. Yet it illuminated the titanic Satan/God conflict that will endure through a godless world system dedicated to extinguishing the light of God. For a time it appeared that the world and Satan would have their way. The Temple was destroyed in 586 B.C. Although the light was reduced to a spark, it burst forth again as Babylon was expiring. Empires would live and die, but God was dedicated to the preservation of His light.

Herod's Temple: The Light Defined (Jn. 8:12)
Then Jesus spoke to them again, saying, "I am the light of the world. He who follows Me shall not walk in darkness, but have the light of life."

In the courts of Herod's Temple, the light took shape and form with Jesus' declaration. Ironically, it happened in a place bearing the name of one of the era's foulest tyrants, illustrating emphatically that God's light would overcome Satan and his emissaries.

Jesus announced His deity at Israel's fabled Feast of Tabernacles (Jn. 7:1—10:21). The commemoration began with a nightlong service, during which the sons of Jacob celebrated in the Temple Court of the Women around four massive candelabra.

The Feast of Tabernacles' nocturnal-light aspect carried the idea that the light of God was shining from the Temple courts, reflecting off the Temple's gold façade. It shone across the Kidron to the Mount of Olives, the city beyond, and to the vales of Israel. Then it leaped off into the far reaches of the world to invite every child of Adam to come to the light shining forth from Jerusalem. Come to the light. That light was now defined—the Light of the world is Jesus.

The Tribulation Temple: The Light Denied (2 Th. 2:4)
Who [the Antichrist] opposes and exalts himself above all that is called God or that is worshiped, so that he sits as God in the temple of God, showing himself that he is God.

Satan's last-gasp effort to extinguish the light will come when, in the person of a counterfeit Christ, he will enter the Tribulation Temple and declare himself God. Satan sees it as the door to fulfilling his manic aspirations. In reality, it is his entrance to Armageddon and the lightning-flash radiance of

God's light from Heaven—the Messiah—who will seal his doom.

The Millennial Temple: The Light Diffused
(Ezek. 40—48; Zech. 14)

It shall be one day which is known to the LORD— neither day nor night. But at evening time it shall happen that it will be light (Zech. 14:7).

The light will be diffused during the Millennium as an emblem of the consummation of all things that God has purposed through giving us the light. All nations will see it and move in reverence toward the Temple Mount in Jerusalem to pay homage to the King—the true Light of the world.

So, while religions and nations fight over the Temple Mount on Mount Moriah in Jerusalem, those who know Him look for the One who will grace its brow.

The Center of the Action

Although the contest over the Temple Mount has important ramifications, the future now coming into focus tells the rest of the story. Evangelical Christians who are turning away from the study of Bible prophecy are unable to discern why our relationship to the State of Israel, the Jewish people, and the land of Israel is of any importance. Replacement theologians have pressed the debilitating fiction that we Christians are, after all, the true "Israel of God." Sadly, many believers are convinced prophecy is merely the stuff of allegory or ancient fulfillment, without practical meaning for us. This position flies in the face of clear biblical revelation, historical reality, and world conditions that are spiraling out of control. The Scriptures teach that a literal Temple will stand on Moriah during the Tribulation.

In 2 Thessalonians 2:4, the apostle Paul undoubtedly spoke of a future event, a specific place, and a personality

(Antichrist) not yet revealed to the world. History obviously is moving toward cataclysmic events. Many question how and when the Dome of the Rock will be removed to make way for the Tribulation Temple. But one thing is sure: When the time comes for the Temple to be rebuilt, if the structure needs to be taken out of the way, it will be.

The Tribulation Temple, of course, is not the last chapter in God's plan for the threshing floor King David purchased from Araunah the Jebusite. Scripture contains a lavishly detailed account of the future Millennial Temple that will grace the Temple Mount when Messiah reigns on Earth. Ezekiel 40—44 lays down the dimensions and details of a structure never before seen on this planet. Into this house, prepared for the King of kings, will enter the glory of the Lord, which left Solomon's Temple and never dwelled in the second Temple:

> And the glory of the LORD came into the temple by way of the gate which faces toward the east. The Spirit lifted me up and brought me into the inner court; and behold, the glory of the LORD filled the temple (43:4–5).

God does not view His land as belonging to Islam. It belongs to Him. He gave it to the Jewish people, and He has plans for it. God's Word tells us of the day when the Messiah will return, ascend His throne, and welcome the masses of mankind that will come up to Jerusalem to observe the Feast of Tabernacles:

> And it shall come to pass that every one who is left of all the nations which came against Jerusalem shall go up from year to year to worship the King, the LORD of hosts, and to keep the Feast of Tabernacles (Zech. 14:16).

As Scripture indicates, future history focuses on the land He has chosen (Israel); the city where He has placed His name (Jerusalem); and the Temple Mount, the site of His House. No conflict over those issues is inconsequential. And those who take it on themselves to drive the Jewish people from their holy place, efface Jehovah's name from the landscape, or impose their will to dictate who will have dominion there will suffer grave consequences.

ENDNOTES

[1] Martin Gilbert, *The Routledge Atlas of the Arab-Israeli Conflict*, 7th ed. (London: Routledge, 2002), 1.

[2] Josephus, *Wars of the Jews*, 5.5.6.

[3] Gershom Gorenberg, "Power of Myth," *The New Republic* 223, no. 23 (2000): 15.

CHAPTER 13

THE SHRINKING STATE OF ISRAEL

To hear the Arabs tell it, Israel is a behemoth whose tentacles have spread far and wide to snatch Arab lands from their rightful owners and subjugate the Arab people. Their tale is a mastery of fiction and a far cry from fact. History reveals quite another story.

> *I have much pleasure in conveying to you, on behalf of His Majesty's Government, the following declaration of sympathy with the Jewish Zionist aspirations which has been submitted to, and approved by, the Cabinet.*
>
> *His Majesty's Government view with favour the establishment in Palestine of a national home for the Jewish people, and will use their best endeavors to facilitate the achievement of this object.*
> —Excerpt from the Balfour Declaration,
> November 2, 1917

The Jewish people had traveled a tortuous road for the better part of two millennia before French Baron Edmond James de Rothschild received, on their behalf, this official letter sanctioning a national home for them in their ancient land. For 400 years (1517–1917) the Ottoman Turks had controlled an immense area in the Middle East, including all of what had briefly been called Palestine, where Jewish people have lived since the days of Joshua. In A.D. 70 the

Romans sacked Jerusalem and burned the second Jewish Temple. Three million Jewish people remained in the land. Later, around A.D. 135, after the Jewish revolt against Rome in which 600,000 Jews perished, many Jewish people still remained in the land, while others migrated away.

The Romans had allowed the center of Jewish life to relocate to the Galilee. Wrote Joan Peters: "The result was that the Jewish identity with the Jewish nation remained steadfast. As the British Royal Commission would report in 1937, almost 2,000 years afterward, 'Always . . . since the fall of the Jewish state some Jews have been living in Palestine. . . . Fresh immigrants arrived from time to time . . . [and] settled mainly in Galilee.'"[1]

Jewish people continued to live in Palestine under the Ottoman Turks, who oppressed them mercilessly. In fact, several well-known Israelis, including the late Gen. Moshe Dayan, were born in the land during that time. Unlike the Palestinians of today, the Ottoman Turks were not Arabs. They were, however, Muslims, which underscores the point that the conflict between Israel and the Arab world is not over ethnic Arab claims to Palestine. It is, rather, an extension of the Islamic worldview toward Jews, Christians, and other "infidels"—a worldview that confiscates lands in the name of Allah.

In 1917 the British defeated the Ottoman Turks in World War I and received a mandate over the area from the League of Nations (precursor to the UN). Because the people of the land had not ruled themselves but had been ruled as part of a greater kingdom, the League of Nations deemed the local population unable to govern itself. Article 22 of the Covenant of the League of Nations established the mandate system, which gave administrative control of such areas to a more advanced nation until the population there was considered capable of taking over. This fact alone drives a stake through the heart of the current argument that there had been a nation of Palestine that succumbed to Israeli occupation.

The mandate, approved at the San Remo Conference on April 24, 1920, stipulated that Britain was to create a national home in Palestine for the Jewish people. Article 2 of the mandate instructed the British to "secure the establishment of the Jewish national home, as laid down in the preamble"; and Article 6 instructed them to "facilitate Jewish immigration under suitable conditions and . . . encourage, in co-operation with the Jewish agency referred to in Article 4, close settlement by Jews on the land, including State lands and waste lands not required for public purposes."

The territory designated for the Jewish state approximated the boundaries established in God's Word (Gen. 15:8; 23:31; Dt. 11:24; Josh. 1:4). It extended from the Mediterranean Sea to Iraq and included all of what is now the country of Jordan.

The Whittling Begins

Contrary to the popular myth propagated by anti-Semites, Arab apologists, and the majority of international news agencies, Israel has never been an expansionist state. From the days of the original land grant under the British Mandate, Jewry's national homeland has continued to shrink rather than expand—and it is still shrinking today.

The whittling began one year after the British Mandate went into effect. The original allotment for Israel was 45,560 square miles (118,000 sq. km.), an area slightly smaller than the state of Pennsylvania. In 1921, to appease the Arabs, the British arbitrarily gave Saudi Arabian Emir Abdullah 77 percent of the territory (35,125 square miles) that had been set aside for the Jewish people. This new Arab country of Transjordan lay east of the Jordan River, extending to the Iraqi desert. Abdullah, grandfather of the late King Hussein, then established the Hashemite Kingdom of Jordan.

The creation of this Palestinian state sliced the Jewish homeland to a mere 23 percent of the original allotment. Now it was down to 10,478 square miles, of which 4,500 square miles were the Negev desert. Furthermore, the Jews who had been living east of the Jordan were forced to leave. None were allowed to settle in Transjordan. But the Arabs were freely allowed to move west of the Jordan River into what was left of the Jewish national homeland.

Then, through a succession of infamous "White Papers," Britain turned its back on its responsibilities to facilitate Jewish immigration under Article 6 of the mandate and virtually closed Palestine to Jews desperate to escape Adolf Hitler's "Final Solution" of torture and death in Nazi concentration camps and ovens. Yet it let Arabs from other countries illegally flood the area. Wrote Joan Peters:

> *While the Jews were working furiously at clearing land that had been ignored or dismissed by Government "authorities" as "uncultivable," and creating places that Government insisted "did not exist," those opened-up places . . . were taken by illegal Arab immigrants. Having cleared those places only to have them expropriated by the Arab in-migrants and immigrant community—Syrians, Egyptians, Hauranis, Algerians, Hejazis, and others camouflaged as "natural indigenous Palestinian population since time immemorial"—the Jews yet continued their efforts, lest the British halt Jewish immigration entirely, which Government on more than one occasion had threatened to do. . . . Had those places in the country been left open for the Jews instead of being usurped by illegal Arab immigrants falsely represented as part of the "original" and "existing" Palestinian population for "thousands of years"—many factors would have changed.[2]*

That said, Ms. Peters continued:

*The British virtually signed the death warrants for
countless Jews in mortal danger by engaging the
might of the British Empire to enforce strict laws
against Jewish immigration. . . . Government not
only encouraged or winked at, but officially enacted
the illegal immigration of thousands of Arab
indigents from neighboring and more distant lands,
to take jobs in the Jewish National Home that might
have saved the lives of Jewish concentration camp
victims.*[3]

"The land being cleared by Palestinian Jews, for Jewish
victims of persecution in Europe," she wrote, "had been and
still was being appropriated by Arabs." It was the Arabs who
were usurping Jewish land, not the other way around. The
travesty, wrote Ms. Peters, was that "thousands of Jews
would be prevented from entering what was to have been
their sanctuary and thus be condemned to the fateful inferno
of the Nazis. And that White Paper would be justified by the
premise that the Jews were usurping the Arabs' places in
'Palestine.'"[4]

In the aftermath of World War II and the near annihilation
of European Jewry, the matter of a Jewish state was thrown
into the hands of the newly formed United Nations.

Two years after the war ended, the borders of the Jewish
national homeland shrunk even further. On November 29,
1947, the UN General Assembly decided to partition the
remaining 23 percent of the mandated Jewish homeland into
three parcels.

(1) A Jewish state would control the Negev to the south; a
strip along the coastline running from Rehovot to the Haifa
area; and a parcel adjacent to Lebanon, Syria, and Jordan,
which included the Sea of Galilee.

(2) Yet another Arab state would be constructed using the
Gaza Strip; the area west of the Jordan River now known as

the West Bank; and a wedge of land in the north, bordering on Lebanon, between the Mediterranean Sea and Israeli territory.

(3) Jerusalem would become an international zone.

So Israel received the barren, largely uninhabitable Negev and two other parcels of land, for a total of 5,500 square miles. The future State of Israel had shrunk to a sliver of territory—only 11 percent of the land the League of Nations had mandated it to have. The rest all went to the Arabs.

No Negotiations. No Recognition. No Peace. No Borders.

Clearly, the Jewish people ended up on the short end of the stick. When the UN General Assembly voted on the Partition Plan in 1947, the Palestinian Jews, however, complied with the resolution. As tiny as their thrice-torn piece of real estate had become, they were willing to take anything that would promise them a haven after the misery of the Holocaust.

The Arabs, however, were intransigent. Unwilling even to recognize Israel's right to exist, they rejected the plan out of hand. As far as the Arab and Islamic worlds were concerned, there was no Israel; therefore, there could be no talk of peace. Their credo became, "No negotiations; no recognition; no peace."

So on May 14, 1948, when the modern State of Israel was born, five Arab armies swept down on the fledgling nation with a ferocious determination to destroy it, along with all its Jews. Certain of victory, Arab leaders counseled their brethren living within Israel's borders to leave their homes. In a few days, they were assured, Allah's armies would finish off the pestiferous Jews. Then they could return in triumph to their properties with the added bonus of enjoying the spoils of their Jewish neighbors. No doubt, some Arabs also departed for fear of what might befall them during the fighting.

The Jewish Palestinians tried their best to keep the Arabs from evacuating. They even drove through the territory on trucks, shouting their assurances of safety through bullhorns and begging the Arabs to stay and live with them in peace. But most would not.

When the war began, Arab leaders woefully underestimated the courage, determination, and ingenuity of a people who had been pressed against the wall before and decided that, this time, they would not kneel to die; they would stand to fight. And fight they did. Against all odds, the Jewish people won. The Israeli War of Independence lasted a year, from May 1948 to May 1949. When it ended, Israel found itself with 2,500 more square miles than allotted in the UN partition. But it had lost the Jewish Quarter of the Old City of Jerusalem and, with it, the Western Wall—a retaining wall of the second Temple—the holiest site in all of Judaism.

During the fighting, the Jordanians, who had received the lion's share of the Jewish homeland, crossed the Jordan River and seized Judea and Samaria (West Bank)—the area apportioned by the UN for yet a second Arab state. They also laid siege to the Old City of Jerusalem, expelled the Jewish population there, and tore all of the ancient Jewish synagogues down to the ground. Meanwhile, the Egyptians, attacking from the South, overran the Gaza Strip, which also was to have become part of that second Arab state. Thus the people who captured the West Bank and Gaza in 1948 were not the Jews. However, the Jews managed to hold on to their land plus gain some territory.

Now the Arabs faced an immense problem. Their leaders had encouraged a massive exodus from what was now, in fact, Israel. Where were these Arabs to go? Afraid to return to their homes, they were now refugees, "confined to refugee camps by their fellow Arab hosts and deliberately cut off from the economic development of the States in which they lived."[5] And so they would remain for at least another half-century. Meanwhile, the 160,000 Arabs who remained in Israel became Israeli citizens and received the same economic and material benefits as the Jews.

Early in 1949, when it became apparent that the Arabs could not drive Israel into the sea as they had promised, they signed armistice agreements. These documents were just that and no more; they were armistice agreements for ceasefire lines. The Egyptians made it abundantly clear that they regarded this arrangement as neither satisfactory nor permanent. According to the UN, "The armistice demarcation line is not to be construed in any sense as a political or territorial boundary, and is delineated without prejudice to rights, claims and positions of either party."[6]

In 1950 Jordan annexed the territory it had captured during the war and announced it was reserving the rights to territorial development. In other words, both Egypt and Jordan held the land they had seized by weight of arms—a situation that would prevail until the Arab states tried again, in 1967, to destroy Israel. So from 1949 to 1967—18 years— Jordan held Judea and Samaria (West Bank), and Egypt held the Gaza Strip.

In the 1967 Six-Day War, the Arabs again failed to destroy Israel and, in the process, lost Jerusalem, the West Bank, Gaza Strip, Sinai, and the Golan Heights to the Israel Defense Forces.

By rejecting the reality of Israel and the UN offer of another Arab state in 1947, the Arab Palestinians authored their own dilemma. And their claim that Israel occupies land located within the legitimate borders of "Arab Palestine" is utterly untrue.

The Population Exchange

In the haggling over Arab Palestinian rights, a central issue is the Arab claim that their brethren (and their descendants) who were displaced in 1948 and 1967 should be granted the "right of return" to their previous homes. Their arguments are buttressed by images in the Western media showing the deplorable conditions of these "refugees" who must live in Arab countries, mainly Lebanon, Syria, and Jordan.

What much of the world has chosen to forget is that 800,000 Jewish people were also displaced. They were forced to flee from Arab countries where their families had lived and owned businesses for years, and they became refugees after the Jewish state became a reality in 1948. Considering threats from Arab leaders, these Jewish people had good reason to flee. During the 1947 UN debates on partition, the Egyptian delegate told the General Assembly, "The lives of one million Jews in Muslim countries would be jeopardized by partition."

The 586,000 Jewish people who opted to immigrate to Israel arrived practically penniless in a struggling, newborn country that could promise only hard work and a daily fight for survival. These Jewish people had to leave everything behind and start over with nothing. The Arab governments of the countries where they had lived confiscated all their possessions, and not a single one offered them any compensation.

This much-ignored fact is one of the sticking points in a final settlement of the refugee problem. The war produced refugees on both sides. And Israel maintains that if it compensates Arabs for their former properties within Israel, then the Arab nations must compensate Jewish people for their former properties and funds in Arab countries. And the demand is justified. For example, in March 1950 the Iraqi government announced the "Special Law Authorizing the Emigration of Jews." It was a euphemistic name for a law that enacted government confiscation of all the assets of Jewish émigrés. In order to qualify to leave, Jewish people had to renounce their Iraqi citizenship and take no more than $16 per person out of the country; children were allowed even less. At least 121,000 of the 130,000 Iraqi Jews chose to leave everything behind and get out.

Despite these facts, it is extremely rare to hear anyone mention the Jewish refugee situation, the reason being that the Jewish people did not endure refugee status for very long. At great hardship, Israel assimilated all returning sons and daughters of Abraham into the life of the nation as quickly as possible. So quickly, in fact, did that tiny nation smaller than the state of New Jersey settle so many refugees that the feat endures as one of the great miracles of modern history.

The number of Arabs who left what is now Israel during the 1948 War of Independence was placed at 472,000 by a UN mediator at the time, although the figure was considered high. In 1967 another 150,000 left what is known as the West Bank. For these refugees, however, life turned out far different than for the Jewish refugees. Even though the surrounding Arab nations urged Arabs to leave Israel, they refused to extend the courtesy of a warm welcome to the refugees they had created. In 1948 Palestinian Arabs fled to Lebanon, Iraq, Syria, Jordan, Egypt, the West Bank (held by Jordan), and Gaza Strip (held by Egypt), where they found conditions far less than desirable. These unfortunate people immediately became political pawns in a "maintain the problem" scenario that would last for decades. Although the oil-rich Arab countries had more than enough resources to resettle their kinsmen and assimilate them into their nations, they did not. Their failure was deliberate and, by any measurable standard, less than humane.

The idea was that if these displaced people were kept in overcrowded, squalid refugee camps like rats in a cage, they would become a problem that would remain an issue in the international community and pose a serious difficulty for the Israeli government. In so thinking, the Arab leaders were, of course, correct. The problem of what to do with these people has, by design, festered for decades. The tragedy is that these

Palestinian refugees are being manipulated for political purposes by a callous, radical element that pursues a win-at-any-price strategy, teaches them that Israel is the source of all evil, and molds them into perfect candidates to become terrorists and suicide bombers.

It is no secret that rich Arab nations have invested megamillions in funding terrorism. When the late founder and leader of Hamas, Sheik Ahmed Yassin, went on a fund-raising tour for his terrorist organization in the spring of 1998, it was reported that he raised $300 million from Arab Gulf states. He also received a pledge of $15 million a month from Iran. The stated purpose of the support was to help Hamas carry out terrorism against Israel and its allies. Yet these same nations that so generously dole out funds for terrorism leave their Muslim brethren in miserable refugee camps with inadequate housing and grinding poverty. Why? Because their goal is not to help their people; it is to seize the land of Israel from the Jews. And to accomplish that end, they are willing to pay almost anything.

Land for Paper and Promises

Israel has repeatedly done something unprecedented in the history of this planet: It gave back land it won in wars of self-defense. Consider the facts.

This tiny nation has been attacked repeatedly—five major wars and two intifadas—by those intent on driving the Jewish state into the sea. Each time, the Arab aggressors were defeated by numerically inferior forces—and lost territory in the process. Afterward, they loudly bemoaned their plight, accused Israel of stealing their land, and demanded that every square inch be returned. One would expect Israel to do what other nations have done over the centuries: simply say, "You lost it; we have it; don't try it again."

The Russians, who now demand that Israel return "occupied lands," think differently about their own self-proclaimed property rights. Their attitude is the norm for nations that succeed in defeating their enemies—especially those who strike first. In a commentary in *Pravda* (September 2, 1964), then a state-run newspaper, the Russians stated their case:

> *The borders of the State have become sanctified in the efforts of the settlers in the border villages and by the streams of blood which they have had to shed in their defence [sic]. A people which has been attacked and which defended itself and emerged victorious has the sacred right of establishing for itself such a final political settlement as would permit it to liquidate the sources of aggression . . . a people which has acquired its security with such heavy sacrifice will never agree to restore the old borders.*

But what's good for the Russians, in their view, is not good for the Jews. Israel has returned land to its attackers, only to have them, in one way or another, attack again.

After the 1967 war in which Israel recaptured the Old City of Jerusalem, it turned over control of its venerated Temple Mount to the Jordanians and made the sacred hill off-limits to religious Jews who wished to establish a presence there. The Jewish state was, of course, concerned over the possibility of a holy war erupting in the Arab world. In the intervening years between 1967 and today, however, Israel's sensitivity and deference to Muslims, save for rare exceptions, have not been returned in kind.

During negotiations with Egypt, Israel agreed to return to Egypt the Sinai, captured in 1967. In exchange for a peace that has been cold but is, nonetheless, a peace, Israel removed Jewish settlements, factories, hotels, and health facilities from the Sinai. In a major sacrifice, Israel turned over the oil fields it had discovered and developed and that supplied one half of the nation's energy needs. Militarily, Israel forfeited its early-warning facilities, strategically important airfields, and direct control of its shipping lanes to and from Eilat.

The Map Tells the Story

Although Israel has stuck to the agreements forged under the failed Olso Accords of the 1990s, the Palestinians have been much less forthcoming. Their steadfast unwillingness to rescind elements in the Palestinian Charter calling for Israel's annihilation is a stark indicator of the fundamental attitude of a large and powerful segment of Israel's "partners" in the peace process. And although many of the issues seem profoundly complicated, there is one simple indicator that reveals true intent at a level all of us can understand.

At this writing, not a single map produced in the Arab/Muslim world contains the State of Israel. Not the map on the wall of the Palestinian president. Not the maps hanging on the walls of schools where Palestinian children are taught. Not the map issued by the Palestinian Ministry of Tourism. It certainly is not on the maps stuck to barrack walls in any Arab or Muslim nation's military installations. Every Arab world map marks all of Israel with one word: *Palestine*.

All you have to do to verify this fact is examine the official Palestinian Authority's *Atlas of the Arab Homeland and the World* published in Nablus, Israel. This atlas (4th edition for 1998–99) is used at all educational levels. Its rendering of the political map of the region does not show Israel as a country but, rather, displays it as "Occupied Palestine." In the listing of "The World: Countries and Capitals," Israel is not mentioned. Jerusalem is listed as the capital of "Palestine." In November 2005 the UN held a "Day of Solidarity With the Palestinian People." Hanging prominently between UN and Palestine Liberation Organization flags at UN headquarters in New York was a map labeled "map of Palestine." Israel was gone completely, even though it had been a UN member at the time for 56 years.

Simply put, Israel does not exist in the minds of the overwhelming majority of the 1 billion Arab and Islamic people on this earth. Most Arab Palestinian leaders have made their ultimate goal unmistakably clear. It seems that the only people who do not take them seriously are Western politicians who insist on writing off bellicose Muslim statements as mere rhetoric born out of legitimate "Palestinian rage." Such Westerners are naïve wishful-thinkers.

Consider a few of these "rage-induced" declarations, some made by the late PA chairman, Yasser Arafat.

> *The struggle will continue until all Palestine is liberated.*
> —Arafat, Voice of Palestine Radio,
> November 1995

> *When we stopped the Intifada we did not stop the jihad [Islamic holy war] to establish Palestine with Jerusalem as our capital. . . . We know only one word: jihad, jihad, jihad. . . . We are in a conflict with the Zionist movement, the Balfour Declaration, and all imperialist activity.*
> —Arafat in a speech near Bethlehem,
> October 1996

> *Whoever has occupied part of Palestine or Jerusalem faces jihad until Judgment Day. Our destiny is jihad.*
> —Sheikh Muhammad Hussein in a
> sermon at the al-Aqsa mosque on the
> Temple Mount in Jerusalem, May 15, 1998

> *We carried out the longest intifada [uprising] in history. They [the Israelis] should know that we can start it again if they try to prevent us from exercising our rights. The state will be established with Jerusalem as its capital whether they like it or*

*not. If they don't like it they can drink from the
waters of the Dead Sea. We, the Fatah and the PLO
are ready to fight a new battle . . . every single day.*
—Arafat in a speech in Ramallah, March 1999

Arafat made that comment following his 1998 Wye
Memorandum promise to "take all measures necessary in
order to prevent acts of terrorism, crime and hostilities
directed against the Israeli side . . . and to prevent
incitement."

*We do not and will not recognize a state called Israel.
. . . This land is the property of all Muslims in all
parts of the world. . . . Let Israel die.*
—Hamas's Mahmoud Zahar in a
newspaper interview, August 2005

Survival Through Strength

The plan to sweep away the whole of Israel is still very
much alive. In fact, it may be more alive than ever. To prevent
their nation from shrinking into a literal nothingness, Israelis
ask two things from the peace process.

Security. They want secure, defensible borders as
guaranteed in prior UN resolutions. To achieve this, Israel is
willing to relinquish land and withdraw from territories that
many feel are vital to Israel's future security. Such was the
reasoning under former Prime Minister Ariel Sharon's unilateral disengagement from the Gaza Strip and parts of northern
Samaria on the West Bank. And his successor, Ehud Olmert,
said Israel must be willing to make even more territorial
concessions.

Reciprocity. When Israel keeps a promise, so should the
Palestinians. That has not been the case thus far. Therefore,
the notion that Israel should continue making unilateral
concessions in the hope that the Arabs will begin to adhere to

their agreements as well simply does not hold water.

All parties attempting to help Israel and the Arab Palestinians make peace should insist on these two vital elements. Furthermore, in the hostile environment that will continue to constitute life in the Middle East, democratic nations, particularly the United States, must do all they can to ensure that Israel remains strong.

The majority of the Muslim world has proven that it is no friend to America. Israel, however, will be loyal to the end.

ENDNOTES

[1] Joan Peters, *From Time Immemorial* (1984; Chicago: JKAP Publications, 1993), 147.

[2] Ibid., 381.

[3] Ibid., 381–82.

[4] Ibid., 233.

[5] Martin Gilbert, *The Routledge Atlas of the Arab-Israeli Conflict*, 7th ed. (New York: Routledge, 2002), 55.

[6] *United Nations General Progress and Supplementary Report of the United Nations Conciliation Commission for Palestine*, General Assembly, 5th sess., 1951, supplement no. 18, (A/1367/Rev.1), chap. 2, par. 17 <http://domino.un.org/unispal.nsf/0/93037e3b939746de8525610200567883? OpenDocument>.

CHAPTER 14

⌀

THE MANY FACES OF PALESTINE

Since many people today are anxious either to rewrite history or ignore it, it is important to look at the origin of the terms *Palestine* and *Palestinian.* An early Zionist leader was fond of speaking of the land that was to become the State of Israel as "a land without a people for a people without a land." Although his observation was, in large measure, accurate, it was not quite the whole of the reality that would become the Jewish experience. Although the majority of Jewish people live outside the land, in what is commonly called the Diaspora, Israel has never been bereft of Jews. They have lived there since the days of Joshua, despite all attempts to obliterate them. Joan Peters' book *From Time Immemorial* extensively documents this irrefutable fact. So we will not deal with it much here. When Diaspora Jews began to return to the land of their fathers, the Arab presence proved as hostile to them as it was to the Jews already in the land.

The conflict has been in existence longer than the State of Israel. Like it or not, there eventually will be a State of Palestine. And with Hamas in charge, few can doubt that it will become a launching pad for what Arabs hope will be the final annihilation of the Jewish state.

Why "Palestine"?

Where did the term *Palestine* come from? The word *Palestine* occurs in neither the Old nor New Testaments.

Scripture refers only to Israel, Ephraim and Samaria (in the north), and Judah and Judea (in the south).

The Greek historian Herodotus (485–425 B.C.) was the first to call the area Syria Palestina. The time corresponds to Israel's return from the Babylonian Captivity, when the land was under the authority of the dominant world power of Persia. Herodotus lived during the events in the books of Esther and Nehemiah, under the reigns of Xerxes (also called Ahasuerus, 486–465 B.C.) and Artaxerxes I (464–423 B.C.). However, the name did not really catch on; and in A.D. 26, when Jesus walked the earth and the Roman Empire ruled the ancient Mediterranean world, the land was still called Judea. History records that Pontius Pilate was the prefect, or governor, of Judea—not Palestine. And the Jewish people were still the main settled population in the area.

After the Romans destroyed the second Jewish Temple in A.D. 70, the area continued to be called Judea. Historians say that Roman Emperor Hadrian adopted the name Syria Palestina around A.D. 135 as a way of erasing the memory of the Jewish people and their association with the land. The word *Palestina* comes from the name Philistine, referring to the people who occupied parts of the region as hostile contemporaries of ancient Israel. Subsequently, the name was shortened to Palestina, and eventually, Palestine.

In approximately A.D. 390 the Byzantine Empire divided the area into three units called the three Palestines: Judea, Samaria, and Perea. Perea is the territory the Bible calls "beyond the Jordan [River]," which today would be the country of Jordan. (See Joshua 13:8; 18:7; Matthew 4:25.) When the Crusaders arrived in 1099, they referred to the entire area as Palestine. Interestingly, the Crusaders were so barbaric and cruel to the Jewish people in the Holy Land that the Jews united with the Muslims to fight them.

After the Crusader kingdom fell in 1291, Palestine was no longer an official designation. The name, however, continued to be used informally for the land on both sides of the Jordan River. The Ottoman Turks conquered the area in 1517 and ruled for 400 years until they lost it to the British in 1917.

Under Ottoman rule, the territory was never a separate administrative unit; it was part of the province of Syria. Wrote Joan Peters:

> *As many, including Professor [Bernard] Lewis, have pointed out, "From the end of the Jewish state in antiquity to the beginning of British rule, the area now designated by the name Palestine was not a country and had no frontiers, only administrative boundaries; it was a group of provincial subdivisions, by no means always the same, within a larger entity."*
>
> *In other words, it appears that Palestine never was an independent nation and the Arabs never named the land to which they now claim rights.*[1]

The British received the mandate over the area from the League of Nations in 1920. By naming the territory the British Mandate for Palestine, "the area that is today Israel and Jordan became the first and only geographic division with the name Palestine since before the Ottoman Empire controlled the area."[2]

After Britain gave the land east of the Jordan to Abdullah, the name only referred to the land west of the river, which is now Israel—including the West Bank.

This historical information is important when approaching the problem of establishing a Palestinian state because a completely new national entity is being formed. Contrary to Arab claims, there has never been an Arab state of Palestine. And the Jewish people never commandeered the "Arab country of Palestine" and turned it into what the media loves to call "occupied territory."

The late David Bar-Illan, former executive editor of *The Jerusalem Post*, addressed the subject in an article first published in November 1998 in *The Los Angeles Times*. He wrote:

> *In a recent speech to the United Nations General Assembly, Yasser Arafat talked of "the need to realize justice for the Palestinian people, to restore their international status and their seat in the United Nations." He referred to "our country, Palestine" and expressed the hope that it would be "restored its freedom."*
>
> *The meaning of this message is clear: Palestine is a country that belonged to the Palestinians until it was invaded and usurped by the Jews. Jerusalem was the Palestinian capital now being Judaized by Israel. Justice will be served only if the Palestinians are allowed to re-establish their sovereignty in it.*
>
> *That all this is unadulterated fiction has not prevented many governments from accepting it. Nor has it deterred pundits from upbraiding Israel for failing to "give back" Palestinian land.*
>
> *In fact, there never has been a state called Palestine, nor have the Palestinian Arabs ever been an independent people, and Jerusalem never has been an Arab or Muslim capital. Jerusalem has had an absolute Jewish majority for more than a century (and a plurality before that), and for the last three thousand years, only the Jewish people have called it their capital. . . . To inveigh against "Judaizing" Jerusalem is like protesting the Arabization of Cairo.*

Who Are the Palestinians?

The word *Palestinian*, as commonly employed today, is a relatively recent term. Until the end of the British Mandate over Palestine in 1948, all inhabitants of the area west of the

Jordan River were known as Palestinians. In other words, a Jewish person living in what is now Israel was referred to as a Palestinian Jew. An Arab living in the same area was a Palestinian Arab. Likewise, a Christian was known as a Palestinian Christian. It was as simple as that. Jewish people from the area carried British passports with the designation "Palestinian Jew."

Palestine ceased to exist as a legal entity after 1948, when Britain relinquished the mandate and Israel became a modern state. The Arab Palestinians joined the rest of the Arab world in rejecting the UN Partition Plan of 1947 and moved to destroy the fledgling State of Israel. After failing to do so, and following five attempts to wipe out the Jewish state, the Arab Palestinians decided to change their tactics, if not their final goal, and begin negotiating with Israel.

The Right of Prior Claim

Arab leaders settled on a rather ingenious and deceptive plan that sprang from the idea that, as "Palestinians," they had a legitimate prior claim to the Holy Land. Historically, the Jews had the prior claim. But the very name the Arabs assumed as their "birthright" seemed to many to legitimatize their rhetoric. They were even willing to go so far as to say the Jewish people had no ancient presence in the land or on the Temple Mount that predated the Arab Palestinians.

Then Yasser Arafat added insult to injury by telling the biggest lie of all: He claimed that his people, not the Jews, were the original brethren and followers of Jesus of Nazareth. Jesus' lineage is recorded in the Bible for all to see and is traced directly from Abraham, Isaac, and Jacob to Judah and King David of Israel. (See Matthew 1:1–17; Luke 3:23–38.) Arafat claimed that Jesus was a freedom fighter against the Romans (also untrue), just as he himself was a freedom fighter attempting to break the hold of the Israelis on his people. As bizarre as this scenario seems to those of us who are biblically and historically literate, these preposterous claims have been certified by many agenda-driven politicians and members of the secular news media who now argue that the Palestinians have a right not only to a state but also to Jerusalem as their capital.

Changing Strategies

At first, the strategy of the Arab world and the Palestinians was simple: militarily destroy the Zionists and drive them into the sea. Doing so did not appear to be a problem. After all, millions of hostile Arabs surrounded a tiny area no larger than the state of New Jersey. In spite of their numerical superiority, however, the Arabs were not successful. Although Israel paid a high price for its survival, it remained intact as a sovereign nation.

Phase two then became the negotiation track. First, the idea was to push Israel back to the 1967 armistice lines, then back even farther—to the 1948 lines. All the while, Arafat and his cohorts were assuring the Arab world that negotiating was only a tactical maneuver—first '67; then '48; then, for the Zionist Jews, the Mediterranean Sea. It seemed for a time that this strategy would work. "Land for peace" platitudes were flying like kites in the wind. Israel conceded land it could not afford to give away. This was real progress for the Palestinians because all they needed was patience A little piece here, a little piece there, and soon they would have it all. Prior to 2005, in fact, 98 percent of all Arabs on the West Bank and in Gaza were already under Palestinian control. In 2005 Israel gave away Gaza, rendering 8,000 Israelis homeless. Now Israel is talking about giving up most of the West Bank, where 260,000 Israelis live in towns they built from the dust of the ground. Not one was constructed where Arabs were living.

Encouraged by steadfast friends in the U.S. State Department and the European community, the Arabs will not stop trying to devour Israel a piece at a time. Recently, in an act of feigned magnanimity 50 years after the fact, the Arabs decided to accept UN Resolution 181 (the original Partition of Palestine), which they soundly rejected in 1947 because they preferred to go to war rather than accept its terms. At one point the Arabs attempted to dissect little Israel still further, proposing to hack it into six small portions—three for Israel and three for the Palestinians—with Jerusalem becoming an international city controlled by "benevolent" Gentiles. The Europeans loved the idea. Israel was revulsed and legitimately cited the irrevocable facts that have made Resolution 181 null and void.

But this was not the last word. Retreating again to the UN decisions of 1948, the Palestinians have championed the Arab "Right of Return" embodied in UN Resolution 194, dated December 11, 1948, which states,

> *[The General Assembly] resolves that the refugees wishing to return to their homes and live in peace with their neighbors should be permitted to do so at the earliest practicable date.*

Such a return would, by Arab estimates, give 3 million to 4 million "refugees" the right to move into Israel proper—that is, the miniscule portion left after the dissection of the Jewish state. A UN mediator in 1948 estimated the original number of Arab refugees to be around 472,000. These are people who voluntarily left their homes when Israel declared statehood in May 1948 because they believed their Arab brethren would drive Israel into the sea during the Israeli War of Independence. Few are still alive. Today's "refugees" are their children and grandchildren, who have been forced by the Arab countries to languish in refugee camps.

In championing the so-called right of return, the Palestinians and their apologists are willing to forget at least two things. First, they unanimously rejected this resolution when it was originally offered; and second, there is no mention of the right of return for Jews who were expelled from Arab countries after 1948.

The Israeli position is that if Arab "refugees" are to be compensated for the loss of property, as Israelis have agreed should be the case, then Jews expelled from Arab countries are entitled to the same treatment. It seems to have escaped Western negotiators that 800,000 Jews were driven out of Arab countries at the same time, suffering the loss of homes, businesses, and bank accounts. Fair is fair; and if Israel is to compensate Arabs, the Arabs are obligated to return the favor.

The so-called Palestinians have less of a claim to the land of Israel than do the Jews. The facts are the facts, despite what revisionists are doing to try to change them.

ENDNOTES

[1] Joan Peters, *From Time Immemorial (1984; Chicago: JKAP Publications, 1984)*, Ibid., 139. Bernard Lewis quoted from Bernard Lewis, "The Palestinians and the PLO, a Historical Approach, *Commentary,* January 1975, 32–48.

[2] "World War I British Mandate" <palestinefacts.org/pf_ww1_british_mandate.php>.

CHAPTER 15

❦

MUHAMMAD VERSUS
THE MESSIAH

Former Iraqi President Saddam Hussein's ill-fated exercise in aggression against "brother" nation Kuwait in 1991 shook a largely passive global population with the facts of the perilous realities of life in the Middle East. Americans quickly took notice of the Iraqi invasion because, within hours, prices at the gas pumps began to spiral upward. Our much-taken-for-granted Mideast oil source was once again prey to the designs of a tyrant intent on controlling price and supply in order to equip and maintain a foreboding military strike force. Hapless Kuwaitis were intended to become a showcase to whip Arab nations into line and recognize the "butcher of Baghdad" as the undisputed leader of the Arab world.

The War Option

Iraq's military buildup and aggressive ambitions opened a new chapter in the never-ending struggle to survive in the Middle East. And, of course, Israel was at the epicenter. Hussein's threat to "scorch half of Israel" with poison gas was backed by his track record in Iraq's war with Iran and against Kurdish people in his own country, which demonstrated emphatically that his threats were much more than rhetoric. Military experts confirmed that Iraq in those days could have massed 100,000 troops on Israel's borders within 24 hours. Arab allies could have swelled that number to a huge strike force. Arab nations that opposed Saddam's suppression of Kuwait were generally divided on a multitude of issues but, as always, united in their desire to destroy Israel. Iraq, Jordan, and Syria possessed a combined tank force that far exceeded the numbers maintained by NATO. Had Arab militants believed the time was right, they could have attempted to strike a deathblow for Allah and his prophet Muhammad against Israel and the hated Jewish presence in the Mideast.

Saddam Hussein followed the classic behavioral pattern spoken of in Genesis to describe the character and methods of his progenitor, Ishmael: "He shall be a wild man; his hand shall be against every man, and every man's hand against him" (16:12). This verse ensures that the strongest and most brutally aggressive will always be the force to be reckoned with in the Arab world.

Abraham or Allah

The impetus behind the Arab determination to destroy Israel cannot be narrowly defined as a family affair, even though both entities are direct descendants of Abraham. Yes, there was the matter of engendered jealousy over Ishmael's being passed over as the recipient of the Abrahamic Covenant. That blessing and the promise of perpetual ownership of the land of Israel fell to Isaac and his heirs (Gen. 17:19). But Ishmael was also given the promise of becoming "a great nation" (21:18)—a nation so great, in fact, that its descendants "shall not be counted for multitude" (16:10). God has faithfully fulfilled that promise. Tiny Israel floats in the middle of a sea of Arab nations scattered across a large portion of the globe.

There are basically two differences between God's covenants with the Jews and the Ishmaelites. Israel, of course was specifically given the land of Israel (13:14–17; 17:6–8; 17:19–21; 28:3–4). However, the paramount difference

188

is engendered in the words of the Abrahamic Covenant: "And I will bless those who bless you, and I will curse him who curses you; and in you all the families of the earth shall be blessed" (12:3). This promise is further defined in Genesis 22:18: "In your seed all the nations of the earth shall be blessed." That "seed" of blessing delivered to the Gentile nations—including the Arabs—through the Jewish people was the Messiah. "Now to Abraham and his Seed were the promises made. He does not say, 'And to seeds,' as of many, but as of one, 'And to your Seed,' who is Christ" (Gal. 3:16). Jewry's presence and assigned mission was, therefore, uniquely set apart in marked contrast to those described as characteristic of Ishmael's seed and national legacy.

The "seed" component in God's program for humanity surpasses every other aspect of history. In addition to being a Savior of men, Messiah is to be King. When His Kingdom finally arrives, He will establish and enforce stability. Delivery of the one who could so bless mankind was the exclusive province of Abraham's seed through Isaac. The promise is specific. The Abrahamic Covenant provided:

1. A King for the throne: "Kings shall come from you" (Gen. 17:6).
2. A land for the King: "Also I give to you and your descendants after you the land in which you are a stranger, all the land of Canaan, as an everlasting possession" (v. 8).
3. A people for the King: "And I will be their God" (v. 8).

Unfortunately, it was the "blessing" aspect of the covenant that developed the same animosity in Esau's posterity; the blessing fell to Jacob rather than to Esau, who fathered their people. Had the Arabs embraced obediently the Savior and kingly aspects of the blessing of the Messiah, history would have taken another course.

These residual resentments became deeply ingrained in the attitudes of the Arabs toward Israel, and those resentments spun off in manifold and discernible ways as the centuries passed. Scripture is replete with accounts of those heirs of Ishmael who warred against Israel while growling their determination to destroy it: "'Come, and let us cut them off from being a nation, that the name of Israel may be remembered no more.' For they have consulted together with one consent" (Ps. 83:4–5). Their "one consent" was the extermination of the nation of Israel.

Since the days of the psalmist, Arab determination has not wavered. However, the entrance of the *new* religion, Islam (7th century A.D.), refined and sanctified the rationale. It became incumbent to subjugate or exterminate the Jews "in God's name." A man named Sheikh As'ad Tamimi who claimed leadership of the Islamic Jihad Beit al-Maqdis, focused the issue in a statement lauding Saddam Hussein's tirade in the first Gulf War about unleashing chemical weapons against Israel: "I hope he is as good as his word," Tamimi said. "The killing of Jews will continue, killing, killing in God's name until they vanish."

Thus the Allah created by Muhammad, who was familiar with both Judaism and Christianity, was a very different god from the God of the two great religions found in the Bible. Muhammad's religion, which he had intended to replace Judaism and Christianity, would also have a new book (the Qur'an), a new look, and a new center of worship (Mecca).

The word *jihad* became enshrined in the ecstatic vocabulary of the Muslim believer. To kill in the name of Allah, in jihad (holy war), became a privilege. To die in jihad is to be assured a place in Allah's heaven. Consequently, military conquest became a theological pursuit, and conquered people became the subjects of Allah.

The religiously fired law of conquest swept Islamic armies into Syria, Israel, Mesopotamia, Egypt, North Africa, and Spain. The advance was finally stopped by Charles Martel, grandfather of Charlemagne, outside Paris in 732. Later, Muslim hordes encompassed Europe, moving as far west as Austria before being defeated in the late 17th century.

Subsequently, many of these areas, through erosion or military actions, were delivered from Muslim domination. The ultimate affront to Islamic ambitions was the deliverance of Jerusalem from the Muslim Ottoman Turks by the "Christian" British Expeditionary Force in 1917 and the return of Jewry to the land after 1948. Symbolically, the modern State of Israel stands as a constant reminder to rabid fundamentalist Muslims of their humiliation before the "infidels." It is a condition they believe can only be remedied through conquest.

This is a fact of life people restrained by Western beliefs and standards often misunderstand, for the issue of land in the Middle East is not primarily a territorial matter. It is a question of religious dominance—the lack of which is intolerable to the Muslim who is taught that Allah is all and is to possess all. This is precisely why the rise of militant Muslim fundamentalists in Iran was viewed with such deep concern— a concern borne out more vividly when 52 Americans were taken hostage November 4, 1979, from the American Embassy in Tehran during the administration of President Jimmy Carter. They were not released until 444 days later, on January 20, 1981, after Ronald Reagan took office.

An abiding tenet of Islam is that all lands are to be subject to Allah. Therefore, once a territory is taken, it must remain under Muslim domination. If land is lost, jihad becomes necessary. Any concessions or treaties made with enemies under conditions making it impossible to restore dominion by force are observed only until means are available to remedy the situation.

For this reason, as Arab spokesmen have repeatedly avowed, any negotiated peace agreement with Israel will only provide a staging area from which to pursue total elimination of the Jewish presence from land claimed to be sacred to Allah. In such a perpetual state of conflict, Israelis know all too well what the Western world must learn or live to regret: survival against the Muslim onslaught means having superior strength and the will to use it.

The Second Wave

Make no mistake about it: Militant Muslims are bent on possessing this planet for Allah, either by coercion or persuasion. And while, in the first wave, the swords of Islam were wet with the blood of vanquished "infidels," a great second wave is now moving across the Western world in the form of Muslim missionary crusaders. In 1974, at a meeting of the World Muslim League, an Islamic World Mission Board was formed. Successes have mounted, and today Islam is one of the fastest growing religions in the world. The Islamic population worldwide now is estimated to exceed 1 billion— one of every five people on Earth.

In France, Islam ranks second only to Catholicism. England has received a massive influx of Muslims, so many in fact that the face of the landscape has literally changed. In 1945 there was one mosque in England; in 1989 there were over 1,000. London is the site of the largest mosque in Western Europe. Note the following from Islam-online.net:

> *The number of Muslims praying at British mosques will be double the number of church goers by 2040, according to a study by the British-based association Christian Research.*
>
> *The study, The Future of The Church, said that there will be nearly twice as many Muslims at prayer in mosques on Friday as Christians attending*

Sunday services, reported the Telegraph *on Sunday, September 4 [2005].*

British government and academic sources said in 2004 that some 930,000 Muslims go to the mosque at least once a week against 916,000 regular worshipers in the Church of England, the mother church of the Anglican communion.[1]

The story is the same in North America. The first mosque in the United States was built in Cedar Rapids, Iowa, in 1934. Today there are well over 1,000. Muslims lay claim to more than 5 million adherents to Islam in North America. If present trends continue, eventually Muslims will outnumber Jewish people in America (the Jewish population is approximately 7 million).

Dr. Ismail Faruqui challenged Muslims to pursue a goal of 50 million to 75 million new American converts to Islam. "Only from massive conversions," Faruqui said, "can we hope to elect Muslim politicians, appoint Muslim judges, and incorporate the *shar'iah* into the judicial system. We must transcend our minority status to make Islam a dominant force in America and the West." Students from Islamic countries now form the largest group of international students in North American universities and colleges.

For the most part, complacent Christians in North America have taken little or no interest in Islam's advances. Many, in fact, see the strange-looking buildings that are popping up everywhere with their curious little crescents as another denomination—just neighbors who take a strong stand for morality and against some of the things that we, too, are against. Such is not the case. Islam is not just another religion in town. Islam is not pluralistic. While Christians or Jews may lament the loss of one of their own to another religion, Muslims who convert to another religion can be killed for their transgression. British Muslim author Salman

Rushdie did not convert but merely questioned Islam and in 1989 was put under a perpetual death sentence from his brothers in the faith. Rushdie went into hiding for a while, and in 1998 the Iranian government said it would not carry out the sentence. However, Iran's Revolutionary Guards renewed the *fatwa* in 2003. When Islam perceives that it has sufficient strength to take control, it will attempt to seize it one way or another.

Years ago Louis Farrakhan of the Nation of Islam led a meeting in Washington, D.C., with a defiant, foot-stomping, fist-waving demonstration before 15,000 mesmerized followers. While he was not taken seriously in many quarters at the time, Farrakhan and his ilk should have been a warning of the potential danger of things to come. They should have caused people, particularly Christians, to awaken. *Time* magazine warned, "For them [Farrakhan's Muslims] mainstream American values are inherently oppressive and racist, to be rejected at root." That leadership used to be fringe. It is fringe no longer. Farrakhan types and militant Muslims are growing in numbers and influence.

Louis Farrakhan has embodied the white-hot zeal of the anti-Semite that today continues to enflame committed Islamists. "Zionism is racism; smash Zionism," runs the theme. "God is going to defeat the United States government!" Farrakhan ranted at a rally in Washington, D.C., in July 1990.[2] Quoting the late chieftain of the Nation of Islam, Elijah Muhammad (born Elijah Poole in 1897, the son of a Baptist preacher), Farrakhan shouted, "If they [black politicians] sell us out, they should be killed."[3]

Is this the raving of a fringe lunatic? No! It is the rationale of jihad.

The Ultimate Conquest

The Word of God has forewarned us of the human heart's capabilities and Satan's bellicose attempts to thwart the gospel and destroy the Jewish people. Militant Muslim intentions—military or missionary—should not surprise, discourage, or distract us.

The point must be made—and reconfirmed—that in the abiding conflict among the world's three major religions, there is only one transforming option. The Jewish people, in concert with biblical Judaism's declared directive, saw the Messiah enter the world. Sadly, the Jewish Temple leadership took a wrong turn on the identity of the Messiah, while Islam has missed completely the point of what God accomplished in Him. The ultimate conquest is not territory, nor is it the satisfaction derived from destroying or subjecting people deemed weaker or inferior. It is, rather, the liberation that comes through faith in the Messiah.

Muhammad sought an alternative to Judaism and Christianity. He succeeded only in leading millions deeper into spiritual darkness. The knowledge that fresh millions are being led along the same path should awaken Christians to the need for increased efforts to demonstrate God's love to Muslims as well as to all people in the world. As I looked at a huge picture of countless thousands of Muslim pilgrims falling on their faces to worship around the sacred Kaaba in Mecca, I was moved with a deep sense of sadness. They were kneeling in the wrong place, before an inanimate object that can bring neither light nor life nor peace. Better they should bow in homage at the feet of Jesus Christ—the King of kings and Lord of lords.

> *And being found in appearance as a man, He humbled Himself and became obedient to the point of death, even the death of the cross. Therefore God also has highly exalted Him and given Him the name which is above every name, that at the name of Jesus every knee should bow, of those in heaven, and of those on earth, and of those under the earth, and that*

*every tongue should confess that Jesus Christ is
Lord, to the glory of God the Father* (Phil. 2:8–11).

ENDNOTES

[1] "UK Mosque Goers to Double Church Attendance: Study," September 4, 2005 <islam-online.net/English/News/2005-09/04/article06.shtml>.

[2] Andrew Sullivan, "Call to Harm," *The New Republic* 203, no. 4 (1990): 13.

[3] Ibid., 14.

CHAPTER 16

❧❦❧

THE COVENANT WITH ISAAC

It is increasingly clear that the major roadblock to peace between Israel and the Palestinians is not Israel's alleged refusal to make concessions to Arab demands. In fact, the more land Israel concedes, the louder the Palestinians cry for more. Islamists view concessions as a sign of weakness and evidence that they will eventually destroy the Jewish state entirely. The Palestinians have not negotiated in good faith, and that reality can no longer be written off as an exhibition of Arab rage. Hamas, Hezbollah, Islamic Jihad and the rest have made their intentions clear: They want to destroy Israel.

Palestinian and the vast majority of Islamic leaders want the Jews out of Israel, which they claim is the sole property of the followers of Allah. Consequently, it is important to understand what the Bible has to say on the issue. This is not a frivolous matter better left to religious philosophers and theorists. It is substantive and must be brought into the discussion regarding Jewish land rights in the Middle East. Indeed, the rationale for creating tyrannical Islamic regimes, such as Iran and Sudan, is based on an interpretation of the Qur'an, which endorses jihad as an instrument for creating an Islamic world.

Islamic leaders say Israel has no legitimate claim to a region that historically is infinitely more Jewish than Muslim. But despite cold, hard facts that confirm Jewry's biblical, historical, moral, and legal rights to the land of Israel, the major authoritative source comes to us from the pages of the

Bible. It is there that covenants, grants, and promises for the future were recorded that are irrevocable. Several factors are basic to understanding God's relationship to the Jewish people and their association to the land of Israel.

Identifying Israel

Conflict between Muslims and Jews often arises over the identification of who the Chosen People are: the rightful heirs to the covenant promises delineated in Scripture:

> *Then God said: "No, Sarah your wife shall bear you a son, and you shall call his name Isaac; I will establish My covenant with him for an everlasting covenant, and with his descendants after him. And as for Ishmael, I have heard you. Behold, I have blessed him, and will make him fruitful, and will multiply him exceedingly. He shall beget twelve princes, and I will make him a great nation. But My covenant I will establish with Isaac, whom Sarah shall bear to you at this set time next year"* (Gen. 17:19–21).

Here God spoke to Abraham regarding the future of his sons Isaac and Ishmael. Most Arabs trace their lineage to Ishmael; the Jewish people, to Isaac. Notice that the covenant promise was bestowed on Isaac and his heirs, not on Ishmael. This is an important truth that is not in any sense discriminatory. Ishmael received sweeping promises, great lands, and the assurance of kingdoms. A look at a map of the Middle East today confirms that the landmass controlled by Arab and Muslim countries far exceeds that held by Israel.

The Promised Land

When God promised a land to Abraham, Isaac, Jacob, and their posterity, the grant was given unconditionally. Whether the Jewish people were in the land or suffering through the many expulsions from it, the territory of Israel, as well as what is now referred to as Gaza, the West Bank, and the Golan, was and is the land of the Jews:

> *On the same day the LORD made a covenant with Abram, saying: "To your descendants I have given this land, from the [little] river of Egypt to the great river, the River Euphrates"* (15:18).

An important element in establishing ancient Israel's possession of the land is Jerusalem. After David ruled from Hebron for seven and a half years, he moved the capital city of the Jewish state to Jerusalem. A key factor in the move was his purchase of the Temple Mount from Araunah the Jebusite. Incidentally, Israel and the Jewish people have never since offered that sacred site for sale. Although Muslims claim it belongs to them, it was legally deeded to Israel well before Islam came into existence; and it must be so regarded today.

Preservation of the Jewish Nation

It is one thing to lay claim to a land on behalf of an ancient nation; it is quite another for that nation to be on the scene thousands of years later to implement the transaction. In the case of the Jews, this is one of the most enigmatic of historical occurrences. How could a people, so minuscule in number, survive after being the subject of an unbroken succession of attempts to wipe them from the face of the earth? Expulsions, pogroms, inquisitions, and the infamous Holocaust inundated Jewish people in their own blood time and time again. Adolf Hitler was not alone in announcing "a final solution to the Jewish problem." In spite of this, Israel has survived. Scattered among the nations as they were, the fact that the Jewish people were not wiped out or assimilated—as were most of their ancient contemporaries—

FOR THE LOVE OF ZION

is in itself the singular mystery of history. How could they have survived?

Although the issues of Jewish survival are indeed complex, the source of their preservation can be explained simply. Anticipating all that would befall the Jewish people across the millennia, the Bible makes a prediction that only God Himself would be qualified to articulate:

> *Thus says the* LORD, *who gives the sun for a light by day, the ordinances of the moon and the stars for a light by night, who disturbs the sea, and its waves roar (the* LORD *of hosts is His name): "If those ordinances depart from before Me, says the* LORD, *then the seed of Israel also shall cease from being a nation before Me forever." Thus says the* LORD: *"If heaven above can be measured, and the foundations of the earth searched out beneath, I will also cast off all the seed of Israel for all that they have done," says the* LORD *(Jer. 31:35–37).*

We would do well to remember that this statement is an against-all-odds declaration. God alone is powerful enough to bring it to pass.

The Return to Eretz Yisrael

For 2,000 years, around every Passover table the world over, Jewish people have intoned the solemn words, *Next year in Jerusalem.* Few ever believed their words would come to pass. And I suppose, in a very real sense, we who have lived to witness the Jewish return to Jerusalem can say, in truth, "We have seen a miracle." Biblically, it was never in doubt:

> *The* LORD *your God will bring you back from captivity, and have compassion on you, and gather you again from all the nations where the* LORD *your*

200

> *God has scattered you. Then the* LORD *your God will*
> *bring you to the land which your fathers possessed,*
> *and you shall possess it. He will prosper you and*
> *multiply you more than your fathers* (Dt. 30:3, 5).

The undeniable fact we live with every day is that Israel is, after all of these centuries, home—just as the Bible said it would be.

A Future Day of Restoration

There is another fact that cannot be discounted. As emphatically as the Bible has outlined Israel's ancient past and present situations, it has sketched Israel's future. All that is developing around us is moving toward a consummation. For those of us who wrestle from day to day with such questions as how to deal with the likes of Iran, Syria, and other nations hostile to Israel, there is hope on the horizon. The same God who pronounced and then performed acts far beyond our capacity to create or circumvent has made another declaration:

> *They [Israel] shall be My people, and I will be their*
> *God; then I will give them one heart and one way,*
> *that they may fear Me forever, for the good of them*
> *and their children after them. Yes, I will rejoice over*
> *them to do them good, and I will assuredly plant*
> *them in this land, with all My heart and with all My*
> *whole soul* (Jer. 32:38–39, 41).

This is the passage referred to in the New Testament as the "all Israel" that "will be saved" (Rom. 11:26). Yes, a national day of reconciliation is prophesied for Israel, but that will also be an era when "the LORD shall be King over all the earth. In that day it shall be 'The LORD is one,' and His name one" (Zech. 14:9).

In all of this, there are some facts we must keep in mind.

First, these Scriptures represent only a sprinkling of texts on these subjects. The Bible is weighted down with statements regarding the future of Israel and the Jewish people.

Second, we must not neglect—for it would be to our peril—a word from Scripture that has been scrupulously borne out by many Western nations, especially the United States of America. This great passage is the Abrahamic Covenant.

> *I will make you [Abraham] a great nation; I will bless you and make your name great; and you shall be a blessing. I will bless those who bless you, and I will curse him who curses you; and in you all the families of the earth shall be blessed* (Gen. 12:2–3).

The Covenant Promise

Question 20 people on the street about why America has become a land of such power and plenty and you are likely to hear 20 different answers. There can, of course, be little doubt that the reasons for this country's rise are many and varied. However, two underlying factors cannot be ignored.

First, America has been the land of the Bible. Freedom to preach, teach, and distribute God's Word has been a central fact of life for successive generations. Our sons and daughters have been sent to carry the Word of Life to people scattered in the remotest regions of the world. Contributions from American Christians provide the means for sending Bibles and literature to established and emerging nations. Believers in the United States finance, equip, and staff organizations that proclaim God's Word and have made it possible to beam the message via radio to people who would never otherwise hear the truth. Our freedom to transmit God's Word has been a vital element in the flood of blessing upon this nation.

The second reason God has held open the door of divine favor and long-suffering is that the Jewish people have found in America a safe haven from persecution. Certainly there has been a measure of anti-Semitic injustice, even in the land of the free. And the recent upsurge in anti-Semitic activity is deeply troubling. Still, Jewish people have been unhindered here in their pursuit of prosperity and happiness.

By and large, America has adhered to the biblical principle laid down in Genesis 12:2–3, and God has lavished His favor on this country.

Most Americans, even many believers, fail to recognize the sweeping implications of the Abrahamic Covenant and its promises, which passed from Abraham to Isaac to Jacob and to all the Jewish people. Too often we reduce the words *I will bless those who bless you* to a balance-sheet evaluation that goes something like this: Be kind to Jewish people, and God will be kind to you. This is clearly a shortsighted and deficient view. We must understand who these people are and what, in the economy of God, their future holds. The Jewish people are:

- A covenant people—Genesis 17:1–21
- A beloved people—Jeremiah 31:3
- A divinely preserved people—vv. 35–37
- A blessed people—Deuteronomy 30:1–10; Romans 11:25–29. These verses show they have a radiant future.

In fact, the standard God will use when He calls the nations to the bar of divine judgment will be their treatment of the Jewish people (Joel 3:1–3; Mt. 25:31–46).

Thus the presence of the Jewish people in any Gentile country is a matter of critical concern for that nation's future. So far America has been good to the Jewish people. And it certainly is true that the Jewish people have been good for America and the world. Unfortunately, this fact has often been buried under the petty insinuations that have made Jewish people the butt of jokes and mindless accusations. In reality, we are all daily beneficiaries of the rich legacy that Jewry offers a nation.

In the field of medicine alone, Jewish people have made contributions that have touched us all. Here are a very few examples:

Albert Sabin, a Polish immigrant, and Jonas Salk, son of a New York manufacturer, eradicated polio as a national problem with their vaccines.

Bela Schick, who came to this country from Austria, delivered thousands of Americans from the scourge of diphtheria.

Ernest Boris Chaim developed the penicillin that was manufactured in the United States for worldwide distribution.

Fernand Widal's typhoid fever vaccination spared the Americans in Europe during World War I from the ravages of the dread disease. He was the same man who discovered the damaging effects of too much salt in the body and instituted the low-salt diet that has extended the life expectancy of many of you who are reading this book.

The list of Jewish people who have contributed to our health and welfare seems endless. As a matter of fact, 20 percent of the 768 Nobel Prizes awarded from 1901 through 2006 have gone to Jewish people: 49 in biomedicine, 27 in chemistry, 20 in economics, 44 in physics, and 12 in literature.[1]

The Greatest Gift

There is, however, a resident reality that outstrips every other contribution these gifted people have made to our world:

> "Behold, the virgin shall be with child, and bear a Son, and they shall call His name Immanuel," which is translated, "God with us" (Mt. 1:23).

Jesus of Nazareth, the Christ (Messiah), entered our world through the womb of a Jewish virgin, walked on Earth as a

Jew, and finished the work of sacrificial redemption on a Roman cross outside the walls of the Holy City, Jerusalem. To attempt to measure the blessings and benefits flowing from this fountainhead would strain the limits of eternity. He is the fathomless Gift that God presented to us through Abraham and his people.

> *For the wages of sin is death, but the gift of God is eternal life in Christ Jesus our Lord* (Rom. 6:23).

A companion fact is found in the gift given to the Gentiles in the person of Saul of Tarsus, the apostle Paul. He explained his call and the course of his ministry this way: "It pleased God, who separated me from my mother's womb and called me through his grace, to reveal his Son in me, that I might preach him among the Gentiles" (Gal. 1:15–16). Paul saw himself as a man with a debt to pay. "I am a debtor," he said, "both to Greeks and to barbarians, both to wise and to unwise" (Rom. 1:14).

Every church spire in the Western world attests to how well Paul discharged his obligation to evangelize the Gentiles. It is safe to say that there is not a believer on the face of this earth who has not been touched by Paul's life and ministry.

God saved a Jewish man, set him apart for the work of the ministry, and sent him to the pagan nations. In so doing, He transformed history. But the transformation did more than alter the stream of human history. Through the apostle Paul's work and God's Word, our Lord molded the composition of eternity. Heaven today is peopled by millions who have entered there from the Gentile nations along avenues paved with the saving gospel first laid down by a Jewish workman.

A Debt to Pay

If Paul, a Jew, labored under an overwhelming sense of debt to take the saving gospel to Gentiles, shouldn't we feel an equal obligation to take the message of life in Christ to Jewish people? The answer to that question is too obvious for words—a simple yes will do. Fuse unembellished logic with the clear command of Scripture, and you have an intensely personal mandate: "For I," proclaimed Paul, "am not ashamed of the gospel of Christ, for it is the power of God to salvation for everyone who believes, for the Jew first and also for the Greek [Gentile]" (1:16).

Our Lord graciously raised up the people of Abraham to bring blessing and life to pagan Gentiles. The result is the church. Unfortunately, a majority of the people of privilege, with the exception of a believing remnant, missed the essence of the message they were sent to deliver and are included in the mandate given believers to take the gospel to "all men" everywhere.

In a day when many Christians have become too sophisticated to proclaim the simple gospel, we must press the point: We are debtors—debtors who, sharing a sense of obligation born from the privilege of being believers, proclaim Christ to the people who have given us so much, as well as to every Gentile on the face of the earth. To do so is to pay the debt we owe to those from whom we have received so much.

These Bones Shall Live

Every nation on Earth, including the United States, is inexorably linked to Israel and God's plan for the land and its people, the Jews.

When pondering the impact Israel has made on nations that touched it for good or evil, you can begin to fathom how important the entire issue of Israel's place in God's program really is. Those who harbor ill-intended schemes against that nation would be well advised to explore the Scriptures on the subject and carefully study comparative history. After all, the well-worn admonition "To be forewarned is to be forearmed" is certainly applicable when it comes to Israel and the Jewish people. Significant amounts of international misery could have been avoided if the nations of bygone days had somehow understood that God was serious when He inspired Zechariah to say, "He who touches you [Israel] touches the apple of His eye" (Zech. 2:8).

Today's leaders, however, are inclined to do no better than their forefathers; and without spiritual discernment, they seem to keep making the same mistakes. Iraq is a textbook illustration. With the ruins of ancient Babylon within eyeshot, Saddam Hussein insisted on trumpeting his intention to wipe Israel off the map. But his Scud missiles proved of no avail, and in the end, the bedraggled "new Nebuchadnezzar" was dragged from a hole in the ground and taken off the scene.

However, it is generally true that even many who believe the Scriptures and study them do not realize the full extent of God's love for and dedication to His land, Israel. Multitudes who identify themselves as Christians fail to fully appreciate His love for the Jewish people.

The central themes of the Abrahamic Covenant rest in God's promise of the land as a *permanent* possession of Abraham and the physical descendants of Abraham, Isaac, and Jacob.

To Abraham:

For all the land which you see I give to you and your descendants forever. And I will make your descendants as the dust of the earth; so that if a man could number the dust of the earth, then your descendants also could be numbered (Gen. 13:15–16).

To Isaac:

But My covenant I will establish with Isaac, whom Sarah shall bear to you at this set time next year. In Isaac your seed shall be called (17:21; 21:12).
And I will make your descendants multiply as

the stars of heaven; I will give to your descendants all these lands; and in your seed all the nations of the earth shall be blessed; because Abraham obeyed My voice (26:4–5).

To Jacob:

And behold, the LORD stood above it [the ladder] and said: "I am the LORD God of Abraham your father and the God of Isaac; the land on which you lie I will give to you and your descendants. Also your descendants shall be as the dust of the earth; you shall spread abroad to the west and the east, to the north and the south; and in you and in your seed all the families of the earth shall be blessed" (28:13–14).

To all of Israel:

He remembers His covenant forever, the word which He commanded, for a thousand generations, the covenant which He made with Abraham, and His oath to Isaac, and confirmed it to Jacob for a statute, to Israel as an everlasting covenant, saying, "To you I will give the land of Canaan as the allotment of your inheritance" (Ps. 105:8–11).

God's Unqualified Love for the Land

A brief survey of Ezekiel 36 and 37 provides a dramatic perspective on the path the chosen nation is following. Several enormous propositions sweep through these illuminating chapters.

The marvelous prophecy in Ezekiel 36:35 will shade and shape the thinking of those who wish to know the ultimate plan for the land of Israel. The Lord stated it when He said, "This land that was desolate has become like the garden of Eden." His words, which are specifically identified in verse 4 as "the word of the Lord GOD," roll across the land like the waters of righteousness that will cover the earth during the Messiah's reign. Therefore, it is easy to understand the inherent attachment to the land of Israel that has been evident in the character of the Jewish people from time immemorial. Anticipation of this future glory has been written for centuries on the hearts of dispersed Jewry. In Ezekiel 36:1–15, God concentrates on three aspects of His divine program for Israel.

1. *Those who trespass with a desire to possess the land of the Jews will be crushed:*

> *Thus says the Lord GOD: "Surely I have spoken in My burning jealousy against the rest of the nations and against all Edom, who gave My land to themselves as a possession, with wholehearted joy and spiteful minds." Therefore thus says the Lord GOD: "I have raised My hand in an oath that surely the nations that are around you shall bear their own shame"* (vv. 5, 7).

Herein lies God's perpetual warning to nations, ancient and modern. Much like the fence that separated the court of Israel from the court of the Gentiles in the Herodian Temple, telling Gentiles to go no farther, God's Word forewarns trespassers on the land He has chosen for the Jewish people, "Proceed at your own peril."

2. *The land will bear fruit for His people:*

> *But you, O mountains of Israel, you shall shoot forth your branches and yield your fruit to My people Israel. . . . For indeed I am for you, and I will turn to you, and you shall be tilled and sown* (vv. 8–9).

One of the glories of modern Israel is the way the land has flourished when nurtured by the hands of the Jewish people. People in many parts of the world are reaping the benefits of Israeli agricultural innovations. If this is true today, how much greater will be the wonders of the land fully possessed and presided over by the Messiah?

3. *The Jewish people will possess the land that is their inheritance:*

> *Yes, I will cause men to walk on you, My people Israel; they shall take possession of you, and you shall be their inheritance; no more shall you bereave them of children* (v. 12).

God promises that the day will come when Israel's lamentation over its lost land will cease. Ezekiel chronicled the final fulfillment of ecstasy emanating from the hearts of returning exiles:

> *When the LORD brought back the captivity of Zion, we were like those who dream. Then our mouth was filled with laughter, and our tongue with singing. Then they said among the nations, "The LORD has done great things for them." The LORD has done great things for us, and we are glad* (Ps. 126:1–3).

Far better things are promised for reconciled Israel: "I will multiply men upon you, all the house of Israel, all of it; and the cities shall be inhabited and the ruins rebuilt. . . . I will . . . do better for you than at your beginnings" (Ezek. 36:10–11).

Ezekiel 36:16–24 treats us to a grand exposition of the theme of the glory of God. The passage draws the bottom line as to why Israel is so blessed and the land He has set aside is so favored. Israel exists as a witness to the faithfulness, might, and majesty of Jehovah. Isaiah 43:10 eloquently explains:

> *"You are My witnesses," says the LORD, "and My servant whom I have chosen, that you may know and believe Me, and understand that I am He. Before Me there was no God formed, nor shall there be after Me."*

With that truth in mind, Ezekiel 36:22 pointedly explains why God will restore the land and the people: "I do not do this for your sake, O house of Israel, but for My holy name's sake." God was witnessing to His own glory through the witness nation He had chosen.

At the root of Israel's cyclical dispersions from its land is the fact that the nation profaned God's holy name and that Israel's sin caused the surrounding nations to mock God and make light of those who were His designated people:

> *So I scattered them among the nations, and they were dispersed throughout the countries; I judged them according to their ways and their deeds. When they came to the nations, wherever they went, they profaned My holy name—when they said of them, "These are the people of the LORD, and yet they have gone out of His land." But I had concern for My holy name, which the house of Israel had profaned among the nations wherever they went* (vv. 19–21).

At issue are the sanctity and honor of God's name. But just as Israel's corrective phase would result in humiliation and derision, her restoration will establish—in even more magnificent ways—the glory of the God who brought it about. His name will, in the end, be sanctified: "'And the nations shall know that I am the LORD,' says the Lord GOD, 'when I am hallowed in you before their eyes'" (v. 23).

Israel was conceived, formed, and fashioned for His glory. And in the end, the Jewish people will indeed glorify Him.

Israel's Reconciliation and Restoration

The story of the Jewish people historically demonstrates precisely how God's integrity will be vindicated and His glory displayed. Ezekiel 36:25–38 structures the process.

1. National Repentance. "I will deliver you from all your uncleannesses" (v. 29). Fundamental to the process is repentance: "Then you will remember your evil ways and your deeds that were not good; and you will loathe yourselves in your own sight, for your iniquities and your abominations" (v. 31). The result, as in all true repentance, is a turning to God from idolatry and sin.

2. Revival. A revival that goes far beyond anything known in the history of Israel or Jewry will take place, related to the yet-future phase of reconciliation to the Lord. The reality of the revival relationship will be a new heart, a new spirit, and a new condition: "I will give you a new heart. . . . I will put my Spirit within you. . . . You shall be My people, and I will be your God" (vv. 26–28).

3. Restoration. "For I will take you from among the nations, gather you out of all countries, and bring you into your own land" (v. 24). Once the Jewish people are securely in the land, they will no longer suffer or bear the reproach of the nations. Cleansed, secure, and satisfied, Israel will dwell in the land promised to Abraham for his descendants—a land that "has become like the garden of Eden" (v. 35).

4. Recognition. Israel's repentance, revival, and restoration will be surpassing evidence among the nations of the world of the faithfulness, power, and glory of the God who cannot be corrupted or dissuaded from His purposes by any human contingency. He has made promises; He will keep them. Consequently, the surviving nations will be compelled to acclaim His glory: "Then the nations which are left all around you shall know that I, the LORD, have rebuilt the ruined places and planted what was desolate. I, the LORD, have spoken it, and I will do it" (v. 36).

In a marvelous way, chapter 37 colors the picture given in Ezekiel 36 and exposes the process by which all of this will take place. The vivid vision has inspired toe-tapping refrains that have reminded successive generations that one day, the dry bones that constituted scattered Israel will come together, rise up, and walk (37:1–10). That promise is sure. As a matter of fact, as the sons and daughters of Abraham return to Israel from nations around the world, we are seeing harbingers of the climactic regathering described here.

A forlorn question rises from the wondering prophet who stood overlooking the valley covered with the bones of the dead. Ezekiel's query has been asked by every generation that has been touched by the wandering Jewish people during their protracted dispersion: "Can these bones live?" (v. 3). The rational answer would of course be "No!" But the point of the vision is that the God of the improbable can do the impossible. There will be "a rattling" (v. 7) in the valley. Bone upon bone, flesh upon sinew, skin over all; and with breath from the four winds, these bones will rise up and form "an exceedingly great army" (v. 10).

The Lord's explanation of the vision clarifies who these bones represent: they are "the whole house of Israel" (v. 11) and the process by which Israel's "lost hope" will be restored. Verses 12–14 embody three phases of Israel's end-times trek to its destiny under the Messiah.

Phase I: Return to the Land. "Therefore prophesy and say to them, 'Thus says the Lord GOD: "Behold, O My people, I will open your graves, and cause you to come up from your graves, and bring you into the land of Israel"'" (v. 12). The implication, clearly compatible with the vision, is that this return to the land will be in unbelief; it will be a body without breath.

Phase II: Recognition That Their Return Is God's Doing. "Then you shall know that I am the LORD, when I have opened your graves, O My people, and brought you up from your graves" (v. 13).

Phase III: Reconciliation to the Messiah. "'I will put my Spirit in you, and you shall live, and I will place you in your own land. Then you shall know that I, the LORD, have spoken it and performed it,' says the LORD" (v. 14).

To this stunning visual prophecy the Lord adds a verbal object lesson in speaking of two sticks coming together in His hand (vv. 15–28). They represent the reunited nation. When the nation became divided under Solomon's son Rehoboam, the split became irreparable. The northern 10 tribes, called Ephraim, were captured by Assyria in 722 B.C. The southern kingdom of Judah went into captivity in Babylon in 586 B.C. Thus the Babylonian Captivity signaled the end of the Davidic monarchy. However, God left the Jewish people a promise: "Ephraim, and . . . all the house of Israel, his companions [the northern tribes]" (v. 16), will be joined, at long last, to Judah and Benjamin, the southern tribes (v. 17). They shall be united under the regency of "David My servant [who] shall be king over them" (v. 24). Then,

> *They shall dwell in the land that I have given to Jacob. [God] will make a covenant of peace with them... [God] will set [His] sanctuary in their midst forevermore* (vv. 25–26).

At home, at peace, and in the presence of the Lord—who could ask for any more? It could not be better said than in God's own Words: "The nations also will know that I, the LORD, sanctify Israel, when My sanctuary is in their midst forevermore" (v. 28).

ENDNOTE

[1] Israel Science and Technology <scienco.co.il/Nobel.asp?s=lit&sort= y&cit=y>.

CHAPTER 17

$\backsim\!\!\infty\!\!\curlyvee$

ENTEBBE: A LIGHT FOR THE NATION

Although Israel has a bright future after the Messiah returns, it struggles mightily in the here and now. As I write this, Israel is trying to recover from its recent fight with Hezbollah, which fired missile after missile into the city of Haifa, wounding, killing, and crippling Jewish people in an effort to eradicate the Jewish presence in the Middle East. Yet at every turn, the UN condemns Israel and looks the other way as terrorists send suicide bombers into the Jewish state. In August 2005 Israel withdrew from Gaza hoping to promote peace. But peace was not to be. Instead, the Arabs are turning Gaza into a launching platform for terrorism because, as they have told the world time and again, they are not interested in peace. They are only interested in destroying Israel.

In February 2006, WorldNetDaily.com ran an interview with Abu Abir, a spokesman for the Popular Resistance Committees, an amalgamation of Palestinian terror groups. Here, in part, is what he said:

> We are planning to be present all around the West Bank. Every Israeli target is a legitimate target. Wherever there is an Israeli soldier or settler they will find our rockets. Jerusalem, Ben Gurion International Airport, Tel Aviv and every Israeli point can be part of our goals. Whenever it is needed, rockets will be fired against every Israeli settlement, city or neighborhood. . . . We have

succeeded with the help of Allah to start our plan to transfer rocket technology to the West Bank. . . . The lives of Israeli citizens will turn to hell very soon.[1]

The Jewish state, in a sense, is fighting for all of us. It is valiantly struggling to hold its own in a war on terror—a paltry 5.5 million Jews surrounded by 360 million hostile Muslims. Caroline Glick, deputy managing editor of *The Jerusalem Post*, put it succinctly when she wrote, "The British and, to a lesser though increasing degree, the Americans refuse to acknowledge that the war against the Jews and Israel is the same as the war against them." How right she is. Islam plans first to destroy the "little Satan," meaning Israel, then the "big Satan," meaning America.

The brutal fight is taking its toll on the tiny country. Its spirits are sinking. Israel was demoralized once before, in the aftermath of the 1973 Yom Kippur War. But it revived through the miraculous rescue at Entebbe.

From Euphoria to Depression

Doubt and frustration clouded the skies over Israel as 1973 drew to a close. Symbolic of the general situation and national despair was the political demise of Golda Meir who for years had been viewed, both inside and outside Israel, as a pillar of strength and good sense. Purse-clutching Golda, with her grandmotherly visage, had become an adored folk figure to admirers the world over.

Born in 1898 in Kiev, the daughter of a poor carpenter, Golda grew up in Milwaukee, Wisconsin, where as a young girl she became deeply concerned over the terrible plight of the Jewish Palestinians under the Ottoman Turks. After the announcement of the Balfour Declaration and the British conquest of Palestine under General Edmund Allenby, Golda and her husband decided it was time to move. So in May

1921, despite full-scale Arab riots in Palestine, where Jews were being murdered and mutilated and where Arab gangs had raped Jewish women in the Old City of Jerusalem, young Golda set sail on the *S.S. Pocahontas* to become a pioneer in the land of her ancestors.

In 1969 she became prime minister of Israel. She took office in the aftermath of Israel's most glorious moment, the 1967 Six-Day War, which had been a stunning victory for the tiny nation that many people now thought invincible. Arab states were said to "lay at her feet broken and stupefied." This lightening-shaft war had all but broken the confidence of Israel's Arab enemies. Time and time again the Arabs had whipped their people into a frenzy of military and religious enthusiasm before sweeping down on the nation, intent on destroying it. Each time, however, the Arabs' Russian-equipped armies were torn to shreds and sent home humiliated. In the case of the Six-Day War, Israeli intelligence had correctly interpreted its enemies' military buildup and decided to smite before being smitten.

Six years later, however, the 1973 war changed everything. Egypt and Syria stunned Israel with massive surprise attacks on October 6—Yom Kippur, the holiest day in Judaism. On the Egyptian front alone, 600,000 Egyptians attacked 500 Israelis. It was the equivalent of the entire population of Baltimore, Maryland, attacking the congregation of a 500-seat church. The ratio was 1,200:1. Intense fighting produced heavy casualties. Nine Arab nations plus the Soviet Union were supplying Egypt and Syria.

As long as Israel was losing, the UN kept silent. Then the tide turned. By October 12 Israel was within 18 miles of Damascus, Syria, and in the south Israeli paratroopers were almost in Cairo. U.S. President Richard M. Nixon and Congress appropriated $2.2 billion to help Israel and ordered an emergency airlift. On October 21 the UN called for a cease-fire. Predictably, Israel was forced to relent just when it was in position to destroy the Egyptian army.

Israel won the war but plummeted from euphoria to national depression. The cost was 6,000 Israeli casualties, the stinging realization that the vaunted IDF had been taken by surprise, plus $7 billion in expenditures to rescue the nation from annihilation. An economic boom had degenerated into galloping inflation, and large-scale immigration slowed to a trickle. Further aggravating the situation was the fact that many insecure citizens were leaving the country. Although the nation's woes were by no means the sole fault of Prime Minister Golda Meir, she nevertheless was forced to shoulder the responsibility. By April 1974 Golda had fallen from grace and chose to leave office. Moshe Dayan, the one-eyed general who rose to international prominence during the glory days of the Six-Day War, also bore responsibility for the near disaster of 1973. In fact, so many blamed him for the heavy casualties that people would spit on him in bitterness as he walked by.

Things on the diplomatic front wore the same dismal face. Everyone seemed to gang up on Israel. To make matters worse, Yasser Arafat and his Palestine Liberation Organization were stringing together some prestigious victories. In October 1974, the Rabat Conference of Arab Nations granted the PLO recognition as the sole legitimate representative of the Arab Palestinians. Arafat declared as his objective the establishment of a "democratic, secular Palestinian State." Within the next three years he and his cohorts won recognition in one form or another from more than 100 nations.

But the indefatigable terrorist won his most spectacular victory when he was invited to speak to the UN General Assembly in November 1974. As he mounted the rostrum to address delegates to the world's most recognized body, one supposedly working to promote world peace, Arafat was decked out in what became his familiar military garb and was swathed in a kaffiyeh. Inexplicably, the man whose business for decades had been killing and fomenting war was allowed to wear his sidearm to the podium. Ludicrous though it seems, his appearance at the UN did much to legitimatize him and recast his image as one of the world's premier merchants of peace.

His carefully orchestrated performance in New York had an extremely depressing effect on Israel's delegates and the nation in general. After centuries of persecution, the Jewish people had become good at reading the warning signs. And when a murdering terrorist suddenly becomes hailed as a peacemaker, the handwriting is clearly on the wall.

In 1975 the UN General Assembly took yet another step into the Muslim camp. It passed an infamous resolution branding Zionism as "a form of racialism and racial discrimination." In short, the UN said it was okay for Muslims to have as many countries as they want, but it was not okay for the Jewish people to have even one. Furthermore, the UN passed this resolution knowing full well that Muslim countries persecute non-Muslims and expel Jews, whereas Israel is a democratic nation with freedom of religion and Arab members of parliament.

Yet the UN said that Zionism—the belief in the right of Jewish people to have a national homeland in the Middle East—was racism. Without a doubt, racism was a valid issue at the UN that day. But the racists were not the Jews.

Insult was added to injury when, in the summer of 1975, the UN came within a whisker of expelling Israel altogether. To its credit, the United States blocked the effort by warning of dire consequences should the UN uphold its resolution.

Terror on the Loose

Most Israelis say they regard UN resolutions as rather abstract non-events. Daily life in Israel is more closely focused on the immediate problems of survival than pieces of paper floated at the UN. And for good reason.

Several months earlier, on April 11, 1974, three terrorists, all members of the Popular Front for the Liberation of Palestine (PFLP), crossed the border from Lebanon and entered the northern Israeli town of Kiryat Shmona. The hit squad hid out near a school until morning and then launched a random attack on apartment buildings on the edge of town. First the terrorists entered two ground-level flats where they murdered five people. After running to the next building, they systematically broke into apartments and shot residents at close range. After reaching the fourth floor they found an empty flat and began shooting at people on the street from open windows. Finally, Israeli troops stormed the building and exploded a bomb in the room, killing the PFLP members. The IDF action, however, came too late to prevent the slaughter of 16 men, women, and children who had arisen that morning thinking they faced a routine day. Two Israeli soldiers were also killed.

Little more than a month later, another squad of murderers slipped into northern Israel from Lebanon. They began by attacking a van filled with women who were returning home after finishing their night's work at a textile plant near Haifa. Two of the women were killed; six others were wounded.

Then the terrorists proceeded to bang on doors of apartments in the town of Ma'alot, demanding in Hebrew to be allowed in. They claimed to be searching for the terrorists. Believing them, a resident named Zion Cohen opened the door and was slain by a hail of gunfire that immediately killed him and his four-year-old son; his five-year-old daughter was seriously wounded. Mrs. Cohen, seven months pregnant, ran from the apartment screaming for help. Her cries were in vain, as one of the gunmen caught up to her on the stairs and killed her.

While the Cohens were being murdered, 110 children on an overnight outing were sleeping in Ma'alot's Netiv Meir School. At 4 A.M. on May 15 the PFLP terrorists entered the school and took the children hostage, along with their adult chaperones.

The entire nation was awakened by a shock wave of horror as news spread that the children were being held for ransom. Defense Minister Moshe Dayan and other military leaders rushed to the scene. They were soon bombarded by demands from the killers and a list containing the names of 20 top terrorists being held in Israeli prisons, whom the terrorists demanded be released. Unless they were released by 6 P.M., the PFLP would blow the school and the hostages to bits. For Israel, compliance was not an option. Yielding to demands of terrorists was not a road Israel was willing to travel.

To prevent the mass slaughter of the children, Israeli military leaders made an agonizing decision. They would storm the building. Moving with all possible speed, they succeeded in killing the three terrorists before the PFLP men could trigger their explosives. Unfortunately, in the shootout that preceded, 22 Israeli children were killed and 70 wounded. The terrorists had lost their lives but in the process had lifted the spirits of Islamic fanatics and traumatized the people of Israel.

By 1975 Arab terrorists had changed their pattern of operation. Rather than attacking mainly from southern Lebanon, they began entering Israel from multiple locations and attacking random sites. On March 6 a terrorist team landed on the beach in Tel Aviv and attacked a hotel in the city. Their day's work netted 11 dead Israelis. Fourteen more were killed in a July 4 Zion Square bombing in the heart of Jerusalem.

Then, in what seemed like a terroristic masterstroke, on Sunday, June 27, 1976, Air France flight 139 from Tel Aviv to Paris, with a stop in Athens, Greece, was hijacked. For a nation not yet fully recovered from the physical and emotional losses of the 1973 Yom Kippur War, the hijacking seemed like the worst scene of a recurring nightmare. Of the

256 passengers aboard, 103 were a combination of Jewish and Israeli.

A Formidable Dilemma

Lax security at the Athens airport allowed four terrorists to board the plane with a small arsenal of weapons. Two of the hijackers, a man and a woman, were German members of the notorious Baader-Meinhof urban guerilla organization. Their companions were Arabs, members of the PFLP. After taking control of the aircraft and ordering a fuel stop at Benghazi, Libya, the pilots were ordered to chart a course for Entebbe, Uganda, deep in Africa. Once on the ground at Entebbe, additional Arab Palestinians and units of the Ugandan army joined the terrorists. They herded the passengers into the old terminal building at the airport to await the outcome of their grim situation.

On the evening of June 29, Uganda radio made known the hijackers' demands: Fifty-three convicted terrorists held in Israel, Germany, Kenya, Switzerland, and France were to be released or the hostages would die. The terrorists separated the Jews and Israelis from the other passengers, and during the course of the week released the others and had them flown to France. The Jews and Israelis remained at Entebbe. Again the burden of life and death hung over Israeli leaders, and the nation fell once more under a pall of gloom and despair.

The situation the Israeli leaders faced was, to say the least, formidable. How could an elite force reach hostages who were being held 2,500 miles away? Was a rescue attempt even an option? The risk appeared too great. Such was the conviction of Prime Minister Yitzhak Rabin who at first refused to consider the rescue plans put in motion by Lt. Gen. Mordechai (Motta) Gur, Israel's chief of staff. Gur's plan called for flying a crack paratroop force over Lake Victoria, parachuting into the Entebbe Airport, and killing the terrorists while capturing the terminal. The hostages would then be defended until arrangements could be made with Ugandan leader Idi Amin for their return to Israel. It was a mission fraught with danger, and Rabin was understandably hesitant to approve it.

Minister of Defense Shimon Peres took an entirely different view: Israel could not give in to terrorists. To do so would open a Pandora's box of hostage-taking and terrorist atrocities that would invite catastrophic moral and political defeat for Israel. Whatever the risks, Peres argued, something must be done. For his part, Mordechai Gur assured the defense minister that he would not recommend the operation until he was personally assured that the risk was reasonable and the proposal feasible. Yitzhak Rabin informed the cabinet that unless he received a proposal backed by the General Staff, he would advise the cabinet to accept the ultimatum of the terrorists and their conditions in order to secure the hostages' release.

Maj. Gen. Dan Shomron was gripped by a memory. When he heard that the Jewish captives had been separated from the rest of the hostages, he remembered the selection process the Nazis had used in the concentration camps. Shomron, who was chief infantry and paratroop officer in the Israel Defense Forces, immediately began to put together a plan to free the hostages. By any standard it would be a high-risk undertaking. Speed and surprise were absolutely essential if there was to be any chance of success. The slightest glitch or hesitation could cost the hostages their lives. Ten to 13 terrorists were moving freely among the hostages. Surrounding them were hundreds of Ugandan soldiers who, at the orders of President Idi Amin, were cooperating with the terrorists.

The objective of the operation was singular: bring out the hostages alive. There was no margin for error, no backup plan, no room for the slightest mistake. The mission would become either a spectacular success or a catastrophic failure. But Dan Shomron was willing to take the risk.

His plan was to use an airborne assault with Hercules aircraft, which could reach Entebbe from Israel. The strike force would have vehicles adapted to look like those routinely used by Ugandan military personnel. Rescue teams would move immediately to the terminal and make their assault only on the building where the hostages were being held.

When Shomron presented his plan to the General Staff, reactions were mixed. Most gave the mission only a fifty-fifty chance of success. Shimon Peres consented only on the condition that the cabinet approve the plan. Shomron saw only one possible problem: landing the lead plane. If the first Hercules could land without being detected, he was 100 percent sure of success.

Permission was granted to construct a model of the terminal, which was well known to some Israeli officers. They had trained forces in Uganda in earlier years. Two hundred highly trained personnel were chosen to stage a mock attack on the model, should they get the go-ahead for the real thing. Planners learned from home movies taken by men who had been in Uganda training Ugandan pilots that Idi Amin traveled in a black Mercedes accompanied by a Land Rover. The Israelis decided to bring matching vehicles to mislead anyone who discovered their presence. Further details were compiled by questioning the passengers who had been released and taken to France. By the time they were ready, Shomron's men had a detailed picture of the situation on the ground at Entebbe.

When he was given the details, General Gur decided the operation could accomplish its purpose, and he called a meeting of all commanders involved in the mission. Each was asked to assess the chances for success. To a man, they said it could be done. Gur was then prepared to go to Prime Minister Yitzhak Rabin and his cabinet with his recommendations. Gur told Rabin, "I present to you a plan for execution this evening, and the entire operation is now in motion according to a prearranged plan."

Rabin listened intently and then methodically gave his approval, subject to cabinet agreement. At this point negotiations for the release of the hostages were still going on. Under this ruse Israel would consent to the terrorists' demands and exchange the prisoners for the hostages at Entebbe. It was now only a matter of working out the details of the exchange. Actually, the Israelis had something quite different in mind.

The plan required four Hercules aircraft. The first would carry a unit of paratroopers with emergency lighting equipment in case Entebbe's runway lights were off. An assault unit would disembark and take control of both the old and new terminals. Lt. Col. Jonathan (Yoni) Netanyahu and his unit would ride in two Land Rovers and a Mercedes and head directly to the old terminal to free the hostages. The second plane would land seven minutes later with additional forces, two armored cars, and Dan Shomron's jeep from headquarters. The third plane would follow the second in and immediately put two more armored vehicles on the ground that would be used by Netanyahu's men. Also on the third plane was a unit of the Golani Brigade. These men would take control of the area linking Entebbe's two runways and act as a reserve unit to react to unforeseen trouble. Their most important task would be to get the hostages onto the Hercules that was to follow them in. This fourth aircraft carried reserve forces along with a Peugeot tender to evacuate any wounded during the rescue operation. The fourth plane would also carry a medical team and refueling personnel.

When the aircraft took off for Entebbe, the cabinet was still in session debating whether the mission should go forward. The understanding was that if the mission was scrubbed, the planes could turn back and return to base. It was only after the rescue force was on its way that the cabinet unanimously approved the operation.

The Lights of Entebbe

The planes were in the air seven hours before they came in range of the Entebbe control tower. For any chance of success, their approach and landing had to be choreographed perfectly. The first Hercules would tuck in behind a scheduled British cargo plane, landing without lights directly behind the British plane. Fortunately, the British jet arrived on schedule and the Israeli pilot eased his huge aircraft in position behind it. As the planes swung over Lake Victoria, a furious rainstorm erupted, making a visual approach impossible. But as the pilots switched to instruments, the storm suddenly subsided. As they looked down, directly before them were the lights of Entebbe streaming down the runway. The British cargo plane landed without incident. Neither the pilots nor anyone in the control tower was aware of the hitchhiking Israeli Hercules hitting the runway at the same time.

The lumbering aircraft was still rolling when the doors opened and the men with the mobile landing lights leaped to the ground and began placing lights along the edges of the runway. With the planes parked in a dark corner of the airfield, the rest of the landing force disembarked, along with the Mercedes and Land Rovers. Their first impression was that, except for the sound of the British cargo plane taxiing to the terminal, a ghostly silence surrounded them. Maj. Gen. Shomron was elated. The Israelis had arrived unnoticed by Ugandans stationed at the field. "Boys," he said to his men, "this operation is a success despite the fact that not one bullet has yet been fired."

In the next few minutes, anyone looking out the windows of the old terminal building would have seen the beaming headlights of the black Mercedes and Land Rovers moving toward the terminal, perhaps carrying Uganda's flamboyant, megalomaniacal dictator, Idi Amin. The small caravan was within 100 yards of the terminal when two Ugandan guards signaled for them to stop. Netanyahu and the second officer fired their silencer-equipped pistols at the soldiers. Because of this unexpected encounter, the Israelis ran for the building. When they broke into the hall where the hostages were being held, they found them asleep on the floor. One terrorist opened fire and was killed immediately. The others, easily recognizable because they carried weapons, were quickly dispatched. The surprise was complete. From the time the two Ugandan sentries were shot until the four terrorists inside the building had been killed, only 15 seconds had elapsed. Unfortunately, even though the soldiers had shouted in Hebrew and English for the hostages to stay down, one man leaped to his feet and was shot. Four Jewish hostages perished in Uganda.

As Netanyahu approached the entrance to the terminal, he paused in the garden before the entrance. Without warning, Ugandan troops fired on him from the roof. Yoni Netanyahu, 30, the oldest soldier in the operation, was shot. He died a short time later.

With the three remaining Hercules planes safely on the ground, troops continued to mop up what opposition remained. In the course of the skirmish they captured the new terminal and locked the Ugandan troops that surrendered in a room with a warning not to leave. As hostilities subsided, the wide-eyed hostages were hustled aboard a plane for the triumphant flight back to Israel. Originally the plan had been to refuel at Entebbe. But with the mission such a success, they decided not to risk it with more time on the ground. Nairobi, Kenya, could be reached on the remaining fuel. They would land in Nairobi to be refueled for the rest of the flight. Total elapsed time from the beginning of the operation to the takeoff for Nairobi was only

57 minutes. The Israelis' final act was to destroy eight Ugandan MiG fighters parked along the runway. This would insure that no one would pursue the departing aircraft.

July 4—A Day to Remember

News of the rescue electrified the nation early that morning. The sight of the giant Hercules aircraft gliding toward the runway at Ben-Gurion Airport ignited the masses gathered to welcome the hostages and their military heroes home. A crowd delirious with joy mobbed the dignitaries who arrived at the airport, including Yitzak Rabin; Foreign Minister Yigal Allon; Israel's chief rabbi; and Menachem Begin, who later would become prime minister. Little Israel had accomplished the impossible. It had rescued its people from the hands of terrorists. And as Americans celebrated their bicentennial with rousing Fourth of July festivities, Israel had its own Fourth of July bash. It was an event equal to the unbridled joy that followed the stunning victories of the Six-Day War.

Dirty and disheveled, the former hostages emerged from the planes along with their rescuers. Relatives and well-wishers milled about them. Their rescue had turned the tide in Israel, and they returned as symbols of what a determined people could do in the worst of circumstances to withstand terrorism. A July 5 *Jerusalem Post* article summed it all up succinctly:

> *The effect of the successful raid on national morale was electric. Many compared it with the mood of gladness that followed the Six-Day War and hailed it as a turning point. Prime Minister Rabin himself, in a television interview last night, said it had restored national confidence, and demonstrated the "latent power of the nation."*

Aftermath

Although congratulatory messages flowed into Israel from many parts of the world, expressing relief that someone had had the courage and ingenuity to deter a major terrorist threat, others were not pleased—among them, the United Nations.

Secretary-General Kurt Waldheim described the rescue as a violation of Ugandan sovereignty and claimed that the situation created by it was likely to have serious international repercussions, especially as far as Africa was concerned. Few, however, seemed to be listening. Certainly not American President Gerald Ford. Ford sent a message of congratulations that was said to be unprecedented. No American president had ever congratulated Israel on a military action.

In the subsequent debate at the UN, which had welcomed gun-toting terrorist Yasser Arafat, an unsuccessful attempt was made in the Security Council to condemn Israel. Chaim Herzog, Israel's ambassador to the UN, spoke for the nation and most of the world when he said the following:

> *It has fallen to the lot of my small country, embattled as we are, facing the problems which we do, to demonstrate to the world that there is an alternative to surrender to terrorism and blackmail. It has fallen to our lot to prove to the world that this scourge of international terror can be dealt with. It is now for the nations of the world, regardless of political differences which may divide them, to unite against this common enemy which recognizes no authority, knows no borders, respects no sovereignty, ignores all basic human decencies, and places no limits on human bestiality.*
>
> *We come with a simple message to the Council: we are proud of what we have done, because we have demonstrated to the world that in a small country, in*

Israel's circumstances, with which the members of this Council are by now all too familiar, the dignity of man, human life and human freedom constitute the highest values. We are proud not only because we have saved the lives of over 100 innocent people—men, women and children—but because of the significance of our act for the cause of human freedom.

We call on this body to declare war on international terror, to outlaw it and eradicate it wherever it may be. We call on this body, and above all we call on the Member States and countries of the world, to unite in a common effort to place these criminals outside the pale of human society, and with them to place any country which co-operates in any way in their nefarious activities.[2]

It was as though history had repeated itself. Little "David" had faced, and brought down, another "Goliath." Not in this instance with a single stone, but with a few brave sons of Abraham who possessed the courage and determination to fly off into the night and fight for the survival of their people.

Since the days of Golda Meir and later Entebbe, the UN has passed at least 65 resolutions condemning not the terrorists but little Israel—the world's most obvious victim. It wrote a resolution equating Zionism with racism; yet it has not passed even a single resolution condemning anti-Semitism or a country such as Saudi Arabia where Islam is the official and only religion and where Jews are not allowed.

In April 2006, during a brief lull in hostilities before the official war with Hezbollah broke out in July, Sami Salim Mohammed Hammed, 21 years old, from the West Bank, detonated himself outside a fast-foot restaurant in Tel Aviv during the Passover holiday. He killed eight people and wounded 49. And who was blamed? Israel, of course. Hamas called the attack a legitimate response to Israeli "aggression."

What a neat little trick: Hamas does the killing, but Israel is the aggressor!

Is it any wonder the nation may be depressed? In 1976 the brilliant rescue at Entebbe boosted national morale. I can't help but wonder if there is anything today, in the dirty here and now, that is capable of doing likewise.

ENDNOTES

[1] Aaron Klein, "Terror Hell to Rain on Israel/Terror Leader Also Demands Israel Be Relocated to U.S." February 23, 2006 <worldnet daily. com/news/article.asp?ARTICLE_ID=48960>.

[2] "Israel's UN address after the raid at Entebbe: 1976," quoted from Chaim Herzog, *The Arab-Israeli Wars,* rev. ed. (New York: Random House, 1984) <www.warchronicle.com/israel/entebbe/herzog.htm>.

CHAPTER 18

༺◈༻

WHEN FORGETTING IS UNFORGIVABLE

One of the reasons people so willingly swallow lies is because they so easily forget the truth. Or worse, they choose to turn their backs on it. Today Muslims and other anti-Semites are liberally rewriting the history of Israel, the Temple Mount, and even the history of the Holocaust.

On March 31, 2001, the California-based Institute of Historical Review (IHR), a big mover and shaker in Holocaust denial, was supposed to sponsor a four-day conference in Beirut, Lebanon. When the Lebanese government pulled the plug on it, the Jordanian Writers' Federation decided to take up the mantle. After the Jordanian government cancelled it twice, the conference finally took place the same year, with 200 people attending. Wrote Abraham Foxman, national director of the Anti-Defamation League:

> *The persistent drumbeat of Holocaust denial is moving to the Middle East, where the deniers are reaching out to Islamic regimes to find sympathy for their anti-Semitic and racist views. . . . The Holocaust deniers have spread their message in the United States. They have met with like-minded anti-Semites in Europe. Now they are fomenting anti-Semitism in Muslim states where there is a sinister track record for the use of Holocaust denial against Israel. For the Holocaust deniers, the already*

charged Mideast environment is fertile ground for their views.[1]

In December 2005, Iranian President Mahmoud Ahmadinejad made headlines around the world when he called the Holocaust a "myth" and denied that the Nazis murdered 6 million Jewish people during World War II. "They [the Jews] have created a myth today that they call the massacre of Jews and they consider it a principle above God, religions and the prophets," he said.[2]

That anyone could believe Adolf Hitler never exterminated 6 million Jews is completely astounding. The Nazis themselves meticulously documented their atrocities. Yet it is easy to understand why Muslims would want to deny the Holocaust. They want to make themselves the injured party and thereby eliminate all sympathy for the Jewish people, who not only were persecuted and killed by Hitler but who endured persecution and suffering long before Islam was a gleam in anyone's eye. Rewriting history plays heavily and conveniently into Islam's tactics.

What is more surprising and extremely disturbing is that nearly half of the adults in Great Britain—a country that endured merciless Nazi bombings—claim they have never heard of Auschwitz, one of the most infamous of Hitler's death camps.

This was the shocking result of a BBC audience research survey related to a new TV series produced in 2005 to mark the 60th anniversary of the liberation of the Auschwitz death camp.

"We were amazed by the results of our audience research," said series producer Laurence Rees. "It's easy to presume that the horrors of Auschwitz are engrained in the nation's collective memory, but obviously this is not the case."

The survey found that almost half of Britain's adults (45 percent) claim they never even heard of Auschwitz. Among people under 35, the figure soared to 60 percent. And among those who had heard of the concentration camp, 70 percent said they did not know much about it.

A revealing corollary surfaced in another survey by the History Channel, which asked 1,000 Britons to name the most significant events in world history. Twenty-two percent named the day Princess Diana died. Only 8 percent opted for the end of World War II, and 12 percent cited England's World Cup soccer victory in 1966.

Of all the killing stations Adolf Hitler established to facilitate his "final solution to the Jewish problem," Auschwitz, in Poland, was the most notorious. It is estimated that 1 million to 3 million people, about 90 percent of them Jewish, were exterminated there.

Among the most poignant cries still echoing from this dungeon of death are the letters of the children. Before little Liliane Gerenstein was killed, she wrote to God:

> God? How good you are, how kind and if one had to count the number of goodnesses and kindnesses You have done, one would never finish. . . . God? It is thanks to You that I had a beautiful life before, that I was spoiled, that I had lovely things that others do not have. God? After that, I ask you one thing only: Make my parents come back, my poor parents protect them (even more than you protect me) so that I can see them again as soon as possible.

On April 6, 1944, the Nazis seized Liliane Gerenstein and others; threw the crying, terrified children onto trucks bound for Auschwitz; and there killed them all.

"The name Auschwitz is quite rightly a byword for horror," Laurence Rees stated. "But the problem with thinking about horror is that we naturally turn away from it. Our series is not only about the shocking, almost unimaginable pain of those who died, or survived, Auschwitz. It's about how the Nazis came to do what they did."

On January 27, 1945, Russian troops liberated Auschwitz, but not before the Nazis attempted to kill or deport any who might be left to tell the dreadful story of their suffering.

How can people barely a generation away from the events of World War II choose to know so little? Yes, *choose*, because their ignorance is a choice.

It is the choice of the educational system on both sides of the Atlantic. The West buries the grim realities of historical atrocities beneath a gloss of contemporary superficiality. Our obsession to pursue pleasure and venerate pop culture icons, such as Princess Diana, rock stars, Hollywood luminaries, and sports idols, has clouded our thinking—especially when it relates to lessons from the past that should not be forgotten. Unfortunately, many do not want to remember and thus are condemned to experience reruns of the horrific.

Both the Old and New Testaments solemnly warn about the consequences of failing to communicate history's lessons to the next generation. These biblical injunctions are not the mutilations of revisionist docudrama. They are fact.

The era of Hitler, the Holocaust, and the extermination of millions of innocent Jewish people and others is an extremely obvious example of why we must teach the truth. That 45 percent of a nation's population can say it never heard of Auschwitz is a dreadful commentary on how far we have fallen.

Fortunately, there are those who do remember and burn with a desire to enshrine in the minds and hearts of people living today the memory of those who failed to survive. Tears still well up in the eyes of those who languished in the squalor of the camps and watched as friends, loved ones, and neighbors wasted away or were fed to the ovens. The desire for truth is heard in the voices of veterans, now dying at the rate of thousands a day, who urge us to keep alive the memory of what they saw in 1945.

Live And Let Die

A visit to Yad Vashem in Jerusalem, Jewry's memorial to the Holocaust, is a haunting experience. *Experience* is the correct word, because Yad Vashem is something more felt than seen. Words are not enough to convey its full impact. You must go there and see it for yourself.

Many these days are expressing a weariness at being reminded of the murder of 6 million Jews in Hitler's Europe. Perhaps they are reacting to a crime so monstrous their minds refuse to assimilate it. It is a phenomenon not unlike that demonstrated in Europe during World War II when people said they didn't notice what was going on—they simply chose to live and let die. Deniers claim the Holocaust didn't happen and that Yad Vashem is nothing but a monument to Jewish perfidy that perpetuates a lie.

The shame is not that the Jews choose not to forget. Remembering their dead is a virtue, not a vice. No, the shame is that the rest of the world refuses to remember them and the 8 million others who perished at the hands of the Nazis.

Christians owe a great debt of gratitude to these Jewish people with long memories. As history bears out, when Jewish people are crushed by tyrants, true Christians almost inevitably suffer alongside them. This fact is often overlooked in "Christian" America. But the fact is there, nonetheless; and the tragedy can happen again.

The Yad Vashem memorial to the children is particularly compelling. Upon entering, one views a display of pictures suspended from the ceiling—faces of children who were thrown into the ovens simply because they happened to be Jewish.

Beyond the entrance is a large room shrouded in nearly total darkness. Only five small candles burn in the center, their light reflecting in thousands of pieces of glass arranged floor to ceiling throughout the room. The effect is at first disorienting. As the meaning penetrates, it stuns your mind. What appear to be millions of tiny lights reflected from every conceivable angle flicker in the darkness. The heavy silence is broken only by the solemn intonation of children's names being read over a loudspeaker. Names, ages, and places where they lived and died are read—one and a half million helpless boys and girls.

Standing there in the darkness, you are compelled to think of those close to you—children and grandchildren—and how it would be for you and them if it all happened again. And it can. Think back to September 11, 2001, when a group of Muslims snuffed out the lives of thousands of innocent men, women, and children on one horrific morning. How long will self-indulgent Americans choose to be reminded of what happened in New York; Washington, D.C.; and Pennsylvania? Will we, as those of another generation, eventually choose to look the other way?

As it was half a century ago, so it is today. Most among us, I'm afraid, choose not to notice or care about what is going on in parts of the world where we cannot see the carnage being spread, opting instead to live and let die. It's an option we can't indulge in for long with immunity without becoming the next ones doing the dying.

So appreciate the fact that the Jewish people remind us of the Holocaust, and let it serve as a constant reminder to us all. To forget is unforgivable. Sixty, or perhaps only six, years from now, how many Americans will say they never heard of September 11, 2001?

An Old, Old Story

Despite the specter of the Holocaust and anti-Semitism that has ranged across the face of the centuries in an unrelenting effort to destroy the nation of Israel and the Jewish people, it is good to remember that God loves them. Despite the worst that devils and men can do, Jewry has survived. And it will continue to survive. Nowhere is this pattern more clearly seen than in the biblical book of Esther, where the Persian king's right-hand man, Haman, tried to annihilate world Jewry with a single stroke. Although God's name is not mentioned in this account, His dedication to the survival of Jacob's sons and daughters is deeply etched on every page.

The Hatred

And the letters were sent by couriers into all the king's provinces, to destroy, to kill, and to annihilate all Jews, both young and old, little children and women, in one day (Est. 3:13).

The Chosen Person

And Mordecai told them to answer Esther: "Do not think in your heart that you will escape in the king's palace any more than all the other Jews. For if you remain completely silent at this time, relief and deliverance will arise for the Jews from another place. . . . Yet who knows whether you have come to the kingdom for such a time as this? (4:13–14).

The Bold Commitment

And so I [Esther] will go to the king [to intercede for my people], which is against the law; and if I perish, I perish! (v. 16).

The Sword of Truth in the Hand of a Woman

So King Ahasuerus answered and said to Queen Esther, "Who is he, and where is he, who would dare presume in his heart to do such a thing [kill the Jewish people]?" (7:5).

The Justice That Triumphed

So they hanged Haman on the gallows that he had prepared for Mordecai (v. 10).

The Holiday for the Jewish People

Therefore the Jews of the villages who dwelt in the

*unwalled towns celebrated the fourteenth day of the
month Adar with gladness and feasting, as a holiday,
and for sending presents to one another* (9:19).

The Celebration of Deliverance

*These days should be remembered and kept through-
out every generation, every family, every province,
and every city, that these days of Purim should not
fail to be observed among the Jews, and that the
memory of them should not perish among their
descendants* (9:28).

Today, appropriately, Jewish people the world over
observe Holocaust Remembrance Day. As the story of Esther
vividly displays, a day is coming when the nation will come
together under the banner of the Messiah to celebrate
Deliverance Day and begin to live out the glorious destiny
God has promised His Chosen People: "The Redeemer will
come to Zion, and to those who turn from transgression in
Jacob, says the LORD" (Isa. 59:20).

*For he who touches you [Israel] touches the apple of
His [God's] eye* (Zech. 2:8).

Never Forget

Standing on the summit of Masada in Israel, where the
Romans crushed the last remnant of the Jewish rebellion in
A.D. 73, one is gripped by multiple impressions. There is the
seemingly futile determination of the few Jewish survivors
who chose death over capitulation. Yet, by contrast, the still
visible Roman siege encampments, wall, and access ramp to
Masada's summit shout of an empire's commitment to
exterminate a people it loathed.

A sense of solemnity exists here, unlike that at any other
site in all of the Holy Land. The setting is appropriate. The
sun-scorched barrenness of the Judean wilderness falls away

toward a lifeless sea shrouded perpetually by haze and heat. Masada is actually more a cryptic memorial than a site for tourists. It is almost as though the words associated with the place ride the desert winds: *Masada, Never Again.* We used to hear that phrase often when people spoke of Israel's struggle for survival. Now, however, less so.

It is much the same when one walks the paths at Yad Vashem. Levity and laughter quickly turn to silence and tears. Once you visit, you are marked with the indelible memory of it. Then there is the unimpeachable evidence on display. The shrunken bodies; hollow, fear-infested eyes; crematories; and manic sneers of the tormentors imprint images as vivid as the blue numbers the Nazis tattooed on the victims of their atrocities.

Masada, Yad Vashem, and scores of other places in the world solemnly speak their message to us: Never forget. A corollary admonition is, "It can happen again." And if we ignore the admonition to remember, it will most certainly happen again.

Twenty Centuries Haven't Made a Difference

From Masada to Yad Vashem and beyond is a long road. For Jewish people, it has been a road littered with the wreckage of lives, families, villages, and sacred institutions. Hebrews 11: 36–38 tells the grim story:

> *Still others had trial of mockings and scourgings, yes, and of chains and imprisonment. They were stoned, they were sawn in two, were tempted, were slain with the sword. They wandered about in sheepskins and goatskins, being destitute, afflicted, tormented—of whom the world was not worthy. They wandered in deserts and mountains, in dens and caves of the earth.*

When we made the turn into the new millennium, many held high hopes for a more tolerant, just, and equitable global community than the one that gave us Masada and the Holocaust. But nothing has changed. Nothing, that is, except the technological ability to disseminate hatred and bigotry more quickly, widely, and efficiently than ever before. The art of killing is being perfected in ways that outstrip by light-years the World War II gas chambers and firing squads. Now we can snuff out lives by the millions in the blink of an eye. And with violent anti-Semitism rising swiftly in the Middle East, Europe, and North America, there is justifiable foreboding over what the next decades will bring.

For Bible-believing Christians, the story is much the same. The New Testament tells us of the severe suffering first-century believers endured. The emissaries of pagan religions and oppressive tyrannical governments were intent on squeezing the life out of the early church:

> *At that time a great persecution arose against the church which was at Jerusalem; and they were all scattered throughout the regions of Judea and Samaria. As for Saul [who later became the apostle Paul], he made havoc of the church, entering every house, and dragging off men and women, committing them to prison* (Acts 8:1, 3).

Later the oil-soaked bodies of crucified Christians, whom Rome considered a threat, would be set on fire to light the streets of the pagan empire.

During the aptly named Dark Ages, godly men and women were tied to stakes and publicly burned by religionists who knew nothing of true and compassionate Christianity. Times have changed. But mankind has not.

On January 23, 1999, missionary Graham Staines and his two young sons, Timothy and Philip, bedded down for a quiet night of sleep in their Jeep outside a village in India where Graham was planning to minister to lepers the next day. Sometime after midnight an enraged crowd of Hindus stormed the Jeep, trapped the father and boys inside, and set it on fire. All three were incinerated.

Whether hung on a cross outside a capital city of the ancient world, tied to a stake in an unenlightened time of ignorance and religious aggression, or trapped in a Jeep outside a village in India, the flesh burns just as intensely. And the hearts of those who drive the nails and light the torches are equally degenerate and evil.

The Mandate to Remember

Being, of course, fully aware of mankind's propensity to forget what should be remembered, particularly the unpleasant, the Lord commanded that memorials be observed annually. For Israel, Passover is an enduring example:

> *So this day shall be to you a memorial; and you shall keep it as a feast to the LORD throughout your generations. You shall keep it as a feast by an everlasting ordinance* (Ex. 12:14).

The Israelites were told to remember Egypt, to remember the bitterness of servitude and slavery, to remember the deaths of the firstborn. And above all, they were told to remember their deliverance through the blood of the Passover lamb. Like Joseph, who never forgot God's promises and ordered the children of Israel not to leave Egypt without bringing his bones with them to the Promised Land, the Jewish people, too, were to remember and intone annually—over countless millions of Passover tables across the centuries—"Next year in Jerusalem." But in a very real way, they were also saying, "Egypt, Never Again!"

Few modern commemorations in the world equal Remembrance Day in Israel. Remembrance Day reveres the memory of the nearly 20,000 soldiers and security personnel who have lost their lives since the 1948 War of Independence. Stan Goodenough, a South African Christian living in Israel, aptly described the sensation when, throughout the country, the sirens begin to wail, and life comes to an abrupt standstill:

> *Loud. Long. Keen. The rising sirens immobilize the nation, paralyzing movement up and down the land. Vehicles stop, their drivers alighting to stand, heads bowed, in the streets. On the sidewalks, in shops, offices, schools, and cinemas, on beaches and playing fields, people stop dead in their tracks.*
>
> *Life arrested. The world turned to stone. Sirens howl their pain to the skies. And in the howling are a myriad sounds, hard to listen to, impossible to ignore.*[3]

On July Fourth, America comes to attention to observe our own Remembrance Day of sorts. No sirens blare, and we do not stand beside our cars with our heads bowed in memory of the fallen. Instead, fireworks crackle; and triumphal, musical celebrations commemorate the founding of this Republic. But after tumultuous years of fighting a war on terror, it seems another note should be sounded in the ears of the nation in remembrance of our young men and women who crossed oceans to liberate the people of Afghanistan and Iraq and, in the course of doing their duty, gave the last full measure of their devotion. It would be fitting, for all of our celebrating, to hear the sirens wail for them.

I recently drove past Arlington National Cemetery in Washington, D.C. I stopped the car for a moment to gaze across the fields at the neat rows of crosses marking the graves of our fallen heroes. On the drive home, I thought of the white crosses dotting the fields of France and Belgium and remembered the terrible price paid to gain and keep our freedom. And without a doubt, that price will be exacted again and again as history unfolds.

What's the lesson? It's a simple one that we've already

heard: *Remember!* On September 11, 2001, sirens screamed down the avenues of New York City, Washington, and rural Pennsylvania. We must never forget their sounds. Never.

A Word to Christians

Several years ago I visited seven major cities in the United States and Canada doing television appearances. I was interviewed on more than 20 Christian radio stations and networks on the subject of Christian persecution. The discussion focused on two facts: (1) 95 percent of all Christians worldwide suffer some form of persecution and (2) more Christians are reportedly being martyred for their faith today than at any time in the history of the church.

This being the case, why do most evangelicals seem enshrouded in silence and indifference? The first explanation offered by interviewers and call-in contributors was that those suffering are outside our field of vision. Then there was the opinion that American Christians are so comfortable with the status quo that they recoil at entertaining unpleasant subjects—such as missionaries being summarily executed, decapitated, or burned to death in their cars.

A few even offered this rationale: "After all, the Bible says that if we are believers, we are going to suffer persecution. Jesus said, 'If they persecute me, they will also persecute you.' If this is the case, it must be God's will. So why should we be surprised or try to change things? And besides, what can we do to make a difference anyway?"

Well, for starters, we are commanded to remember those who suffer persecution:

> *Remember the prisoners as if chained with them—*
> *those who are mistreated—you yourselves are in the*
> *body also* (Heb.13:3).

Second, we will be held accountable for our conduct toward suffering saints, at home and abroad:

Deliver those who are drawn toward death, and hold back those stumbling to the slaughter. If you say, "Surely, we did not know this," does not He who weighs the hearts consider it? He who keeps your soul, does He not know it? And will He not render to each man according to his deeds? (Prov. 24:11–12).

So where do we start? We start by daring to remember. Ignoring the suffering of our brothers and sisters in Christ blatantly violates God's clear command. And forgetting Auschwitz and what His Chosen People have suffered allows the world to rewrite history and deny the truth of God's holy Word. At the Last Supper, when our Savior instituted the ordinance of Christian communion, He said, "Do this in remembrance of Me" (Lk. 22:19). His suffering, death, and resurrection were all to be remembered. "Never forget," He said, "what I have done for you."

What did He do? He suffered that we might have life. May we be compassionate and obedient enough to remember and reach out to those who share in His suffering, Jew and Gentile alike. And may we also remember that there never again will be a need to suffer in order to redeem us. His suffering alleviated ours and ensured for us an eternally better day, one free of blood and tears.

ENDNOTES

[1] "Holocaust Deniers to Convene in Lebanon" <adl.org/presrele/holocaustdenial_83/3756_83.asp>.

[2] "Holocaust Comments Spark Outrage" December 14, 2005 <news.bbc.co.uk1/hi/world/middle_east/4529198.stm>.

[3] Stan Goodenough, "The Siren Wail," April 29, 2003 <jerusalem news wire.com/editorial/03/04/030429_siren_wail.asp>.

CHAPTER 19

c⟨⟨⟨⟨⟨⟨⟩⟩⟩⟩⟩⟩

ROME AND BABYLON REVISITED

The time of the judges was a period of almost unbroken national depression for Israel. All indicators for the nation's survival pointed downward. The mood swing from Israel's exhilarating entrance into the Promised Land under Joshua to the dismal failures of his successors was one of the most dramatic in the nation's roller coaster ride through history. There were few Calebs who could say, "I wholly followed the LORD my God" (Josh. 14:8). Few were there, indeed, who could raise Caleb's valiant request, "Give me this mountain" (v. 12). The nation had lost its way, and it seemed that survival for Israel was an open question.

The events, in sequence, that contributed to Israel's calamity were disobedience, compromise, and idolatry. They initiated a slide into darkness that opened the door to immorality and virtual anarchy. Judges 10:6 gives us a fair summation of Israel's national and spiritual situation:

> *Then the children of Israel again did evil in the sight of the LORD, and served the Baals and the Ashtoreths, the gods of Syria, the gods of Sidon, the gods of Moab, the gods of the people of Ammon, and the gods of the Philistines; and they forsook the LORD and did not serve Him.*

Israel disobeyed God by failing to carry out His clear command to expel His enemies and theirs from the land: "But the children of Benjamin did not drive out the Jebusites who inhabited Jerusalem" (1:21). The same failing would be ascribed to the tribes of Manasseh, Ephraim, Zebulun, Asher, and Naphtali.

Clearly, as is always true with those who fail to obey, compromising with the ungodly seemed okay: "And it came to pass, when Israel was strong, that they put the Canaanites under tribute, but did not completely drive them out" (v. 28). The results were predictable. Israel's conduct evoked severe rebuke from God. When they "did evil in the sight of the LORD" (e.g., 2:11), He turned the Israelites over to their enemies for correction and rebuke until they were prompted to "cry out to the Lord" for deliverance (e.g., 3:9).

And so it was written, much like an epitaph, "In those days there was no king in Israel; everyone did what was right in his own eyes" (21:25). In other words, men were consigned to finding their own way in a spiritually hostile environment. In the eyes of some, this represented liberation; in actuality, it amounted to their receiving what they deserved rather than what they desperately needed from the God of all grace and mercy.

As has so often seemed true with God's Chosen People, the situation looked hopeless. But it was far from it. In reality, Israel's future would not be dictated by its prevailing circumstances. In the midst of all the national, moral, and spiritual carnage, there rested resources that would carry the nation through its dilemma. When the present had faded into picturesque stories of bygone days, the true substance of the issues would endure to benefit the whole of humanity; for in the midst of all the ruin, there was a remedy; a remnant; and, above all else, a Redeemer.

Although this pattern for preserving the nation surfaces in the book of Judges periodically through the likes of Gideon and Israel's parade of deliverers, it is most clearly portrayed in the book of Ruth, for here we discover an island of spiritual serenity in a sea of national chaos. The setting is Bethlehem, city of David, birthplace of the coming Messiah. The terraced fields on the approaches to the place where Ruth gleaned speak of serenity. Even today, with all of the tension found in Bethlehem, the gentle green patches of earth harboring small vineyards and olive trees within the stone enclosures in the fields once belonging to Boaz give the feeling that all is well. And, as the story unfolds, this well-being is confirmed for us: All is well, because in that place—with a simplicity only God Himself could fashion—grace, love, redemption, peace, and security take the stage to play out before us the fact that at every juncture in history, no matter how confused things seem to be, God has His plan. God has His remnant of faithful people, and through those people, He continues to extend His grace and mercy via redemption.

In many respects, events taking place in America and much of the Western world parallel the condition of ancient Israel during the period of the judges. Moral and spiritual standards have deteriorated at an alarming rate over the past decades. It now appears our nation is being pushed off its traditional course onto a path that will no longer follow the Judeo-Christian way of life.

Admittedly, this nation is not, as was ancient Israel, a theocracy (a country over which God Himself reigns). Israel's experience was unique and has not been duplicated by any other nation on Earth. However, no other nation in history has more solidly built its national structure on Judeo-Christian standards than has the United States of America. For generations, we were able to lay claim to the blessing of a "nation whose God is the LORD" (Ps. 33:12).

Being reared in America used to mean experiencing life where the lines for conduct, ethics, and morals were clearly drawn. You did not have to be a Christian to understand right and wrong, acceptable and unacceptable. Our laws were based on Judeo-Christian values and were enforced accordingly; and, in order to lead a "quiet and peaceable life" (1 Tim. 2:2), one lived within the limits of the law.

America's break with the past came with the change in attitudes about moral absolutes and the determination to make man, rather than God, the center of the universe. Ultimately, God was virtually banned from our public institutions. Particularly devastating has been the banishment of God from our classrooms. Social revolutionaries recognize that controlling the classroom means controlling the future of the nation. Sadly, many Americans now stand shoulder to shoulder with godless systems in the determination to create a society unencumbered by the recognition of Jehovah.

Consequently, what has developed in recent years is a jihad-type war to destroy the Christian faith, with an emphasis on slaying evangelical Christianity in particular and replacing the traditional Judeo-Christian social order with an anything-goes, pagan, secular society. In a March 2006 article titled "The Media's War on the 'War on Christians' Conference," columnist Don Feder wrote:

> *Evangelicals have been described as "a clear and present danger to religious liberty in America" (former Labor Secretary Robert Reich), determined to "Christianize all aspects of American life" (the ADL's Abraham Foxman), "moral retards" and "an ugly, violent lot" (City University of New York Professor Timothy Shortell), possessed of "the same kind of fundamentalist impulse that we see in Saudi Arabia" (Al Gore), and responsible for moving America "each day closer to a theocracy where a narrow and hateful brand of Christian fundamentalism will rule" (a full-page ad in* The New York Times, *signed by Jane Fonda, Ed Asner and other Hollywood savants).*[1]

The strategic word in this litany of vituperation is *theocracy*. Ancient Israel was the only theocracy that ever existed on Earth, and no theocracy will ever exist again until Jesus Christ Himself returns to this planet and sits on His throne in Jerusalem to rule over His theocratic Kingdom. That is the biblical fact. And the idea that evangelicals have a unified, conspiratorial plan to elect an ultrafundamentalist, apartheid-type government to rule over every aspect of American life is utterly ridiculous. It is a lie; but it is a lie that is picking up steam.

The fact that these "intellectuals" publicly make this absurd accusation would be embarrassing were it not for their motives. Certainly, evangelical Christians take their convictions and values into the voting booth. We "render . . . to Caesar the things that are Caesar's" (Mt. 22:21). It is what citizens in democratic societies are expected to do. And it would compound the absurdity to assert that liberals, feminists, gays, abortionists, neoconservatives, Republicans, Democrats, and Independents do not do likewise. Free people have both the right and obligation to vote their consciences.

But determined, minority-driven forces brook no opposition from the vast majority, whom they see as an obstacle on the road to their particular vision of a ruleless, secular nirvana. Many of them (the entertainment industry in particular) assault America with debasing influences and flaunt and wave the First Amendment in our faces to justify their "right" to debauch the nation in the interest of financial gain.

An even more unsettling manifestation of this crusade involves the forces that are casting evangelicals as subversive, conspiratorial members of lobbies that jeopardize the security of America. Two prominent American international relations and political science professors released an inflammatory work in 2006 titled, "The Israel Lobby," accusing Israel of so strongly manipulating U.S. policies that

America has become a virtual puppet of Israeli interests, to its own detriment. Stephen Walt, academic dean at Harvard's Kennedy School of Government, and John Mearsheimer, from the University of Chicago, assert, "The combination of unwavering support for Israel and the related effort to spread 'democracy' throughout the region has inflamed Arab and Islamic opinion and jeopardized not only US security but that of much of the rest of the world."[2]

And who are the members of this "Israel Lobby" that pulls the strings and endangers the world on the chopping block of Arab and Islamic hatred? They are a "loose coalition of individuals and organizations who actively work to steer US foreign policy in a pro-Israel direction."[3] In her *Jerusalem Post* column on the subject, Caroline Glick told us whom Walt and Mearsheimer consider members of this so-called Lobby:

> *Most US media outlets; Jewish American organizations generally and AIPAC [American Israel Public Affairs Committee] and the Conference of Presidents of Major Jewish American organizations in particular; [and]* **pro-Israel evangelical Christians** *[emphasis ours].*[4]

TV commentator Bill O'Reilly was right when he said there is an anti-Christian bias in this country. "Other battle zones," wrote Don Feder, "include Ten Commandments monuments, God in the pledge of allegiance, stigmatizing the Boy Scouts, advances in the culture of death, and attempts to impose homosexual marriage by judicial fiat."[5]

To be sure, these symptoms may seem superficial on the surface. But at the core, they reveal the battle taking place for the survival of the Judeo-Christian values upon which this country was founded.

Rome Revisited

The late Francis Schaeffer articulated the situation years ago. "We are now," he warned, "living in a post-Christian era." He was correct; and his statement, startling as it was, made great table conversation. Practically, however, few Western evangelicals paid much attention. Immersed in our affluent, secular lifestyles, most Christians ignored Schaeffer's fears, which embodied the type of remoteness reserved for philosophers.

But now we've had the much-touted "wake-up call." Rome has returned, and contemporary Christians are confronted with the same challenges our first-century forefathers encountered. We are exactly where the Scriptures declared we would be in the last days. You can confirm this fact by reading Romans 1. And rather than waste time being depressed about what's going on around us, we should redeem the time and be encouraged about what has opened up.

We do not live in a religious-political utopia. America will not be molded into a theocratic nation. Yet, as in the bleak days of the judges, there is a godly remnant that stands like an island of serenity in a spiritual and moral sea of chaos and confusion. As Ruth sparkled against the darkness of her day, so believers stand at this hour as "a light that shines in a dark place" (2 Pet. 1:19). And we have the only true remedy to offer a sick and dying world: the gospel. Paul took it to pagan Rome, and it penetrated the darkness and transformed people who had given up all hope. For people out of options and sinking quickly into the swill hole of paganism, the gospel will triumph again.

Our mandate at this moment is to proclaim and live out a clear contradiction to all of the spiritual and moral corruption that is plaguing the nation. Thank God, there is a Redeemer. Let us pursue, with every fiber of our beings, Paul's pattern for pagan Rome:

So, as much as is in me, I am ready to preach the gospel to you who are in Rome also. For I am not ashamed of the gospel of Christ, for it is the power of God to salvation for everyone who believes, for the Jew first and also for the Greek (Rom. 1:15–16).

Babylon: Mother of Harlots

So as the world careens toward a new order, we "right-wing Christians" will continue to live for Christ and preach the gospel. Meanwhile, we will continue to be vilified by rhetoric that compares us to the jihad-minded of the Muslim world. We also will continue to be accused of everything from pursuing a cultural war of oppression to breeding intolerance, hatred, and division, to undermining national security because we support Israel. And, rest assured, this campaign to discredit us is only beginning. The dreadful spiral of degeneracy delineated in Romans 1 has finally elbowed its way into the mainstream of America's national life. People will say we are bad for the country and bad (in the end, it all boils down to money) for the economy.

As important as economic conditions are, history trumpets realities that are inescapable. In the 1930s, for example, the German people made political choices based on what was viewed as economic expedience. In so doing, they made one of the most catastrophic mistakes in the history of humanity. Adolf Hitler and his legacy of 50 million dead left a ghastly scar on the human record.

Nevertheless, the world is nearing the juncture when economic expedience will instigate a calamitous decision that will make the choice of Hitler pale by comparison. The world is preparing to opt for the Antichrist.

First Corinthians 10:32 reaffirms the segmenting of humanity into three distinct divisions: "Give no offense, either to the Jews or to the Greeks [Gentiles] or to the church of God." Contemporary history is cascading toward a conclusion that involves all three of these participants. End-times Babylon, the Mother of Harlots, is beginning to stir.

Babylon as Satan's Ideal

Genesis 11:1–9 reveals the birth of Babylon and exposes the driving forces behind an ideal crafted by Satan—an ideal designed to be the antithesis of God's plan for humanity. The Genesis account of the fiasco created by mankind's attempt to erect its unifying tower in the place that would become Babylon introduced the Gentile worldview that would plague the earth. The key to understanding the process is found in Ephesians 2:2: "You once walked according to the course of this world, according to the prince of the power of the air, the spirit who now works in the sons of disobedience." The verse refers to Satan, who is also called "the god of this age" (2 Cor. 4:4). He is the instigator of every strategy developed to thwart God's purposes through the Jewish nation and the church. His instrument is the Gentile world system idealized in Genesis 11.

Strategy #1: Redirecting Worship

Satan's plan to deny God His rightful place in human affairs does not involve the elimination of worship. It merely focuses spiritual adoration on other objects and false gods—in short, idolatry. The Scriptures clearly tell us that, though the Devil is a rebel, he is not an unbeliever. This is an extremely important point. Satan is not an atheist. Nor does he desire his followers to be. His entire struggle against God for the hearts and minds of the Lord's creatures is not an effort to eliminate acknowledging deity but to direct worship toward himself.

The Communists' colossal miscalculation was in thinking they could strike the compulsion to worship from the minds of the people under their control. Within a generation, they boasted, no one would believe in the existence of God. The material state would be lord and master wherever atheistic Communism reigned supreme. What they managed to accomplish by suppressing religious belief and expression, however, was to fuel the inherent desire to worship something other than money or machines. In fact, the Russian rush toward gaining knowledge about the Bible and God since the fall of the Soviet Union demonstrates the folly of atheism. People deprived of spiritual light will not gravitate automatically to a permanent state of unbelief. God fashioned people to worship, and they will bow the knee. The only question is, To whom or to what?

The sea of Gentile paganism surrounding Israel across the centuries illustrates redirected worship. The great temptation the Jewish people consistently faced was idolatry. That is why the Lord prohibits worship of anyone but Jehovah:

> *You shall not make for yourself a carved image—any likeness of anything that is in heaven above, or that is in the earth beneath, or that is in the water under the earth; you shall not bow down to them nor serve them* (Ex. 20:4–5).

In other words, don't become a god-maker!

Strategy #2: Creating the Self-God

Idolatry carries an inevitable conclusion. If people can make gods out of images they have carved, what does this say about the god-maker himself? The answer is obvious: The creator of gods must, after all, be a superior form of god. Worshiping creatures—created things—moves toward self-adoration, or, it could be said, human deification.

Need I remind you that this is precisely where paganized Americans are headed at this moment? There is nothing new about the New Age. The dominant features of the system are a fixation with the creatures of "Mother Earth" and the proposition that each of us, in a degenderized way, is a sort of self-god. Thus, getting in touch with yourself and tapping into self-empowering sources, whether it be crystals or psychic-occult energies, simply resurrects Israel's ancient adversary—pagan idolatry.

Strategy #3: Crafting the Grand Delusion

As far as the Devil is concerned, all forms of idolatry are only stepping stones from which to leap to the grand delusion. That will come when the preparatory process has run its full course. The Antichrist will exalt "himself above all that is called God or that is worshiped, so that he sits as God in the temple of God, showing himself that he is God" (2 Th. 2:4). The objective? "So they worshiped the dragon who gave authority to the beast [Antichrist]; and they worshiped the beast, saying, 'Who is like the beast? Who is able to make war with him?'" (Rev. 13:4).

Those two questions, posed by fully paganized earthlings, are the consummate put-down of God and the Messiah-King, Jesus. If the objective of all biblical Judaism is the Messiah and His opening of the way back to God, the Devil's design—through his Baalish-Babylonian style idolatry—will lead to the Antichrist and a demented, God-free, satanic utopia.

In ancient days, humanity consorted with Satan to build a city and a tower—Babel—that would be its gateway to the heavens. Self-conceived, self-constructed, self-fulfilling, the operative phrase was *let us* (Gen. 11:4). Three thoughts dominated the satanic desire to break free from the Creator's dominion: *let us build*; *let us ascend*; *let us establish dominion*. Rebellion was at the heart of the movement.

But there is another *let us* in the passage, and with it comes the clarifying revelation that it is always God who has the last word: "Let Us," He said, "go down and there confuse their language. And from there the Lord scattered them abroad over the face of all the earth" (vv. 7–9). The battle was joined, and it will rage until the final rebellion following the Millennium (Rev. 20:7–10).

Man—Let us ascend
God—Let us descend
Man—Let us build
God—Let us confuse
Man—Let us have dominion
God—Let us scatter

Babylon as an Empire

The ideal born on the plain of Shinar was imperialized in the Babylonian Empire. "The king [Nebuchadnezzar] spoke saying, 'Is not this great Babylon, that I have built for a royal dwelling by my mighty power and for the honor of my majesty?'" (Dan. 4:30). The spirit present in the ideal was embodied in the empire.

In the prophetic scheme of things, Babylon represented a prototype of the imperial structure and design that would rise in the world empires that succeeded Babylon. Although each will display individual characteristics, Media-Persia, Greece, Rome, and Rome's yet future and reconstituted end-times manifestation will all cherish the same desires: *to ascend*, through idolatrous allegiance, to false gods; *to build* grandiose monuments for their own glory; and *to create* dominion by subjugating weaker nations and unifying them in their world system. The root of it all is rebellion against God. And a common thread in Gentile-inspired history seems to be the need to subdue the Jewish people and establish dominion over their land, Israel.

Babylon invaded Israel, devastated Jerusalem, sacked and destroyed the first Jewish Temple in three waves of captivity: 605 B.C., 597 B.C., and 586 B.C.

Media-Persia subdued Babylon in 539 B.C. and, during the reign of Xerxes (Ahasuerus, 586–465 B.C.), ultimately produced Haman who attempted to destroy "all the Jews who were throughout the whole kingdom of Ahasuerus" (Est. 3:6).

Greece, following Alexander the Great's death in 323 B.C., was divided among his generals. The infamous Antiochus Epiphanes (175–164 B.C.)—archetype of the future Antichrist—arose from the Syrian segment of the empire. He attacked Jerusalem, desecrated the Temple, forbade the Jews to worship Jehovah, and attempted to paganize Jewry. In short, he tried to destroy Judaism and repopulate Israel with pagans.

Rome had, by 146 B.C., subdued remnants of the Greek Empire. Daniel 9:26 prophesied that the Romans would subjugate Israel, crucify the Messiah, destroy the Second Temple, and scatter the Jewish people across the face of the Gentile nations.

Babylon as a Global System

The final stage of the Babylon phenomenon moves from imperial to global proportions. The dominant vehicle in the transition is the reconstituted Roman Empire prophesied as the end-times manifestation of the fourth empire revealed to Daniel (Dan. 7).

The important factor is not the city itself; it is the satanically crafted system that will challenge Jehovah and try to consummate what the Devil has attempted through all the lesser empires. Revelation 17 and 18 detail the destiny of the global, Babylonish system that will embody the ideal and imperial designs foretold in Scripture and evidenced through history. On the plain of Shinar in ancient Babylon, those who rebelled against God built their tower of Babel as a gateway to the heavens. Their religious efforts, which have afflicted humanity from that day to this, are traced through the mystery religions that were spawned at Babel and have threaded through apostate religious systems throughout history.

Full fruition of the satanic masterpiece is described in Revelation:

> *The woman was arrayed in purple and scarlet, and adorned with gold and precious stones and pearls, having in her hand a golden cup full of abominations and the filthiness of her fornications; And on her forehead a name was written: MYSTERY, BABY-LON THE GREAT, THE MOTHER OF HARLOTS AND OF THE ABOMINATIONS OF THE EARTH* (17:4–5).

This "woman" rises as the consummate manifestation of apostate religion without reality—a religion "drunk with the blood of the saints and with the blood of the martyrs of Jesus" (v. 6). This harlot system will bring together world religions that oppose Christ and His program. Apostate and ecumenical Christianity, as well as Islam, the Eastern religions, and the Earth worshipers, will eagerly consort with the Mother of Harlots to form the "Church that Satan Built."

The Beast (Antichrist) will carry the harlot; that is, he will ally himself with the church for a time to give the appearance that religion is calling the shots. This fiction will end when "the ten horns which you saw on the beast, these will hate the harlot, make her desolate and naked, eat her flesh and burn her with fire" (v. 16). Intriguingly, it will be God who will put it in the hearts of these kings (the ten horns) to destroy the religious harlot and give total allegiance to the Beast, who will lead the world religious system into catastrophe (v. 7). For when the Antichrist destroys his religious competitor, he will declare himself divine and institute a cultic Devil worship such as the world has never seen (2 Th. 2:3–4).

Thus the stage is set for Satan's ultimate assault on his one remaining enemy: the Messiah he is attempting to dethrone:

"These [the Antichrist and his cohorts] will make war with the Lamb, and the Lamb will overcome them, for He is Lord of lords and King of kings; and those who are with him are called, chosen, and faithful (Rev. 17:14).

Babylon as Dust

Three things are worthy of note, as a "stone . . . cut out of the mountain without hands" crushes political Babylon (Dan. 2:45).

(1) **Lamentation.** "The kings of the earth who committed fornication and lived luxuriously with her will weep and lament for her, when they see the smoke of her burning, standing at a distance for fear of her torment, saying, 'Alas, alas, that great city Babylon, that mighty city! For in one hour your judgment has come,'" (Rev. 18:9–10). The tenor of the Earth dwellers' lament is that their economic losses were more than they could endure. "The merchants of these things [gold, precious stones, pearls], who became rich by her, will stand at a distance for fear of her torment, weeping and wailing" (v. 15).

The calamity of seeking affluence and economic security devoid of any association with or recognition of a beneficent God reaps the final catastrophe. A world long adrift on a sea of greed and materialism is finally exposed for what it is, and it is brought down by God.

(2) **Retribution.** "Rejoice over her, O heaven, and you holy apostles and prophets, for God has avenged you on her! . . . Babylon shall be thrown down, and shall not be found any more" (vv. 20–21).

There is a pervasive feeling in our blood-sodden world that one day, accounts will be settled once and for all. Righteousness will triumph, and God will make an end of all the machinations of a God-hating world system bound to work its own will and build a religious, political, and economic utopia apart from Him. The summary phrase is found in the stark statement, "Babylon the great is fallen, is fallen, and has become a dwelling place of demons" (v. 2). God hasten the day!

(3) *Bankruptcy.* Perhaps the most cryptic words are found in 18:5. Remembering the objectives embodied in the empires and the global phenomenon Babylon represents, the words reflect the pathetic bankruptcy of Satan's grand delusion: "For her sins have reached to heaven, and God has remembered her iniquities."

Perhaps this is the most fitting epitaph for the headstone of all nations and individuals, who seek a "better way"—one devoid of "the way, the truth, and the life" (Jn. 14:6).

The High Cost of God-Making

The question we must ask is, "Where are we positioned today?" Clearly, we are squarely in the stage that is producing frantic, satanic efforts to divert and redirect worship. And the primary point of attack is to direct worship away from Christ. Jesus, the Messiah, in His First Coming, began what will be finalized in His glorious Second Advent. Therefore, Satan, whom the apostle Paul called the "god of this age" because he has blinded the minds of those "who do not believe," must concentrate on distraction and diversion until his Antichrist can come to the stage (2 Cor. 4:4). And to this end, he must have a host of contemporary human assistants.

Over the last 100 years there has been a concentrated assault on the integrity and identity of Christ. A survey of the multitude of American-bred religions is evidence of the growing obsession to discredit the deity of Christ and offer palatable alternatives. Mormonism, for example, converts Jesus into "a god" and anoints its followers as "gods." So the Messiah becomes merely a god among gods. Liberal Protestant theologians have stripped mainline denominations of the very core of their spiritual existence by proposing that Jesus was the illegitimate son of Mary and a Roman mercenary. Adolf Hitler's mania for divorcing Jesus from any attachment to Jews or Judaism reduced Him to a Germanic Gentile. H. S. Chamberlain, Hitler's theological voice, stated emphatically, "Whoever claimed that Jesus was a Jew was either stupid or telling a lie. . . . Jesus was not a Jew . . . He was probably an Aryan!"

Hans Kerrl, Minister of Church Affairs for the Third Reich, said, "Faith in Christ as the son of God. That makes me laugh." Incidentally, all forms of revived Nazism, from the sheeted members of the Ku Klux Klan to the pseudo-Christian Identity Church, share the Hitlerian view of the non-Jewishness of Jesus. They thus reduce the New Testament, from which they often quote, to little more than a fictional novel.

Yasser Arafat promoted the idea that Jesus was his "freedom-fighting" Palestinian forebear. Closer to home, but equally ominous, is the anti-Semitic, anti-Christian, Black Muslim leader Louis Farrakhan who heads the Nation of Islam. He would have us believe that Jesus was a black revolutionary.

We could go on, but these examples will serve the purpose. Each of these groups or individuals has recast Jesus into a humanized instrument to serve their prejudices and purposes in implementing their nefarious agendas. And they do so with an obvious objective in mind: Jesus divested of His deity is used to play a humanly designated role; that is, to promote causes that are, in essence, evil.

Such god-makers are only doing what has been done since that first ignoble encounter in the Garden of Eden. They are doing what the pagans did who tried to construct the Tower of Babel. They are buying into—and holding out to others—the ancient, satanic, seductive promise that people can "be as God."

What is the final word in all of this? Simply this: At all

costs, avoid the god-makers. Idolatry in any form leads to destruction. It destroys nations, and it destroys human beings. Paul said it in extremely dynamic words.

> *For even if there are so-called gods, whether in heaven or on earth (as there are many gods and many lords), yet for us there is one God, the Father, of whom are all things, and we for Him; and one Lord Jesus Christ, through whom are all things, and through whom we live* (1 Cor. 8:5–6).

Let His Word be the last word.

ENDNOTES

[1] Don Feder, "The Media's War on the 'War on Christians' Conference," March 31, 2006 <frontpagemagazine.com/Articles/ReadArticle.asp?ID=21871>.

[2] Caroline Glick, "Column One: The Jewish Threat," March 23, 2006 <jpost.com/servlet/Satellite?cid=1139395665010&pagename=JPost%2FJPArticle%2Fprinter>.

[3] Ibid.

[4] Ibid.

[5] Don Feder, "Christmas—Going, Going . . . Gone?" <donfeder.com/filecabinet//12022005.doc>.

CHAPTER 20

❦

THE COURAGE TO STAND UP

While at lunch with an Israeli diplomat in Washington, D.C., we discussed, among other things, the inescapable tensions that often arise between the Christian and Jewish communities. And he made an observation I had never considered. Although Israel is an ancient people with a deep well of experiences, as a nation it is still young. It arrived on the international scene in 1948 and is virtually in its infancy.

In relationship to the State of Israel, evangelical Christians have always been perceived as friends and reliable allies. Even prior to the first Zionist Congress in Basel, Switzerland, in 1897, a strong core of evangelicals had the courage to stand up and lend its influence and support to the cause of the Jewish people's right to a homeland in the Middle East—in a word, *Zionism*.

Men like the venerable British clergyman, William Hechler, stood by the early Zionists. Later he became a confidant of Theodor Herzl and introduced him to many European heads of state. The Christian Restoration Movement in England, allied with Prime Minister David Lloyd George and Foreign Secretary Lord Arthur James Balfour, was instrumental in forging the Balfour Declaration. Before the violent assaults on the fledgling state in 1948, men like the revered British Army Captain Orde Wingate helped teach Israelis how to defend themselves against Arab aggressors.

It was said of Lawrence Oliphant that he acted from a "biblical point of view." Oliphant was a well-known Christian

Zionist whom Israel honored by naming a street after him in Jerusalem.

These Christians and thousands more can be credited with an unfailing commitment to the Jewish people and the plight of Israel. The common thread binding them together was a belief that the Bible provided the divine rationale for establishing a modern Jewish state. In their minds, the land belonged to Jewry because God declared it. It's as simple as that.

It should not be surprising, then, that the leaders of successive Israeli administrations have had a high regard for evangelical Christians committed to the biblical principles basic to the Zionist dream of Israel returning to its land. Israel's physical rebirth brought millions of Christians, ardent believers in a Jewish return, into the public arena to support the fundamental belief that the Jewish people possess irrevocable rights to the land occupied by their patriarchs. Bible-believing Christians, who were awakened to the historical reality of the prophetic Scriptures, have always been and will remain a valuable asset to the old, yet new, nation of Israel.

The Gulf Between Old and New

Israel's perception of evangelical Christians, however, is quite different from that widely held among Jews of the Diaspora (those still dispersed among the Gentile nations). If Israeli leaders have taken a new look at these Zionist Christians, world Jewry has tended to cling to an old perception that associates all Christians with past atrocities. Although the situation is definitely improving, there still remains a misperception of what Christianity is and what design Jesus' followers have for Judaism and Jewish people in general.

In many Jewish minds the record speaks for itself, as I discovered in a conversation with a young Jewish intellectual in Israel some years ago. I asked him what he knew about

Christianity. He replied that he knew a great deal. He had studied Christian relations at Hebrew University. I asked him what he thought about Christians based on his studies and personal observations.

"You don't want to know," he said.

"Yes, I do," I replied.

"Okay," Yoram responded, "but you're not going to like it.

"When Christian Crusaders came to this city, Jerusalem, to create a kingdom for Jesus, they cut down Jews in the streets, locked some in synagogues, and burned them alive.

"A Jew thinks of the year 1492 in an entirely different way than you Christians do. You associate it with the discovery of the New World. We remember it as the year that Christian King Ferdinand and Queen Isabella said to every Jew in Spain, 'Get out,' and the Inquisition began.

"During the Black Plague that killed millions of people in Europe, Jews were accused of poisoning wells and were expelled from their homes to suffer great persecution.

"That's not all. There were the pogroms in Russia, ghettos in Europe, and blood libels. How would you like to be forced to wear a pointed hat or tags on your garments that say, 'Here comes a Jew. Watch out'?

"And then there is the matter of the Holocaust. Six million of my people perished in the greatest bloodbath we have known. Where did it originate? In Germany, the country that had been the seat of Christian theology. And what about Adolf Hitler? Wasn't he, after all, himself a Christian?"

To a Bible-believing Christian like me, the young man's views were shocking, as they would be to most genuine believers. His perception was molded by the pseudo–Christian political and religious elements operating far outside the realm of true biblical mandates. His vision of our history was tied to forced conversions, mockings, murder, and mayhem. He had never been personally exposed to true Christianity.

FOR THE LOVE OF ZION

Aiding and Abetting Enemies of the Jewish People

Unfortunately, the same satanically driven forces that shaded my young friend's vision of Christianity are still shaping the minds of many Jewish people. I recently viewed a map of the United States that showed the locations of neo-Nazi cells, Ku Klux Klan elements, and assorted groups of militantly anti-Semitic organizations. Most of them tag themselves as "Christian" and claim to be protectors of the name of Jesus. These people are anything but Christian, and their blasphemous rhetoric and militant conduct feed the perception that, for Jews, things haven't really changed. The obsession to rid the world of the sons and daughters of Abraham is still a potent force in the world of Gentiles.

Admittedly, these elements, coupled with old torments, are extremely formidable obstacles to overcome. But we have clearly reached a juncture in history when fanatics who aid and abet the enemies of God and His Chosen People cannot be allowed to win the day. Christians have a biblical mandate, not only to "pray for the peace of Jerusalem" (Ps. 122:6), but to recognize that God has not changed His mind nor diminished His love for Abraham's children. Speaking explicitly of Jewry, to whom so many divine gifts have been given, the Scripture says, "For the gifts and the calling of God are irrevocable" (Rom. 11:29). This being the case, all true Christians are charged to agree with our Lord and conduct themselves accordingly.

Showing the Best Christianity Has to Offer

Thankfully, despite what fringe fanatics manifest, there are millions of living, breathing contradictions to all that they represent. Many may be less visible than they should be, but they are there nonetheless. Allow me to present a case in point.

For many years I had a friend, now in heaven, who had a profound influence in my life. I admired him greatly. Gordon was a man who taught me and scores of others what it meant to be a true friend of Israel and the Jewish people. He believed implicitly that the Bible was the authoritative source for accepting the fact that God's promises to the Jewish people were literal and historical and that the land of Israel was theirs by divine right. Whenever an anti-Israel sentiment was voiced in the local newspaper, there would be an opposing letter to the editor from Gordon.

In churches where he had considerable influence, he was always quick to make people aware of the proper place the Jewish people had in God's economy. And it was always done in a way that encouraged as well as challenged. He was an ever-present face at local synagogue bazaars and public events in the Jewish community. Gordon constantly reminded his circle of Christian friends that they should be supportive of the synagogue and show solidarity with the Jewish people.

Although he faithfully maintained an unwavering relationship with the Jewish community, he was never reticent to share his faith in Christ and never lost sight of his responsibility to fulfill Jesus' commission to make Christ known. And he did so, always mindful to be sensitive to the old perceptions that so often cause Jewish people to shrink back from the message of the gospel.

When Gordon died, representatives of the synagogue attended his funeral, which I was honored to conduct. After the ceremony, they approached me and asked if I would attend their Sabbath service the next Friday evening. Of course, I said I would. When the meeting began, it was announced that the service would center on a tribute to Gordon and his multiple accomplishments among and on behalf of Israel and the Jewish people.

In closing the eulogy, the speaker said, "I could only wish that every Christian could live up to the standard that this man consistently observed in his own life. Without question, Gordon showed us the best that Christianity has to offer." Today there is a plaque on the wall of that synagogue honoring the memory of this Gentile who had such a large heart for God and His people.

I close this story on an optimistic note. Although the shadows of distrust remain, they seem to be slowly fading. There are many reasons for this, not the least of which is the cultural revolution that threatens our Judeo-Christian way of life. Consequently, concerned Jewish people and evangelical Christians are coming together with a new sense of understanding. And, in the spirit of people like Gordon on both sides of the line, that understanding is bridging some of the significant obstacles of the past.

Where Do We Sign Up?

Another man I admire is the late Col. Teddy Roosevelt, later to become the 26th president of the United States. Roosevelt was certified as an American icon during the Spanish-American War of 1898. The Spanish presence in North America, especially in Cuba, was one of iron-fist suppression and brutal efficiency. An officer commonly known as "Butcher" Weyler because of his ruthless tactics commanded the Spanish garrison.

America's conflict with the Spanish was its first major step into the international arena. Roosevelt, a vigorous patriot and champion of American values, entered the war in the lead column of his Rough Riders—men who were destined to ride into the lore of American history on their bloody but victorious charge up Cuba's San Juan Hill.

For his part, the colonel chose to lead from the front. It exposed him to great personal danger, but he insisted that leadership meant just that—leading men, not bringing up the rear.

Along with portraits of his great courage and penchant for the derring-do, the colorful Rough Rider left a catalog of quotations worthy of applying to the current situation facing America and those individuals who believe in solid principles to live by. For example,

> *Far better it is to dare things, to win glorious tri-*
> *umphs, even though checkered by failure, than to*
> *take rank with those poor spirits who . . . live in the*
> *gray twilight that knows neither victory nor defeat.*

It seems that we are sliding into a national and cultural vortex drawing us into what Roosevelt aptly described as "the gray twilight that knows neither victory nor defeat."

Here in the affluent, self-absorbed West, there exists a near obsession with maintaining the status quo, an unwillingness to confront tyranny, injustice, and evil beyond a certain point. When ultimate triumphs are marred by checkered, temporary failures, we hear the cry to settle for the existing state of affairs. But the cold fact is that there is not, nor will there ever be, a "good enough." The status quo, although deceptively attractive, is the Never Never Land of people trying to preserve a fantasy.

It is a real-time issue that we have a great deal of difficulty comprehending. Yet the answers to the problems at hand are not hard to come by. At the core is the fact that, for our enemies, there is no status quo. They are not satisfied with the way things are, nor will they be until they are in possession of what we have, and have altered it to fit their concepts of what constitutes the "good life."

We may have no desire to confront the bloody realities of terror, war, and mayhem. But we need not be deceived into thinking that we have the ability to talk our adversaries into sharing our perceptions of peace and tranquility. It will not happen. To take this route is intemperate and self-delusional. Our propensity to talk much and dispense random acts of kindness may have the ring of pop-culture political correctness, but it will not placate those whose chief goal in life is to snuff out our lives.

A perpetual failing of free, democratic societies is their

pursuit of the idea that the entire world essentially thinks and reasons as they do. We made this mistake with the Nazis, then went to the edge of a catastrophic nuclear confrontation with the Communists, and are currently repeating the same potentially fatal error with Islamists bent on global domination.

A serious deficiency in American thinking lies in the idea that people are basically good and that a quiet sit-down over a cup of coffee and a season of reasonable negotiation done in good faith will enable us to work out even the most difficult issues to everyone's satisfaction. It doesn't work that way. Men are not good by nature. Some very bad people operate in this arena, and they have no intention of negotiating solutions that will create peace in our time.

Unfortunately, many of those suffering from the give-them-what-they-want dementia need a refresher course in historical reality. Empires and nations afflicted by the status-quo syndrome have consistently passed into the mists of history.

Men like Hechler, Lord Balfour, Oliphant, and others had the courage to stand up for what they believed. Our world has entered the final drama. We face an enemy that will stop at nothing to destroy us. It uses all of Satan's tactics, including deception, hatred, violence, and fear.

Somewhere along the line there is a choice to be made. The old Rough Rider understood the issue. Do we camp with those poor spirits who "live in the gray twilight that knows neither victory nor defeat"? Or do we have the courage and tenacity to take the high road and ride to the front of the column and lead rather than follow?

If the latter option is our choice, perhaps it's time that we signed on.

CHAPTER 21

⚜

O JERUSALEM, JERUSALEM

The modern State of Israel will be 60 years old in 2008. No nation in the history of mankind has been born out of such enormous suffering. And certainly no nation has surpassed Israel in its perpetual struggle to survive against seemingly insurmountable odds.

With the dawn of May 15, 1948, a dream became a reality. Israel was miraculously reborn. But clouds wafted on the horizon, and the tiny nation, fresh from the rigors of the Holocaust, had precious little time for celebration. Its enemies in the Arab world were set to annihilate the fledgling state and drive the Jews into the sea.

A new generation of Jews fought for their lives. It was something the Arabs had not expected, nor were they prepared to accept. They sued for a cease-fire.

By January 7, 1949, all hostilities concluded. The War of Independence was over, and the State of Israel was now a fact. But Jewish forces had paid a high price for their homeland. Some 4,000 soldiers and 2,000 civilians had been killed. Financially, they had taken a heavy blow—$500 million. But the state had survived. Little Israel was at center stage. And six decades later, it is still in the international spotlight.

At the first meeting of the Provisional Council of State, Chaim Weizman, Israel's first president, summed up the import of the nation's rebirth:

273

This is a great day in our lives. Let it not be regarded as undue arrogance if we say that it is also a great day in the life of the world. There is recompense for a righteous struggle. If we, the suffering and wretched people, impoverished and downtrodden, have been privileged to celebrate this occasion, there is hope for all those who aspire for justice and righteousness.

His words had the ring of the voices of the prophets:

If I forget you, O Jerusalem, let my right hand forget its skill! If I do not remember you, let my tongue cleave to the roof of my mouth— if I do not exalt Jerusalem above my chief joy (Ps. 137:5–6).

It is impossible to assess the love for Jerusalem embodied in the Jewish people. It is equally difficult to fully compute the anxiety felt when the War of Independence ended, and they had to face the fact that the Old City of Jerusalem was firmly in the hands of the Transjordanian Arab Legion.

Following the war, Jewish people were ecstatic over the establishment of the State of Israel. Yet, for all of their astonishing accomplishments, they could never feel fully satisfied as long as the Jordanians held their beloved city. Israel was a nation whose heart was now held by another.

Israeli Palmach troops had been within the walls for a brief time during the battle for Jerusalem. They were forced to leave, however, when it became apparent that they were no match for the Jordanians. For 19 bitter years thereafter, Jewish people were denied access to their homes, places of worship, and above all, the sacred Western Wall. All of that changed on a June day in 1967.

Reunified at Last

On that fateful day in June, battle-begrimed young paratroopers stood looking up at the Western Wall, the last artifact of the Herodian Temple. Their faces graphically mirrored the awe engendered in the heart of Jewry as they reverently touched the wall referred to by a prominent Israeli of that day as "our place of places." There was a look of relief on their faces, too, because on that day Jewry sensed, as did much of the rest of the world, that something momentous had happened—something that gave rise to the hope that things would be all right now. The 2,000-year trek of foot-weary Jews across inhospitable nations had finally come to an end. The waves of people making *aliyah* had followed circuitous paths back to the land and had finally reached Israel's high place—the Temple Mount and the ancient city of David. The "wandering Jew" finally had a place to go; he could go home.

Jewry's passion for the city of Jerusalem is difficult for most Westerners to comprehend. Ancient Jewish rabbis viewed Jerusalem as the precise center of the earth. "The world," they said, "is like an eye. The white of the eye is everything else. The iris is Israel. The pupil is Jerusalem. But, ah, the gleam in the center of the pupil, that is the Temple Mount—that is Mount Moriah."

Thus it was that at 9:40 A.M., Wednesday, June 7, 1967, Israeli paratroopers altered history. The hope, born of desperation and fanned through 2,000 years of debilitating dispersion, was now attained; wonder-struck Jewish paratroopers were standing on the Temple Mount. And, to Jews the world over, the "gleam in the center of the pupil" was shining around them for all the world to see. On June 27, 1967, Israel officially annexed the Old City and began the long-sought task of reclaiming the city of its fathers.

Reclamation of the Old City was an immense undertaking.

The years of Jordanian occupation had wreaked havoc on what had historically been the Jewish sector of Jerusalem. Muslims had vented their animosity toward the Jewish presence by destroying Jewish synagogues in the quarter. The base of the relic, the Western Wall, revered by Judaism as the most important visible remnant of the Temple complex, had been turned into a receptacle for animal dung. When Jordan captured the Old City in 1948, it drove out all the Jews and erected fences to prevent the Israelis from entering the sector where the historic Jewish presence had endured over the centuries. Tearing down those fences was a symbolic act, one that demonstrated the Jewish determination that, for all the days to come, the new Israeli Jerusalem would be a city open to all. Jews, Christians, and Muslims alike could come to their holy places unmolested. And Israel has kept its word.

It is doubtful that any city in the world has had more love lavished on it than has Jerusalem since 1967. People sometimes wonder why those who visit wish to return year after year. Many reasons can be given, of course. But a compelling one is the city's beauty, which draws people like a magnet. During his decades-long tenure as mayor (1965–1993), Teddy Kollek led world Jewry in the effort to transform Jerusalem from a place of shabby, narrow streets, rock-strewn lots, and garbage-infested alleys to a city reflecting the glories embodied in psalm, hymn, and story across the centuries.

An Act of the Heart

Israel's enemies have stridently continued to raise the accusation that Israel's projects in Jerusalem are little more than wanton acts of aggression designed to blot out Muslim identity. While it is true that the Jewish people, with a just and historic claim, wish to identify with Jerusalem and have the city properly reflect its Jewishness, endeavors there go far beyond politics or spite. To the contrary, what is unfolding between Jerusalem and its Jewish sons and daughters is more of a love story, for there is something inexplicably etched in the Jewish heart that demands a presence there. Jews are bonded to the place in a tenacious demonstration of union, passion, and permanence—in other words, the best of everything genuine that love embodies. And this is not the exclusive domain of religious Jews; it is inflexibly resident in the vast majority of Jewish people regardless of their religious persuasions.

So they dig there. Jewish archaeologists sift ancient ruins down to bedrock in search of Jewish origins. Archaeologists, in fact, are there in profusion at Solomon's city, David's city, the city streets where Jesus walked. Long centuries before Islam was a flicker in Muhammad's mind, the Jews were there.

And the Jews build there. The reclamation of the Jewish quarter of the Old City is a tribute to the tenacity and commitment to permanence that links Jewry to the place. Jerusalem stone, once only a segment of the landscape, is transformed daily into beautiful edifices that have changed the skyline of the city of David.

And Abraham's sons and daughters plant there. Reforestation, parks, gardens, and flower-strewn hillsides grace the eyes of those who come to the city. Indeed, one of the finest experiences visitors enjoy is spending an hour on one of Jerusalem's hillsides, planting a tree or shrub that will grow as a memorial to having walked there.

Israel invites the world to come and see. Although tourism constitutes a major portion of the nation's economy, the invitation involves much, much more than income. Christians can come to be spiritually refreshed at the empty Garden Tomb and walk where the Savior ministered and purchased our redemption. Muslims are free to go to their al-Aqsa mosque and the Dome of the Rock to share prayers and listen to Islamic sermons. Jews are urged to come, see, and leave a bit of themselves, or to stay and experience—as the words of "Hatikvah" so beautifully put it—the dream of living upon the hills of "Zion and Jerusalem."

Shadows of Hope

As Israel continually celebrates its reunion with the city that holds Jewry's heart, we will hear intoned with perhaps more passion than ever before, "We are here to stay!" There seems to be a Masada-like determination among the vast majority of Israelis that Jerusalem will never again fall into the hands of interlopers. As Masada symbolizes this commitment, Jerusalem stands as an enduring symbol that Jewry's heart and home are in the right place—the City of Peace, the City of Shalom.

But most of the world does not agree. Many nations, including the United States, have demonstrated their displeasure by refusing to recognize Jerusalem as the legitimate capital of the State of Israel. Islam lays claim to Jerusalem, and the major powers' increasing penchant for coddling Israel's (and the West's) Muslim enemies will assure the growth of controversy over the right of dominion in the Holy City.

The issue, however, reaches beyond the Islam/Israel conflict. It is rooted in a desire as old as the creation of nations—particularly Israel, with its glowing biblical promises granting Jews the land of Canaan in perpetuity.

When the UN on November 29, 1947, voted to grant the Jewish people a portion of their homeland in the Middle East and to recognize the legitimacy of the tiny state under international law, Jerusalem was declared an international city. This action implied that the city would be under UN control and that the UN's role would be to oversee Jerusalem's affairs and stifle the passions of the various elements representing the tapestry of religions in the area. The point is that a Gentile world body, the UN, was determined to exercise control over Jerusalem. That desire has not changed. And you can be sure that when the question of rights in Jerusalem is addressed during any future peace negotiations, the UN will insist on internationalizing the city, thus placing it under UN control.

If this scenario sounds all too familiar, it is. Jerusalem, rightfully the city of the Jews, has been prized by virtually every significant Gentile power since she rose from the dust of the Judean hills.

From Babylon to Bethlehem

Jerusalem will be trampled by Gentiles until the times of the Gentiles are fulfilled (Lk. 21:24).

Lord Byron, in "The Destruction of Sennacherib," caught in vivid poetic form not only the essence of a battle long gone, but also the final convulsions of the Times of the Gentiles that stretch from 586 B.C. until the Lord Jesus returns:

> *And there lay the rider distorted and pale,*
> *With the dew on his brow, and the rust on his mail:*
> *And the tents were all silent, the banners alone,*
> *The lances uplifted, the trumpet unblown.*
> *And the widows of Ashur are loud in their wail,*
> *And the idols are broke in the temple of Baal;*
> *And the might of the Gentile, unsmote by the sword,*
> *Hath melted like snow in the glance of the Lord!*

First published in 1815, this poem portrays the prophetic declaration of Gentile domination until, in the words of Jesus, "the times of the Gentiles are fulfilled." That the conclusion of the Gentile era is related to Jerusalem being "trampled by Gentiles" clarifies the importance of events taking place in the Middle East and shapes the entire prophetic program set forth in the Scriptures.

God has provided precise information concerning the course and destiny of the Gentile empires that followed Nebuchadnezzar and the first worldwide kingdom, Babylon. Few areas of human history are more intriguing than the development and demise of successive empires that all conspired to dominate the world and capture its most prized possessions: Israel and Jerusalem. Herein lies the surpassing story of supreme human aspirations and Jehovah's divine dedication to the land, its people, and the City of Peace. The battle lines are drawn between Satan and God, darkness and light, chaos and peace.

Parade of the Nations

The four great empires—Babylon, Media-Persia, Greece, and Rome—have been there and are gone. In their turn, they all came to the land of the Jews. A reconstituted form of Rome will make a return trip in the days ahead.

Prior to these great empires, the likes of Egypt and Assyria planted banners and left monuments to the gods they believed crafted their triumphs. When Rome crumbled as a viable force in the ancient world, lesser invaders— Byzantines, Arabs, Seljuks, Crusaders, Mamluks, Ottoman Turks, the French, and others—vied for supremacy in *Eretz Yisrael*. Names like Napoleon and Britain's Edmund Allenby turn up in the latter stages of the countdown for the return of the Jewish people in our time.

Over the centuries, little Israel and its capital city of Jerusalem have been at the center of the great international tug-of-war that someday will consummate where so many have struggled: near the hill Megiddo in the Jezreel Valley— Armageddon. At the moment, we seem to be warming up for the political and military convulsions that will dwarf all that has gone before. At Armageddon there will be no limited engagements; the conflict will be a winner-take-all contest of global proportions.

The return of the Jewish people and the rebirth of Israel sent a wake-up call to the nations of the Middle East, and the area that had been viewed as a rather slow-paced region of the world began to stir perceptibly. Arab-Muslim neighbors began their frenzied military attempts to rewrite the map and, for that matter, the history of the land. Indeed, big things began to develop on the world stage in proximity to the new national reality in the Middle East. When the Lord began to stir the heart of Jewry for its land, Satan sent an alarm out to his troops and launched the great counterstrategy that is now unfolding at an ever-increasing pace.

Europe, fragmented for centuries, began what many prophetic scholars believe to be the move toward reconstituting the Roman Empire. Echoes can be heard of Daniel's prophecy of an end-times entity in Europe that will produce the world's most colossal dictator, the Antichrist. The United States, Russia, and successive legions of greater and lesser nations in the UN wrangle and vote over issues related to Israel with a heat of passion seemingly reserved for it alone.

It is fascinating to observe that, as the world makes obvious moves toward a one-world system, the UN seems preoccupied with minding the business of everyone else on the planet. With the UN secretary-general and the General Assembly posturing to call the shots for all possible military intervention, the United States has gone all out to send troops to bring down tyrants and spread democracy. Consequently, from the prophetic point of view, things are heating up.

Jerusalem: A Thermometer of the End-Times

When talk first began about peace in the Middle East, Jerusalem was a subject everyone wanted to keep on the back burner. So volatile was the issue that, not only did no one want to open a Pandora's box of problems, but people made rather bizarre decisions in an attempt to avoid trouble. As part of its resolution plan for Palestine, the UN in 1947 proposed that "the City of Jerusalem shall be established as a *corpus separatum* under a special international regime and shall be administered by the United Nations." The rationale was not applied to any other city in any other nation created from the mandatory system. Bottom line: Gentiles would rule the place God had long since designated as the undisputed capital city of the Jewish nation.

When Arab Muslims rejected the partition plan and waged war to eliminate the newborn state, they seized Jerusalem (in open defiance of the UN) and promptly closed the city to Jews. For 19 years Jerusalem endured a squalid situation, and no one in the UN seemed to notice.

As a result of the Six-Day War in 1967, Jerusalem was united, the barriers were taken down, shrines of all faiths were opened for free access, and all residents—Jews, Arabs, and Christians—were allowed to pursue their lives in relative security. The UN did notice this time, however, and time and time again called for sanctions against the "occupation."

For Israel's part, the city was at last united and declared the undivided capital of the Jewish state. Randolph Churchill and Winston Churchill (son and grandson respectively of the late British Prime Minister Winston Churchill), commented on the reunification: "Three laws were passed through the Knesset on June 27 annexing the Old City of Jerusalem and reuniting it with the New on the next day. Whatever else Israel may be prepared to negotiate we may be sure Jerusalem is not included."

In another rather strange twist of international thinking, only two nations, Costa Rica and El Salvador, recognized Jerusalem as the capital of Israel. One wonders when any sovereign state was refused "permission" from the UN to designate its own capital. But under firm and fair Israeli control, Jerusalem has flourished and remains for most Jewish people the nonnegotiable center of the Jewish world.

Then a man in a kaffiyeh, toting an automatic rifle,

came to the stage. Arafat settled for limited autonomy—temporarily. He made no secret of the fact that the "peace process" concocted in the doomed-to-fail Oslo Accords of the 1990s was only the first step on the road to Palestinian statehood. The capital city of that state was to be Jerusalem. It was his settled agenda, and even today the world seems to assume this will ultimately be the case.

Dr. Baruch Goldstein brought the issue of Jerusalem to the front burner in 1994 when he shot nearly 30 Arab worshipers in Hebron. In the wave of emotional hysteria that followed, the UN sought someone to blame for the misdeeds of one unbalanced man. Predictably, Israel was the culprit. To assuage the rage of Muslims and, in the process, throw another concession their way, the world body voted to label Jerusalem "occupied territory." For the first time in the history of the modern State of Israel, the United States forfeited its moral obligation to veto such rancorous nonsense and consequently contributed significantly to more trouble for Israel and, for that matter, the peace process. You might say the Gentile nations were once again exercising their intention to place a firm foot on Jerusalem.

The Vatican stated as much with its decision in July 1994 to establish full diplomatic relations with Israel. The Vatican's primary objective was to position itself to exercise authority in the "final status" negotiations, which you can be sure will not designate Jerusalem as the united capital of Israel but, rather, as a divided hodgepodge that will satisfy no one. We can learn one great thing from all of this: The nations are on the move, and they are moving toward the eventual showdown in the Middle East.

A Cup of Trembling

Today every major political element on the international scene feels that it holds vested interests in the Middle East and the fate of Jerusalem. During the Cold War, Israel and

Jerusalem were seen as a democratic buffer against Communism in the region. Communists themselves dreamed of seizing Israel and Jerusalem. The consistent obsession reflects the biblical reality. The Lord said, "Behold, I will make Jerusalem a cup of drunkenness [trembling] to all the surrounding peoples" (Zech. 12:2). The nations will attempt to seize Jerusalem, and she will prove to be a trembling cup and a very heavy stone in their hands—an emblem of disaster:

> *And it shall happen in that day that I will make Jerusalem a very heavy stone for all peoples; all who would heave it away will surely be cut in pieces, though all nations of the earth are gathered against it* (v. 3).

This situation has been true of Gentile nations across the centuries. The context of Zechariah 12 speaks of the final day when "all nations of the earth" will be gathered together against it. As Jesus said, "Jerusalem will be trampled by Gentiles until the times of the Gentiles are fulfilled (Lk. 21:24)." In the last gasp of the last days, control of Jerusalem will once again be wrested from the Jewish people, and they will be in their beloved city at the sufferance of Gentile overlords. In charge will be the infamous Antichrist, cited in both the Old and New Testaments as the last human antagonist of Israel and the Jewish people. The Bible teaches—and history increasingly affirms—that the clouds of battle are forming above Jerusalem. One day the storm will break with sound and thunder the likes of which the world has never heard.

Across the decades since the War of Independence, Israel has faced the constant threat of assault. Five times since the state was born, Arab nations have attacked Israel in an attempt to finish what they started in 1948. Today they strap bombs on themselves and blow themselves up in their ongoing war against the Jews. In 2006 they initiated an all-out attack through Hezbollah. And what they cannot accomplish on the battlefield, they take to the acquiescing, pro-Palestinian corridors of the UN, which is anything but united—except when it comes to condemning Israel.

The UN's position only confirms past history and sheds significant light on Zechariah 14:2: "For I will gather all the nations to battle against Jerusalem." Jerusalem indeed is destined to become a cup of trembling to all people (12:2).

So far the United States stands with Israel. The day will come, however, when there will be no friend to help the tiny nation—no friend, that, is, except One. When Israel stands alone before those bent on its destruction, help will come from the Lord Himself, who will reconcile the nation and deal with its satanically driven enemies:

> *Then the LORD will go forth and fight against those nations, as He fights in the day of battle* (14:3).

He will indeed, and Israel will at last know, in full measure, His lasting peace.

Bethlehem's Answer to Babylon's Dream

The good news for all of us is that God has anticipated the Gentile obsession to dominate and then subjugate His creatures and creation. Consequently, His response has been determined and is in motion. It became physically visible in Bethlehem when, by way of a virgin's womb, deity took on humanity. His birth was the living embodiment of all that the prophets had promised the Messiah would be.

Near the completion of His redemptive work at Calvary, the Messiah revealed the full scope of His earthly mission to, oddly enough, Pontius Pilate, the prefect of Judea and emissary of imperial Rome in Jerusalem nearly 2,000 years ago:

> *Pilate therefore said to Him, "Are You a king then?"*
> *Jesus answered, "You say rightly that I am a king.*
> *For this cause I was born, and for this cause I have*
> *come into the world" (Jn. 18:37).*

At the hour of His greatest humility, He exposed His coming majesty.

Appropriately, Jesus mapped the future course laid down by the prophet Daniel who, when outlining the phases of the Messiah's ministry, wrote: "And after the sixty-two weeks Messiah shall be cut off [crucified], but not for Himself" (Dan. 9:26). In other words, this cutting off would occur before the city was destroyed in A.D. 70 and before the Messiah would receive His Kingdom, according to Daniel's prophecy.

Thus the Messiah was telling Pilate, "Yes, I am a King, but a King for another time, if not another place." Jesus was telling Rome's man in Jerusalem that they would meet again one distant day, but under far different circumstances. So, while we scan developments in the Gentile plan to sweep the planet with its marauding hordes, seize Israel, and triumph over Jerusalem, we confidently look for that promised Kingdom and pray for its coming:

> *I was watching in the night visions, and behold, One*
> *like the Son of Man, coming with the clouds of*
> *heaven! He came to the Ancient of Days, and they*
> *brought Him near before Him. Then to Him was*
> *given dominion and glory and a kingdom, that all*
> *peoples, nations, and languages should serve Him.*
> *His dominion is an everlasting dominion, which*
> *shall not pass away, and His kingdom the one which*
> *shall not be destroyed (Dan. 7:13–14).*

All believers who long for true peace can confidently look forward to the day when they will walk in white on the streets of a Jerusalem fit for the King.

You see, the issue of control of Jerusalem is not simply Gentile nations against Jewish dreamers. Jerusalem is the city of the King! God is sovereign over His eternal city. And the Messiah-King will one day come to His city, "and in that day His feet will stand on the Mount of Olives, which faces Jerusalem on the east. And the LORD shall be King over all the earth" (Zech. 14:4, 9). And He will do so from Jerusalem.

For those who will heed the call to prepare to meet the Messiah, there will be a grand celebration to enjoy. Reconciled Israel will have its city—just as He promised. And the years will pass as quickly as a dream interrupted by a new morning. Jerusalem, the city of gold, will be the shimmering possession of Israel's sons and daughters forever and forever and forever.

CHAPTER 22

⟡

ASSESSING THE GOD FACTOR

Although I am not an avid viewer of television preaching, I've made a notable exception: a program broadcast from a church in Brooklyn, New York. The pastor, now retired, was a stately, dignified minister of a black congregation and was gifted in oratory, knowledge of the Scriptures, and the application of biblical truth to everyday circumstances. In one of his memorable sermons, he touched on the current state of world and national affairs, exposing the futility of searching for human answers to profound questions, as well as the downward spiral of moral and spiritual rectitude. The developing state of misdirection and creeping chaos was due, he said, to the absence of any consideration of the God Factor. Without it, humanity is doomed to a state of perpetual, Babel-like confusion.

The pastor was correct. And when the God Factor is merely peripheral to our assessment of where we are, how we've arrived, and where we're headed, we're on a collision course with catastrophe.

This condition was demonstrated during the 2006 Hamas and Hezbollah attacks on the Jewish state and by the general uncertainty of military affairs in the Middle East. As the dismal situation progressed and things looked bad for Israel, some evangelicals began to tilt toward the Replacement Theology fantasy or, at least, adopt a silence-is-safest posture in case the Islamo-fascist fanatics achieved their stated goal of dismantling the Jewish state and driving the Jewish people into the Mediterranean.

These evangelicals either minimized or failed to consider the God Factor. Television talking heads, secular political analysts, and belligerent anti-Israel activists both inside and outside the evangelical community have tainted the environment and caused people to back away from a public commitment to Israel. The syndrome—so prevalent in our time—that blames the victim for the misdeeds of the perpetrators seems to have taken its toll.

Of course, the problem is nothing new. Israel's history is awash with religious advisors who counseled kings to play it safe; conciliate; appease; or simply believe that, despite the obvious and perilous signs, everything would turn out okay. The stance was an ancient variation of the cop-out evasion by today's "pandispensationalists" who disdain prophetic teaching and dismissively claim there is no need to consider seriously what God lays before us in the prophetic Scriptures because everything will pan out all right in the end. They ignore the historical essence of the God Factor.

An Irreducible Promise

The Israelites appeared to be in a tight spot some 3,400 years ago when they languished in the Sinai between Egypt and the Promised Land. The minds and hearts of many were still in the land of the pharaohs. Visions of fish, cucumbers, leeks, onions, garlic, and melons danced in their heads as they gathered the tasteless, daily stock of manna. Others, wearied with the journey and its scorpions, snakes, spiders, and insufferable heat, verged on open rebellion and spent their time carping about the so-called ineptitude of their leaders and the prospect of perishing in the wilderness.

But through all of the dark days and seemingly endless wanderings, there was a promise, one that a steadfast remnant of true believers kept ever in their range of vision. It was the carpet of truth laid for them in Deuteronomy 6:23:

> *Then He brought us out from there [Egypt], that*
> *He might bring us in, to give us the land [Israel] of*
> *which He swore to our fathers.*

Here was the key that opened the door to their future. No matter how dark or cold the nights, how weary the days, or how fierce the pursuit by their enemies, there was a promise. It did not originate with Moses; it came directly from the throne of God, Israel's sovereign Commander-in-Chief. He did not purpose to bring His people out of the cauldron of suffering in Egypt merely to allow them to perish in the desert. They were a people of destiny. Israel was meant to be brought into permanent possession of the Promised Land.

If there was ever a time in modern history when this lesson should be learned and applied, it is now. Israel's precarious condition is not terminal. Nor is it God's intent to allow Gentile hate mongers to plague and persecute His Chosen People forever.

In studying prophecy, one must never fall into the trap of placing undue emphasis on the darkness through which Israel and the world must pass during the prophesied Time of Jacob's Trouble. To be sure, the Time is in the Book; and we see harbingers of that future trauma even today. However, there is an end in view that we must never neglect. As believers, we endure trials and suffering, knowing they are but comparatively short-term affairs; better things lie ahead. So it is with Israel. Tribulation is merely a short-term means to an end—one that will manifest His mercy, grace, and ever-abiding love for His people and the land He has given them forever.

A People Unto Himself

Deuteronomy 7 sets the tone:

> *For you are a holy people to the LORD your God; the*
> *LORD your God has chosen you to be a people for*

Himself, a special treasure above all the peoples on the face of the earth. The LORD did not set His love on you nor choose you because you were more in number than any other people, for you were the least of all peoples; but because the LORD loves you, and because He would keep the oath which He swore to your fathers, the LORD has brought you out with a mighty hand, and redeemed you from the house of bondage, from the hand of Pharaoh king of Egypt. Therefore know that the LORD your God, He is God, the faithful God who keeps covenant and mercy for a thousand generations (vv. 6–9).

These incomparable verses do not contradict what our New Testaments tell us of His covenant-keeping promises to Israel. In a few brief words amid a lengthy exposition of Israel's past, present, and future glory (Rom. 9—11), the Lord presses the point:

"For this is My covenant with them [Israel], when I take away their sins." . . . *For the gifts and the calling of God are irrevocable* (11:27, 29).

God does not change His mind! Not toward His promises for Israel or toward His promises for the church. If He could break one promise, all of them would be in jeopardy. But thanks be to God, He has not and will not.

A Chosen City for a Chosen People

Have you ever wondered why Jerusalem has so often been—and will be in the future—a "cup of trembling"? It is because of the God Factor. God chose Jerusalem as His. It is the one city on all of the earth that He has chosen to name as His own.

> *And to his son I will give one tribe, that My servant David may always have a lamp before me in Jerusalem,* **the city which I have chosen for Myself, to put My name there**" (1 Ki. 11:36, emphasis added).

It was there His Temples stood and will again stand in the future. It was there His kings reigned. It was there all males were called to worship three times each year at the great feasts. And there the Messiah shall hold sway over reconciled Israel and all the nations in the Kingdom Age:

> *And the* LORD *shall be King over all the earth. In that day it shall be "The* LORD *is one," and His name one* (Zech. 14:9).

There are few places in God's Word where this truth is expressed with more passion than in Isaiah 62:

> *For Zion's sake I will not hold My peace, and for Jerusalem's sake I will not rest, until her righteousness goes forth as brightness, and her salvation as a lamp that burns. The Gentiles shall see your righteousness, and all kings your glory. You shall be called by a new name, which the mouth of the* LORD *will name. You shall also be a crown of glory in the hand of the* LORD, *and a royal diadem in the hand of your God. I have set watchmen on your walls, O Jerusalem; they shall never hold their peace day or night. You who make mention of the* LORD, *do not keep silent, and give Him no rest till He establishes and till He makes Jerusalem a praise in the earth. Indeed the* LORD *has proclaimed to the end of the world: "Say to the daughter of Zion, 'Surely your*

*salvation is coming; behold, His reward is with Him,
and His work before Him.'" And they shall call them
The Holy People, The Redeemed of the* LORD; *and
you shall be called Sought Out, A City Not Forsaken*
(vv. 1–3, 6–7, 11–12).

So, there we have it. The God Factor makes it clear to us.
We are not victims, but victors. Israel will do much, much
more than survive; it will endure to become a light to the
nations.

Thus, while we slog through the muck of the present—
and slog we must—there is a city whose Builder and Maker
is God. There is a Kingdom that will surely come and an
eternal, new heaven and new earth awaiting us.

What could be better? We should not shrink from moving
toward all of this for the love of Zion and with allegiance to
the One who makes it all possible.